ROUAULT:

A Vision of Suffering and Salvation

To the memory of my sister Virginia Faith,
who loved Christ and therefore all of God's gifts

Preface

The painter Georges Rouault enjoyed the gifts both of faith and of delicate artistic expression. <u>He was a man with a keen sense of human misery, but also with a healing sense of the presence of God.</u> He seems a particularly important artist for a North American audience, for Americans have a hard time accepting the darkness of human evil. We like to think there is no problem, not even this one, that we cannot solve with hard work and good sense. The continued force of this debilitating illusion may be one reason we no longer experience much of the healing and reconciliation of the Christian Gospel.

The present study was undertaken as a doctoral thesis for the Protestant Theological Faculty of the University of Strasbourg, France. I should like to express my appreciation to that faculty for their kindness and especially to my professor, Dr. Pierre Burgelin, now Professor and Director of the Institute of Philosophy at the Sorbonne.

The literature on Rouault is limited when compared to that on other contemporary painters. His religious preoccupation seems to have made him especially difficult to interpret. Lionello Venturi, Bernard Dorival and Pierre Courthion are among the critics who have undertaken significant studies of Rouault. Courthion has written what must be considered, despite its weakness in organization, the most complete critical work, and we shall use the classified catalogue which he prepared with Isabelle Rouault, the painter's daughter, when we discuss specific paintings. The present work, a study in Christian aesthetics, should be read in the light of such critical studies. This study also needs as a complement a thorough, historical study of the painter's life, which in this writer's judgment remains to be written. On this centennial anniversary of Rouault's birth, I hope that this modest study will help create a deeper appreciation for this important twentieth-century painter who endowed his canvases with something of the faith and grandeur of the medieval cathedrals.

The author is happy to record here certain personal debts accrued in the course of study. Mr. Michel Hoog of the National Museum of Modern Art in Paris has been generous both with his time and with the resources of the museum. His counsel has been especially valuable in regard to the periods of Rouault's development. Professor H. R. Rookmaaker of the Free University in Amsterdam has also read the manuscript and offered helpful suggestions. The Rouault family, especially Miss Isabelle Rouault and Mrs. G. Nouaille-Rouault, have given kind attention to the project. They must not be blamed, however, for any of the shortcomings of the present work. Finally I must say how much I owe to my wife, Grace, who has looked on this endless affair as a family project, typed the manuscript, and translated the Spanish; and to my dear friend in Christ, Mr. Richard L. Benware, without whom this book would not have been written.

We close with the words Rouault so liked to quote: *Non nobis Domine, sed nomini tuo da gloriam.* Not to us, Lord, but to thy name be the glory.

                                    —W. A. D.

Zandvoort aan Zee, The Netherlands

Contents

List of Paintings

1. General Introduction

Since the breakup of the medieval synthesis, man has struggled to find a lasting alliance between the heavens and the earth. The history of religious art has been a graphic reflection on this struggle. After the Reformation, Alfred North Whitehead believes, the Protestants recoiled from the thought that aesthetic effects were dependent on a material medium. They had come to the recognition of the independent, substantial existence of each entity as distinct from any outside relationship. But such recognition, Whitehead reasons, ignored the manifold interrelationship of all things, and carried Protestants away from the realm of values altogether. They ascribed value to what is in itself valueless, namely, the independent private world of experiences.[1]

One can see the Protestant reaction to art in Zwingli, who outlawed from the church in Zurich anything that turned man's mind from complete trust in God. Charles Garside's study of Zwingli and the arts summarizes: "The prime symbol of true belief is the Word, invisible and heard; the prime symbol of false belief is the image, visible and seen."[2] A gulf was therefore conceived between the two worlds, spirit and matter, the visible and the invisible.

A single important exception must have been in the North where, after 1600, a genuinely Reformed atmosphere produced a unified conception of life and art. Landscapes and genre pieces of the period display an almost divine naturalness.[3] This atmosphere en-

---

[1] Alfred North Whitehead. *Science and the Modern World* (New York: Mentor Books, Macmillan, 1948), p. 174. Says Whitehead: "The heavens had lost the glory of God."

[2] Charles Garside, Jr. *Zwingli and the Arts* (New Haven, London: Yale University Press, 1966), p. 175.

[3] Eric Newton sees the split evident even here. The Dutch, he believes, were so concerned with "the trivial happenings of everyday life that they

abled a genius like Rembrandt to see within the Biblical events a supernatural quality.

The divorce between the two worlds was especially evident in the Catholic art of this period. Paul Claudel points out that Baroque art, especially after the Council of Trent, refused to deal with the concrete, historical facts of the faith, as had Gothic art. It attempted, rather, to make up with flourish what it lacked in substance—in Claudel's words, to "show off with clanging cymbals, with taste, and even with a pathetic air, this void as though it were a medallion, the access to which had been forbidden to our jaded senses."[4] As Eric Newton put it: "Catholicism had little to offer but a set of formulae for religious ecstasy."[5] Once again, because experience had lost its content, value was ascribed to what is without value.

Claudel's observation is directly relevant to the problem of religious art in France in the last century, when the same spiritual poverty was evident. He cites this tendency as one reason for the decadence of religious art in France. The second reason he notes is a certain French school—nourished, he suggests, on Jansenism and quietism—which saw faith merely as a matter of the spirit "stripped of the flesh." These causes combined to bring about a divorce "between the propositions of the Faith and the powers of imagination and sensitivity which are such treasured possessions of the artist."[6]

For our purposes it is sufficient to recognize the divorce; we need not trace the details of its philosophical and historical background. Eugène Delacroix, although he vigorously rejected many of Romanticism's artificialities, can illustrate the same split which that movement exemplified. Nature for him is merely a dictionary from which the artist-poet chooses his "words." All that is outside becomes personal and valuable only within the spirit of the creator. He writes in his journal: "That which is the most real for me is the illusion which I create with my painting. The rest is shifting sand."[7] Later, referring to his travels in Africa, he tells how he had to wait until the details had faded in order to recall creatively. Until

---

were incapable of interpreting the deeper levels of the New Testament." Eric Newton and William Neil. *2000 Years of Christian Art* (New York: Harper Brothers, 1966), p. 182.

[4] Paul Claudel. *Pages de prose* (Paris: Gallimard, 1944), p. 207.

[5] Newton and Neil, *op. cit.*, p. 182.

[6] *Op. cit.*, p. 207. These remarks were made in a letter to Alexandre Cingria on the causes of the decadence of sacred art and was written in July 1919.

[7] *Le Journal d'Eugène Delacroix* (Paris: Plon, 1932), vol. 1, p. 53. The entry for February 27, 1824.

then, he confessed, "I was pursued by the love for exactitude, which most people take to be the truth."[8] But truth is *not* accuracy, nor is beauty representation. Both beauty and truth have their source, as Baudelaire was to show, in taste and imagination. Nature is merely the servant of both.

Subjectivity is the key to Baudelaire's aesthetic. As Henri Lemaître explains in his introduction to Baudelaire's *Curiosités esthétiques,* the spiritual realm for Baudelaire is the point of contact between man and the supernatural. "The aesthetic form of spiritualism is supernaturalism. . . . Art is the passage to salvation."[9] An artist must know nature thoroughly, but in the end he looks within and not without for his inspiration. For the artist's ambition is a large one: "aspiration toward the infinite, expressed by every means that the arts contain."[10] Here, then, is one respite in the grappling of spirit with matter. In contrast to the triumph of matter proclaimed by modern "Pop Art," Baudelaire's Romanticism hails the supremacy of the spirit. Yet the gulf between spirit and matter remains wide.

It is in the Romantic tradition of Baudelaire that Rouault is often placed. Raïssa Maritain, a friend of Rouault and an artist in her own right, applies Baudelaire's phrase to Rouault's work: "The quality of a work does not depend on its subject, but on its spirit."[11] And many would concur with R. H. Wilenski when he writes that he may come to regard Rouault as a great artist:

> But the day will never come when I shall regard him as an artist of the twentieth century. For he is assuredly an artist whose mind is steeped in the nineteenth century—a painter in the tradition of Delacroix, a painter of *Les Fleurs du mal* whom Baudelaire himself would doubtless have admired.[12]

There is no doubt that Rouault has spiritual affinities with this tradition. He was not, however, consciously Baudelairean, nor was he an adherent of any particular school of aesthetics. He was a practicing artist, and his aesthetics were expressed in the art he created. Later we will examine how Rouault viewed the division between spirit and matter.

We will note that in his own way Rouault may have gone beyond Baudelaire, perhaps even beyond the tension of spirit and matter

---

[8] *Ibid.,* vol. II, p. 92, entry for October 17, 1853.

[9] Charles Baudelaire. *Curiosités esthétiques: l'art romantique* (Paris: Garnier Frères, 1962), p. 11.

[10] *Ibid.,* p. 103.

[11] Raïssa Maritain. *Les Grandes amitiés* (New York: Editions de La Maison Française, 1941), vol. II, p. 47. Cf. Baudelaire. *Curiosités esthétiques,* pp. 85, 86.

[12] R. H. Wilenski. "Georges Rouault." *Apollo.* 1930, vol. II, p. 474.

altogether. Rouault's admiration for Baudelaire is no secret,[13] and his art came straight from the creative soul; but in a deeper sense he penetrated to the very sources of religious faith. This aspect of Rouault's art will lie in the background of the present study.

Our more immediate concern, however, is Rouault as a religious artist. Religious art, as we shall use the term, should be carefully distinguished from what can be called church art. The latter is art designed for use in the church. Such art subjects itself to ends outside itself—ends such as instruction (in which case it is properly referred to as religious iconography) or worship. It is usually commissioned by the church and submits itself to certain stipulations.

The problem of church art is a complex one, and we cannot dwell on it here. It may be instructive, however, to note Rouault's relationship to the Catholic Church. Perhaps in this way we can better understand the subjectivity and independence that characterized Rouault's religious art and set it so noticeably apart from church art.

The ecclesiastical leaders who represented the Church largely passed Rouault by. Though the imagery of its rich tradition and a few of the clergy were influential in his development both as an artist and a person, in the main he worked independently of the Church. Many in the Church were plainly suspicious of the dark and sinister nature of his earlier work.

The root of the problem between Rouault and the Church was revealed in an illuminating exchange that took place publicly in 1937 and 1938. Waldemar George, in the October-December, 1937, issue of *La Renaissance,* wondered out loud why the Church had so ignored Rouault. Referring rather bluntly to the Dominican Fathers who directed the review *L'Art Sacré,*[14] George accused them of searching for a renaissance of Christian art in Picasso and the Surrealists and turning their backs on Rouault. He concluded that the Church ". . . refuses to understand that the Catholic artist is not the one who treats sacred themes, but the one whose every activity bears the imprint of Christian thought."[15]

He had thrown down the cudgel, and it was not long before it was taken up. Father Couturier, writing in *L'Art Sacré* for September, 1938, rejoined that he had never seen anything inhuman in Rouault's violence, and that it is wrong in any case to accuse the

---

[13] In his *Souvenirs Intimes* (Paris: Frapier, 1926), p. 65, he calls him a "brother in spirit" and warmly defends him against the attacks waged against him.

[14] Fathers Régamey and Couturier.

[15] Waldemar George. "Georges Rouault: oeuvres inédites." *La Renaissance.* October-December, 1937, no. 5, p. 10.

Church of the faults of some of its members. The problem, if there was one, was between Rouault and the Church hierarchy—and here Father Couturier admitted that a difficulty existed. For the clergy had never commissioned Rouault to do any work.[16] The reason, argues Couturier, is that Rouault places material objects in the way of spiritual appreciation. The dark and fierce style sometimes blurred the profundity. Here, Couturier sagely notes, is where the problem really lies: in the revival in modern art of deeper values at the expense of secondary factors such as literal realism.[17]

The problem which caused misunderstanding by the clergy also plagued a church public—and a gallery-going public—who had been nourished on idyllic, romantic realism. And the dilemma with which we began this introduction again intrudes: how do we avoid losing the profound in the banal, or the real in the mystical? Waldemar George had called attention to this very problem: "The Church is accustomed to an art rather more governed and conventional. It mistrusts mystical effusions."[18] But Father Couturier is equally correct in calling this more a problem of all modern religious art than a betrayal of Rouault by the Church.

What was Rouault's own view of religious art? Though he would never openly oppose any group, he made it known that he distrusted any organized attempt to 'stimulate' religious art. Bernard Dorival, a reliable student of Rouault's work, records Rouault's feelings toward the movement started by Maurice Denis and Desvallières toward a school of sacred art. Rouault liked neither the spirit nor the productions of such an attempt. For Rouault, Dorival notes, "the sacred is so intimately tied to Christianity, and even more, to the person of Christ himself, that only the epithet Christian can characterize his creations in this realm."[19]

In 1952, a writer for the religious periodical La Croix asked Rouault what he thought of religious or sacred art. As usual, Rouault refused to be brought into a debate. He said simply that, to talk about art in the Church, one must first of all love painting. It is possible, Rouault added, to be religious and not have a deep sensitivity.

---

[16] This remained true until 1945 when Devemy and Couturier asked him to do windows for the Church at Assy. Finally in 1953 Pope Pius XII honored him. Cf. L. Venturi. Rouault: étude biographique et critique (Geneva: Skira, 1959), p. 118. But clearly the recognition by the Church followed rather than led the honor of the world.

[17] M. A. Couturier. "Rouault et le public ecclésiastique." L'Art Sacré. September, 1938, pp. 245-247.

[18] George, op. cit., p. 10.

[19] Bernard Dorival. Georges Rouault: oeuvres inachevées données à l'Etat. Musée du Louvre, June-November 1964 (Paris: Ministère d'Etat Affaires Culturelles, 1964), p. 97.

One can pray for sensitivity, but it is really a gift. "One needs perhaps special gifts, especially in that which concerns sacred art."[20] The gifts of love for painting and a deep sensitivity—hardly theological graces these! Yet they are requisite to religious art.

Here we discover the difficulty of distinguishing Rouault the Christian from Rouault the artist, and questions of iconography from those of aesthetics. We shall notice throughout our study how often critics are forced to speak theologically in trying to understand Rouault as an artist. Perhaps some have refrained from speaking of him at all because they were puzzled by the religious nature of his work. This may be one reason he has not gained the popular recognition of, for example, Picasso or Klee. Other critics, discussing his work, throw up their hands and admit, as did Gustave Coquiot in 1913, that one "must be a monk to understand him."[21] The canons of art criticism often seem to fail in finding the clue to this artist whom other critics called the greatest religious artist since Rembrandt.

Admittedly we intend to undertake this study from a Christian perspective. And with this approach come certain problems. Religious art must be identified, as we have suggested, by its character and inspiration and by its ends.[22] By this standard, Rouault is clearly a religious artist, and most critics are agreed on this point. But we must not equate artistic value with religious meaning. Rouault was a greater artist than, say, Maurice Denis, but as Dom Angelico Surchamp reminds us, we ought not to conclude that he is therefore more religious.[23] We cannot appeal to Rouault as a theologian; his artistic greatness does not make him a prophet. Rouault was an artist and also a Christian. We will explore both of these facets of the man in their interrelationship.

For although we cannot measure Rouault's artistry by his faith, the relationship between the two is nevertheless important. We mean to discover in what way his Christianity was important to him as an artist. But throughout our study we must bear in mind that what an artist believes—about himself, his world and his art—

---

[20] Maurice Brillant. "Ce qu'ils pensent de l'art sacré: Georges Rouault." *La Croix.* May 11, 1952, p. 5.

[21] Gustave Coquiot. *Cubistes, futuristes, passéistes* (Paris: Librairie Ollendorff, 1914), p. 157. Coquiot was, however, an early and much appreciated defender of Rouault's work. Cf. Courthion, p. 74.

[22] Cf. Jacques Maritain. *Art and Scholasticism* (New York: Charles Scribner's Sons, 1962), p. 65. "Christian art is defined by the one in whom it exists and by the spirit from which it issues. It is the art of redeemed humanity."

[23] Dom Angelico Surchamp. "Un Art sacré pour notre temps." *Zodiaque.* October, 1952, p. 14, no. 2.

belongs fundamentally to the realm of the artist's intentions. These must be clearly distinguished from the aesthetic object created by the artist, which must be evaluated on its own merits. Any judgment about the work must be confirmed within the work itself, not justified by appealing to the artist's intention.[24]

What validity is there, it might be asked, in studying the intentions of the artist, his faith and his world view? Henry David Aiken raises just this question in an article entitled "The Aesthetic Relevance of the Artist's Intentions."[25] He notes that, since a work of art is so-called because it is viewed in such a way that it gives pleasure,[26] art calls for concentration of attention on itself for its own sake. Everything then is relevant to art that stimulates attention to the object or heightens enjoyment. While "intentions" must not be relied on to support a particular interpretation, they can enlarge the framework within which a judgment can be made. As Aiken points out, showing the relationship of a work to things outside it need not lessen its integrity. "Intentions," after all, are not privileged information. "They do not take us away from the work, but, rather, bring us in the end closer to it."[27]

In this way we have a response for Coquiot's plea about Rouault. One need not be a monk to understand what this artist does, but one must be patient enough to listen to the man as well as the work. And one must not listen to each alone, but to both together, carefully, and thoughtfully.

Even then, we will not understand entirely. In the end a great part will still be shrouded in mystery. Rouault's work will go on giving its own explanation more clearly than words ever can.

Here lies the most serious difficulty with which we will struggle: Rouault as a painter does not deal primarily with language. He is less able than a writer or a poet to scrutinize and analyze his inner experience. We will need to appeal, as Maritain reminds us, to "external, indirect and so to speak oblique indications, whose

---

[24] Cf. Monroe C. Beardsley. *Aesthetics: Problems in the Philosophy of Criticism* (New York: Harcourt, Brace and World, Inc., 1958), pp. 21-26.

[25] *The Journal of Philosophy*, vol. LII (1955), reprinted in W. E. Kennick, ed., *Art and Philosophy* (New York: St. Martin's Press, 1964), pp. 403ff.

[26] Though a discussion of the nature of aesthetic objects is beyond our scope, it is worth noting that this definition agrees with the scholastic one espoused by Maritain and Gilson: That which being seen pleases. Cf. Gilson, *op. cit.*, p. 178; J. Maritain, *op. cit.*, pp. 23ff., though this has been challenged recently by the formalist school of aesthetics represented by Clive Bell and Susanne Langer; cf. conclusion below.

[27] Aiken, *op. cit.*, p. 412.

complete meaning it is up to us to infer."[28] This inference will be the major task of our study. In Part One we will approach these problems by studying the man as artist and Christian.

In Part Two we will concentrate especially on the iconography of Rouault's work, considering the religious impact of each of the themes he employed and the views of man, nature and God implicit in his work. Then, in the conclusion, we will be ready to consider the hints our study has suggested toward developing a Christian aesthetic.

---

[28] Jacques Maritain. *Creative Intuition in Art and Poetry* (New York: Meridian Books, 1954), p. 185. Cf. chapter 6, below, where we discuss this in more detail.

PART ONE:
The Artist

SECTION A: SOURCES FOR THE THOUGHT
AND WORK OF ROUAULT

* * *

2. Family Milieu and Formal Training

Claude Roulet in his *Souvenirs* of Rouault tells of sitting with the artist in a Parisian sidewalk cafe. The sky was darkened and a fine rain was falling. Looking up into the mist Rouault exulted: "I am a man of the North." Breathing deeply he added, "Ah! I feel like I am in my element."[1]

Though this was an incidental episode, the "element" Rouault mentioned shaped much of the character and spirit of his work. His was a unique heritage, little influenced by schools or traditions. Modern writers and painters have become enamoured with the worker-artisan who is the foundation of any civilization, but this common man has usually been idealized beyond recognition rather than seen in the context of his weary and often hopeless existence. Rouault can help to correct this view, for he is an artist whose roots lie in the drudgery of a worker's life.

Georges Henri Rouault was born on the 27th of May, 1871, in the Belleville quarter outside of Paris. Rouault was not, properly speaking, a Parisian by birth, for his "Belleville Village" was not yet a suburb of Paris. He liked to refer to his beginnings in this humble outlying district in both his writings and his paintings. "In the faubourg of toil and suffering, in the darkness, I was born. Keeping vigil over pictorial turpitudes, I toiled miles away from certain dilettantes."[2]

---

[1] Claude Roulet. *Rouault: souvenirs* (Paris: Bibliothèque des Arts, 1961), p. 234.

[2] Georges Rouault. "Le Pêcheur de perles suivi de bâtons rompus." *Les Saisons*. Summer, 1945, p. 31.

Several commentators on Rouault's life have pointed out the symbolic nature of the "darkness" in which he was born. The times
were sunless. It was the end of the Franco-Prussian war. Paris was
in the hands of the Commune, which was to be suppressed by the
Versailles government the very day after Rouault's birth. On the 27th,
Belleville itself was taken; as Marie-Louise Rouault was feeling the
birth pangs, government troops were bombarding the northern part
of the city. A shell struck the outside of the house and she was
hurriedly carried to the cellar in a bed sheet. There she gave
birth to a frail, light-haired boy. So weak was he that they wondered
for a time whether he would survive. We might call these ominous
beginnings a portent of the darkness of his life and thought, but
(since his life both physically and emotionally was remarkably free
of severe trials after his early years) it would be more accurate to
see them as an indication to Rouault of the tortured fate of a host
of nameless folk, whose lot Rouault felt deeply.

The artist's father, Alexandre Rouault, was a cabinetmaker, a Bréton
from Montfort in Britannia. It was to this nordic strain that young
Rouault owed much of his rugged tenacity. Throughout his life, he
was to acknowledge the importance of this inheritance. "After all,"
he would often say, "it is my nature which directs me."[3] In 1895
when he failed for the second time in his bid for the Prix de Rome,
we would expect that Rouault might have felt long nights of despair.
But he once told Courthion his reaction to the defeat. "I'm made
of Bréton granite, the kind you break your teeth on. You remember
how the Dutch succeeded in salvaging land from the sea? There's
something of that in my nature. If I had been a failure I would
keep at it just the same. I'm hardheaded, with terrible faults."[4]

Here Rouault took after his father. Like his ancestors before him,
Alexandre Rouault was a stubborn individualist. He was a Christian,
if a bit anarchistic in his faith. He was a partisan of Lamennais,[5]
standing against the Pope.[6] For this reason he would not send his
Georges to a Catholic school but had him placed in a Protestant
institution. Soon, however, he took him out because of an overly

---

[3] Quoted in R. Huyghe. "Le Fauvisme: les peintres pathétiques." L'Amour
de l'Art. 1933, no. 14, p. 130.

[4] Pierre Courthion. Georges Rouault (New York: Harry N. Abrams, Inc.,
1952), p. 50. Hereafter listed as Courthion.

[5] H. Félicité Robert de Lamennais (1782-1854) was a sensitive priest who
though ultramontane later was estranged from the Church when his program,
which had for its motto "God and Liberty," was condemned by Rome.

[6] Cf. Jean Grenier. "Idées de Georges Rouault." L'Oeil: Revue d'Art. April,
1957, no. 28, p. 31.

harsh punishment, and young Rouault passed his high school exams in a public school.[7]

Another prominent influence on young Rouault was his maternal grandfather, Alexandre Champdavoine, whom Rouault often recalled. During the week grandfather traveled as the chief in a mail car. On Sundays, in the company of his grandson, he would stroll along the Seine in search of reproductions of Manet and Courbet. Champdavoine lived with his other daughters, who would spend their evenings painting porcelain vases or fans. Rouault spent many evenings with them as a child, making chalk drawings on the floor. Rouault referred to this period of his life when once asked where he first became interested in painting:

> From my first steps I tramped about in colors. My aunts used to paint on porcelain and fans. I would grab the ends of the pencils, old brushes, and tubes that lay about and I too would try to paint.[8]

"In this little milieu," notes Grenier, "everyone had taste—a personal taste."[9] Their taste had no need of newspapers or fashion books.

Georges Rouault's father worked in Paris at Pleyel's, a piano manufacturer, as a finisher and varnisher. He was a true artisan; he grimaced whenever his wife pulled out a drawer abruptly. "They don't realize how they make the wood suffer," he would say.[10] Young Rouault was as proud of his artisan heritage as he was of his nordic ancestry. Vollard records the following exchange which occurred at Rouault's wedding in 1908.[11] One of Rouault's inlaws asked him what his father did.

"He was a worker (ouvrier) at Pleyel's," he answered.

"You mean he was employed at Pleyel's," she persisted, thinking to suggest a somewhat higher position.

"No, Madame," Rouault insisted. Then frowning a bit he asked her: "Are you a Christian?"

"What a question!" gasped the lady.

"Then you should honor my father," Rouault explained, "as you do Joseph the carpenter and his apprentice, the infant Jesus."

The vexed woman exclaimed, "Now I know why the painting of this young man is so ugly!"[12]

---

[7] Courthion, p. 14.

[8] Quoted in Ambroise Vollard. *Souvenirs d'un marchand de tableaux* (Paris: Club des Librairies de France, 1957), p. 161.

[9] Grenier, *op. cit.*, p. 31.

[10] Courthion, p. 13.

[11] On January 27, to Marthe Le Sidaner. They were to have four children: Geneviève, b. 1908; Isabelle, b. 1910; Michel, b. 1911; and Agnes, b. 1915.

[12] Vollard, *op. cit.*, p. 162.

It may seem pedantic to insist so on the importance of these artisan roots, but this aspect of his heritage is essential to an understanding of Rouault. Jacques Maritain has reminded us that the ancients did not have a special classification for the fine arts.[13] In fact, the distinction we make between the beautiful (or fine) arts and the useful arts is not what logicians call an essential division. The differentiation derives from the end pursued and not from the nature of the activity.[14]

Rouault began as an artisan, or more precisely as an artisan's assistant. When his grandfather died following an accident, the 14-year-old Rouault had to find his own spiritual and material support. He was apprenticed to Hirsch, a restorer of stained-glass windows.[15] At this time he was earning about 15¢ a week and doing everything that needed to be done at the workshop. He described his work this way: "My job consisted of watching the firings and especially of sorting the little pieces of glass that would fall from the stained-glass windows brought to us for repair."[16] Working in the midst of precious examples of an ancient art, he had ample opportunity to stimulate his appetite for rich colors. These same colors Rouault later spoke of fondly as "dull or flamboyant reds, golden yellows, ultramarines like those of early antiquity."[17] "It was thus," confesses Rouault, "that I acquired the passionate taste that I have had and always will have for the ancient stained-glass windows."[18]

It was in many ways a fruitless experience. There was not much future to this job, and yet it was to leave a lifelong mark on Rouault. He says of this period in a letter to Suarès: ". . . cherished memory; my time there was short, but it marked me with a seal that was legendary, epical; I would even say traditional.

> I think of the Rose of Chartres
> That I have never seen.
> Shame and misery."[19]

More than the stylistic influence of the windows, it is especially

---

[13] Jacques Maritain, op. cit., p. 21. Cf. J. Huizinga. The Waning of the Middle Ages (Penguin Books, 1965), p. 236.

[14] Maritain, op. cit., p. 158n.

[15] Courthion, p. 14, says first Tamoni, then Hirsch. Venturi (1959, p. 25) and others mention only Hirsch.

[16] Quoted in Vollard, op. cit., p. 161.

[17] Georges Rouault. "Visage de la France." Verve. 1940, vol. 2, no. 3, p. 15.

[18] Quoted in Vollard, op. cit., p. 162.

[19] Georges Rouault/André Suarès, Correspondance (Paris: Gallimard, 1960), p. 199.

the spirit of the ancient glass-makers, whose names no art history book discloses, that has struck Rouault.[20]

In this humble workshop Rouault got his inspiration as an artisan's assistant. Much later he said of such beginnings: "One starts out being a craftsman, then one becomes an artist if he can. But is it not better to be a good craftsman than a mediocre artist?"[21] Rouault longed, nevertheless, to be an artist and a painter. Even as he worked for Hirsch he had begun his second apprenticeship. After work, in the evening, he would race home for a bit of supper and then hurry to the other side of Paris to l'Ecole des Arts Décoratifs, hoping to arrive before the doors closed at 7:30.[22]

Rouault aspired above all to enter l'Ecole des Beaux-Arts. Despite an offer to collaborate in making windows for the school of pharmacy, despite the quadruple raise in salary his boss offered him upon learning of his ambitions, Rouault left his first apprenticeship. He had outgrown its curriculum.

If Rouault's background was among the artisans, his training in art was classical. If his physical inheritance was northern, his artistic heritage was latin. From the time Rouault enrolled in l'Ecole des Beaux-Arts in Paris he was exposed to the riches of a latin cultural history, and his latin sense of composition always set him apart from German or nordic expressionism. He had prepared himself for entry into the prestigious school by spending his Sundays wandering through the Louvre. It was with a whetted appetite that, in December, 1890, he entered the studio of Delaunay.[23]

---

[20] Rouault's frequent references to this period along with the obvious stylistic resemblance, especially in his use of heavy black outlines, have forced many to see a decisive influence of this period in Rouault's painting after 1910. The most intelligent discussion this writer has seen of the subject is that of James Thrall Soby: *Georges Rouault: Paintings and Prints* (New York: Museum of Modern Art, 1945), pp. 11, 12, who is especially helpful in his consideration of how the influence could be latent during his early period and become more prominent later. We shall not venture to judge on this matter except to suggest two points relevant to the issue: (1) As Venturi shows (1959, p. 26), the windows of St. Séverin (with which he was involved) have no rapport with Rouault's work. Besides, with Rouault the contours "have an essentially pictorial function and not the technical function of marking out the colors as did the lead filaments. They have the artistic function of adding value to the colors and making them shine by contrast." (2) As noted in the text, the attachment Rouault felt with the ancient craftsmen was much more than technical. It was almost a mystical one, and as we shall note often in this study, it is the expression of emotion that is prominent with Rouault and is determinative of his style.

[21] Georges Rouault. *Soliloques* (Neuchâtel: Ides et Calendes, 1944), p. 104.

[22] Cf. Georges Rouault. "Souvenirs du jeune âge sont gravés dans mon coeur." *Le Point.* August-October, 1943.

[23] Courthion, p. 15.

In the fall of 1891, Delaunay died and Gustave Moreau was asked by the Academy to succeed him. Moreau's teaching and example were to have a remarkable influence on young Rouault. The esteem in which the latter held his early teacher even to the end of his life, and the impact of Moreau's guidance, can hardly be exaggerated.

In one sense the attachment Rouault felt for his teacher was inexplicable. They did not have a great deal in common. As a painter, Moreau had never abandoned an academic design; Rouault's works were quite the opposite. Moreau sought the "beau idéal" while Rouault was to portray reality in all its atrocities. Rouault's religious faith was strong, almost mystical; Moreau had an intellectual faith in the supersensible. Though Moreau, like Rouault, was a withdrawn person, he felt none of the horrible contradictions in life which his student struggled with all his life.[24] The friendship with Moreau nonetheless was the first of a series of deep and lasting friendships that Rouault enjoyed during his lifetime. For Rouault, one could almost say, defined his life in a few friendships. They were attachments of the spirit that far surpassed mere comradery, unions on which the spirit of the painter could feed and nourish itself. Bloy and Huysmans were among such friends in his early life after the death of Moreau. During the difficult days of the first war, Jacques and Raïssa Maritain sustained the artist. Later writer André Suarès, again unlike Rouault in so many ways, was one with whom the searching, agonizing mind of Rouault could find repose. The last was especially meaningful during the difficult days with Vollard. We will reflect on all of these in greater detail later in our study.

Gustave Moreau was born in Paris in 1826 into surroundings deeply involved in the arts. His father was an architect, and he himself studied painting in the studio of François Picot, and later with Chasseriau. He traveled in Italy, then in Holland, exposing his work from time to time in the Salons in Paris. He was the creator of an imaginary world which was both romanesque and symbolic. He worked alone in his researches, separating himself both from the realists and impressionists, and was known for his independence. "He is the sphinx of painting, it is said, a painter for alchemists." Some supported him, however, for his powerful conceptions and "the glittering mosaic of his palette."[25]

The mixed reaction to Moreau continued into his teaching period. Courthion recounts the excitement that surrounded his *atelier*. During the 1890's his studio was a center of artistic attention, as con-

---

[24] Venturi, 1948, p. 17.
[25] Louis Hourticq. *L'Encyclopédie des beaux arts* (Paris: Librairie Hachette, 1925), p. 74.

noisseurs from abroad used any excuse to get in to see his paintings.[26] Moreau's major importance, however, lies in his inspiration
of future generations of artists. Art historians have debated his part
in the experimentation of surrealism, but his impact on Rouault
is unquestionable. Moreau was a liberal, far-sighted teacher. "I am
the bridge over which many of you will pass," he used to say to
his students. He taught more than the mechanics of drawing. He was
concerned to stimulate in his students a respect for their interior
vision. "The harmony and secret rhythm of life, there is our cer-
tainty," he emphasized.[27]

Because he opened windows in his students that looked in on
themselves, he was never a demanding or overbearing instructor.
In fact, he preferred that students work by themselves. He felt that
art could lead to religion, real religion of the heart. His confession
of faith was later quoted by Rouault:

> Do you believe in God? I am asked. I believe only in God. In fact,
> I do not believe in what I touch nor in what I see. I only believe in
> what I cannot see; solely in what I sense (sens). My mind and my
> reason seem to me ephemeral and of a dubious reality. My inner con-
> sciousness (sentiment intérieur) alone appears eternal and unquestion-
> ably certain.[28]

Here was a plea to the students to turn their attention inward
even before they reflect on an outer reality. It was to the clarifica-
tion of this inner perspective that the artistic means were to be
subordinated.[29] How can this "inner consciousness" be understood?
Michel Puy, in the first monograph published about Rouault, points
out that what predominated with Moreau was what could be called
the poetic imagination. And the confession quoted above, on close
examination, is seen as merely a poetic and artistic sensitivity, a
creative imagination. Puy calls it primarily a "literary sentiment."[30]

Later Rouault was to conceive of faith in a totally different fashion. Faith for him was a firmly religious sentiment, which, even if
not articulated, demanded absolute abandon. But during this impressionable period, the awareness of the inner life brought Rouault
and Moreau together. Rouault tells us that Moreau distrusted all

---

[26] Courthion, pp. 40-46.

[27] Rouault. Souvenirs Intimes (Paris: Frapier, 1926), pp. 19, 20. Hereafter
listed as SI.

[28] Georges Rouault/André Suarès. "Moreau." L'Art et les Artistes. April,
1926, p. 240.

[29] Cf. Michel Puy. Georges Rouault (Paris: Les Peintres Français, No. 8), p.
4. As Puy points out, most of the students rejected Moreau's plea and fell
under the seductive influence of impressionism, but Rouault was an exception.

[30] Ibid.

forms of dogma, which suggested to him earthlike hierarchies.[31] This did not prevent him from adhering to a religion that was, in James Soby's phrase, an iconographic storehouse from which he could furnish the exotic creations of his fertile imagination.

A second point of Moreau's influence upon Rouault follows from this respect for an interior sentiment. One could term it a spiritual humility. There was, Moreau taught his students, an unfathomed depth to reality, an unknown that one must not presume upon. Rouault once recalled a comment Moreau made when viewing a work by Goya which expressed a sense of the tragic: "They say he is a 'little master', but when his subject is magnified and so clearly transcends the anecdote, he joins the 'great masters.' "[32] On another occasion Moreau demonstrated not only his thinking but his pedagogical gift as well, in handing to Rouault a portion copied from Pascal. It read: "Human knowledge is like a sphere that is continuously growing in proportion as its volume increases and multiplies the number of points of contact with the unknown."[33]

From this viewpoint, all of reality takes on—as indeed it did take on for Rouault—a spiritual sense.

A third influence can be discerned as a result of these two. The interior sensitivity and humility suggested to Moreau that only one attitude was appropriate for the artist: a radical independence of spirit. This theme was to strike a sympathetic chord in Rouault. Noble art for Moreau had to free itself from all superficialities— whether of nature, as in Courbet's realism, or of science, as in post-impressionism. In fact, all schools and aesthetic theories must be left to care for themselves, as the artist feverishly, singlemindedly tracks down "those inner feelings by means of plastic expression."[34]

The path of this search is a difficult one, and the road is inevitably lonely. Moreau once spoke to Rouault of the poverty that must accompany many artistic quests: "It is necessary that their art be well grounded in themselves, for they will cross the desert without provisions or baggage."[35] But the way is necessary. "One has to suffer and see for himself."[36] Moreau predicted with uncommon accuracy how this aspect of the artist's life would affect Rouault: "I see you more and more of a recluse. You like a solemn art that

[31] Rouault and Suarès, op. cit., p. 240.
[32] Ibid., p. 248.
[33] Ibid., pp. 231, 232.
[34] Cf. Soby, op. cit., pp. 7, 8.
[35] Quoted in Georges Charensol. Georges Rouault: l'homme et l'oeuvre (Paris: Editions de Quatre Chemins, 1926), p. 21.
[36] Ibid., p. 23.

is sober and religious in its essence. All that you do will be marked with this stamp."[37]

The goal of the quest on which Moreau set his students was an art of integrity. This end was worth the cost. Moreau told them: "Thank God that you do not have success, at least that it is postponed as long as possible. Then it will be possible for you to reveal yourself completely and without coercion."[38]

But references to loneliness and poverty were only prophecies at that time. Those years were happy ones for Rouault. They were days, Roulet records, of gaiety and skirmish, and Rouault, though never an instigator, was a part of it all. Léon Lehmann, a painter and friend of Rouault's, revealed later what his fellow students thought of young Rouault: "Rouault was very well liked, as much for his simple character, which was always warm and lively, as for the pride and exalted joy that his talent stimulated in us. His ardour at work was prodigious."[39]

If Rouault was diligent, it was because there was so much to absorb and make a trial of. Art history was for him a beloved treasure. His writings are filled with references to the masters from Michelangelo to David and Ingres, from the artisans of the middle ages to Delacroix and Cézanne. Certain traditions seem to have made more of an impact on Rouault than others. But here one can depend less on his reminiscing. He himself admits that the mysterious influences of traditions, though no doubt very real, are difficult to trace. In an interview in 1950, Rouault confessed that he left such matters to art critics.[40] For influence is not a matter of one generation copying another. Moreau had taught that the artist must feel his own way. Tradition is in the air we breathe, he would say. "It flowers in different ways."[41] Rouault emphasized this in *Stella Vespertina*, his book published in 1947. "You do not climb aboard Tradition like a city bus, with its route marked on the front. There must be more secret affinities."[42]

All of art history, moreover, simply shows how much there is to learn. Rouault asserted that, despite all the technical perfection of the ancients, we still know very little about form, color and harmony. Their inspiration, therefore, must be only a point of em-

---

[37] Quoted in Luc Benoist. "Georges Rouault." *Les Tendances.* 1965, no. 37, p. 443.

[38] Roulet, *op. cit.*, p. 163.

[39] *Ibid.*, p. 129.

[40] Russell Warren Howe. "An Impasto Dream: Georges Rouault." *Apollo.* 1950, vol. 52, p. 36.

[41] Rouault, *Soliloques*, p. 55; cf. also p. 158.

[42] Rouault, *Stella Vespertina* (Paris: René Drouin, 1947), no pagination.

barkation and not a terminus. For their greatest lesson, he admits in a letter to Suarès, is that one must learn to be himself.[43]

Still there remain particular sources of Rouault's work that are incontestably certain. His affection for Rembrandt was well known in the *atelier*. His "Jesus Among the Doctors" (1894) recalls Rembrandt's dark, rich colors. Moreau noticed the young painter's attachment and once cautioned him not to be caught in a spell by Rembrandt's style. Rouault replied bluntly: "I would rather be under the spell of Rembrandt all my life than make myself up in the mode of the day that hardly suits me."[44]

What impressed Rouault as much as Rembrandt's talent was his spiritual impact. He admitted in a passage quoted by Soby that this was how he judged all the masters:

> However great a talent is needed to produce David's "Leonidas at Thermopylae," for example, many more works (I am thinking of the unobtrusive Chardins, of the "Christ at Emmaus" of Rembrandt, of Poussin's "Diogenes") go far more directly to my heart—I am not afraid of employing this rather old-fashioned word, having been called the last of the Romantics.[45]

Of Rembrandt specifically, Rouault states in his *Soliloques* that this master was able to renew each subject he treated. He always translated into painting an emotion of high quality that was both human and intimate.[46]

That Rembrandt had a strong faith and was a man of the Bible is well known.[47] But we must be careful to note at what point Rouault was struck by that painter. It was neither his beliefs nor anything about his spiritual life that made him impressive to Rouault. It was rather that quality of faith which he was able to incarnate into his paintings. Only this spoke to the heart of Rouault.

One further source in cultural history has already been mentioned and should perhaps be emphasized. Moreau had an attraction for the subject matter of the middle ages. Rouault also found inspiration here, less in subject matter than in the spirit and the faith of those times. For Rouault the value of the "cathedral spirit" is not its skill or scholasticism but the ardor and faith that impregnated everything which that spirit inspired.[48] Rouault liked to

---

[43] *Correspondance, op. cit.,* p. 63, 1913: "The quality of being yourself is only granted to a very few people."

[44] *SI,* p. 34.

[45] Soby, *op. cit.,* pp. 26-28.

[46] *Soliloques,* p. 76.

[47] On this see Visser 't Hooft, *Rembrandt and the Gospel* (New York: Meridian Books, 1960), chapter 2.

[48] Rouault and Suarès, *op. cit.,* p. 248. It is fitting, as one writer expressed

quote the inscription he felt befitted those nameless artisans who toiled for so little earthly reward: *Non nobis Domine, sed nomini tuo da gloriam.* "Not to us, Lord, but to thy name be the glory." But before this spirit could be fully awakened in Rouault, the source to be discussed in the next section was needed.

---

it, to "... emphasize the fact that there is still inspiration to be drawn from a great conception of existence as expressed by its greatest artists (the medievals)." *The Studio,* 1938, no. 116, p. 168. We will leave to others the question of how radically Rouault, and especially Bloy, idealized that misunderstood period. Certainly a man is to be judged by his ideals as much as by his reality.

3. The Religious Reaction of Léon Bloy

One must look beyond the walls of Gustave Moreau's studio for further influences on Georges Rouault. The young painter was passing his impressionable period in the dying years of a tired and disillusioned century. The nineteenth century had witnessed the apogee of the reign of science, formalized as Scientism. In many ways materialism and naturalism had succeeded in draining all spiritual life from literature and culture. One historian has observed that in the nineteenth century materialism had become a science, whereas in the century preceding it had only been a sentiment.[1] The new philosophy had brooked no rivals. The emotional warmth of Romanticism had frozen in the cold objectivity of Positivism. Baudelaire had given way to Rimbaud.

By the 1880's, the growth of ideas had borne the bitter fruit of naturalism. A group of thinkers and writers sparked by the realism of Flaubert and the positivism of Taine gathered around Emile Zola (1840-1902). They sought to portray "reality" in all its objectivity. For them there would be no moralizing, but simply the "science" of examining hereditary and environmental determinism.

The influence of this movement on Rouault was only indirect, partly because the movement had spent itself by the end of the century. Rouault's realism, as we shall notice, springs from entirely different sources. But the group was influential on Léon Bloy,[2] whom we will want to study in some detail because of his affinity with Rouault.

Léon Bloy played a part in one of the most important revivals of religious literature in French history. Near the end of the century, spectacular conversions, coupled with the waning of the century's

---

[1] C. Baumgartner. *Le Dictionnaire de spiritualité: ascétique et mystique* (Paris: Beauchesne, 1932 et seq.), p. 962.

[2] Cf. Mary Rosalie Brady. *Thought and Style in the Works of Léon Bloy* (Washington: Catholic University Press, 1945), pp. 14ff.

intellectualism and the staunchly anticlerical Republican government, stimulated a most violent reactive revolution in religious
literature. Huysmans, Péguy, Claudel, Mauriac and the Maritains as
well as Bloy are often associated with this revival.[3]

Whatever the extent of Bloy's inspiration of Rouault,[4] it is clear
that they share the reactive mentality that gathered strength around
the turn of the century. In many ways, Rouault represents the pictorial expression of this literary revival. A discussion of Bloy can
therefore illuminate in several ways our study of Rouault. The two
share a faith manifesting itself in a consuming and passionate religious sentiment. Venturi mentions that Bloy was the very embodiment of the necessity of faith which Rouault felt; the writer was
for him an "older brother."[5]

Throughout that long century that began with dreams and ended
in nightmares, there were voices speaking for Grace, but only a
few were heeded. One who spoke up loudly was Ernest Hello (1828-
1885). This little-remembered critic and satirist was an early follower of the young Lamennais and Comte Joseph de Maistre.[6] Hello's
learned works of essay and criticism were discordant notes in his
day and went largely unheard. His work on man, L'Homme, trumpets
what has been called Hello's impatience with the patience of God.[7]

Throughout this work one can see gleams of the later work of
Bloy. Its barrages are characterized by maledictory extremes. Writes
Hello: "Nothingness is a root that produces boredom as its flower,
and hopelessness as its fruit."[8] Like Bloy after him, Hello saw everything in the light of God's absolute point of view. "The presence
of God is the aroma that keeps human life from falling into decom-
position." And again: "To find life one must always look above."[9]
Art, for Hello, was to bear the same profile as life. Religious art
"ought to be the magnificent imprint of the traces of light that
traditions have fostered within man . . . the invincible hope of

---

[3] Richard Griffiths entitles his comprehensive work on this revival *The
Reactionary Revolution: Catholic Revival in French Literature: 1870-1914*
(London: Constable, 1966). His is an excellent review of the causes and
nature of the revolution. Since, as Griffiths demonstrates, Bloy so well represents the group, and indeed gives them his spirit, we will limit our discussion of the movement to a study of Bloy.

[4] Courthion cautions vaguely: "It would be a mistake to attribute more
importance to this influence than it had." P. 98.

[5] Venturi, 1948, p. 22.

[6] 1753-1821. One of the founders and certainly the ablest leader of the
Neo-Catholic anti-revolutionary movement.

[7] *L'Homme* (Paris: Librairie Académique, 1921), Lasserre in introduction,
p. xxi.

[8] *Ibid.*, p. 18.

[9] *Ibid.*, pp. 387, 388.

humanity. It ought to keep watch over the cradle of Jesus Christ, and keep close to his tomb."[10] Nor is there any alternative to this art. Art must tell the truth and that means the religious truth. "Art which is associated with degenerate man is obliged to disguise what it persists in painting, for the old man is ugly. Art thus conceived is a falsehood."[11] Hello sums up the path man must take: "Live in the Truth, think as you live and speak as you think."[12]

Bloy found in Hello a spiritual companion, if not a mentor. One commentator claims that "all the ideas were in Hello before they were roared in Bloy."[13] From 1870 to 1880, when the contact between Bloy and Hello was the closest, Bloy also met Father Tardiff de Moidrey (d. 1879) who added to Hello's ideas a theory of exegesis that was to be very influential.[14] De Moidrey taught that every word in the Bible is to be taken as referring to the Holy Trinity. God only speaks of himself. Bloy extended the idea from all of Scripture to all of history. God is to be seen in everything, in good and in evil, in Cain and in Abel. From this, Bloy concluded that all of history is part of the sufferings of God in Christ. This timeless drama reduces all historical events to moments of the divine pathos, spiritualizing not only history but also social conditions.

All of these currents merged in the cold, cynical Bloy. Born in Périgeux in 1846, he worked for a while on the railroads and was converted to Catholicism, as he says, "after ten years in an impure novitiate in the latrines of philosophic examinations."[15] According to Griffiths, this was probably just before 1870.[16]

Bloy's odyssey continued in 1877 when he began to live with the prostitute Anne-Marie Roulet. She soon was converted and began to surpass Bloy in her mysticism. Their bizarre spiritual experiences and Anne-Marie's revelations[17] led them to expect the imminent end

---

[10] *Ibid.,* p. 373.

[11] *Ibid.,* p. 424. Bloy repeats this same thought in *La Femme pauvre:* "When art is conceived otherwise than on its knees, it must necessarily be on its back or its belly. And this is what is called passional art, the only thing that can, at this point, give a semblance of palpitation to human hearts, hung like tripe in the devil's butcher shop." (Paris: Mercure de France, 1937), p. 171.

[12] *Ibid.,* p. 393.

[13] Stanislas Fumet. *Mission de Léon Bloy* (Bruges: Desclée de Brouwer, 1935), pp. 141, 142. Fumet notes their friendship was a close one and though Hello was kept from Bloy for a while by Hello's suspicious wife, their common apocalyptic interests inevitably brought them together. Cf. Seillière, *Léon Bloy* (Paris: Nouvelle Revue, 1936), p. 57.

[14] Griffiths, *op. cit.,* pp. 50, 51.

[15] *Le Désespéré* (Paris: Mercure de France, 1967), pp. 25ff.

[16] *Op. cit.,* p. 11.

[17] Bloy, we learn, was at first cautious about her pronouncements, but Hello urged him to take these things seriously. *Ibid.,* p. 139.

of the world. This period with its horror and its ecstasy is recounted, thoroughly romanticized, in *Le Désespéré* (The Desperate One), which appeared in 1886 and is one of Bloy's most important books.

With the publishing of this autobiographical novel, Bloy launched one of the most unusual literary careers imaginable. "His life," declares one biographer, "was a permanent scandal that suited his century."[18] During most of his life he was kept safely outside the stream of cultured society. He was never decorated or honored in any way. And that suited him well.[19] He did not write his books to sell—he expected they would not (he even entitled one volume of his journal *L'Invendable* [The Unmarketable])—but, in the crude but somehow appropriate words of Rouault, he wrote to vomit his age. Remarks Rouault: "He belched on cheap journalism and all things mediocre."[20]

If his career was eccentric, his impact has been profound, especially in the area of Catholic literature. One writer asserts of Bloy: "He was an initiator of a movement that penetrated to the heart of things Catholic."[21] Some, such as Jacques and Raïssa Maritain, were converted through his influence. Many others—Claudel, Mauriac, Baumann, and even Graham Greene—went to him for inspiration.[22]

We must first examine Bloy's faith, for only through this source can we grasp the meaning of his work. His was a faith at once mystical and supernatural, revolutionary and apocalyptic. Its supernatural character follows from the nature of faith: an alliance frankly divine and super-terrestrial. In 1870 he acknowledged writing to a Miss Delabelle:

> I see that all true Christians can, indeed should, live a completely supernatural life, totally above all earthly preoccupations, and that among them—as among the angels—there is a mysterious bond.[23]

Man is forced, however, to live "in an irreparable deprivation of the view of God."[24] Such existence is only endured, never enjoyed.

Religious experience must then be mystical. For Bloy every encounter with God involves a self-transcending ecstasy. Marchenoir,

---

[18] Prevost and D'Amat, eds. *Dictionnaire de biographie Française, in loc.*
[19] Rouault tells us this in *SI*, p. 58, though Seillière, *op. cit.*, p. 163, records that at the end of his life he was living in Paris as a respectable member of a literary society.
[20] *SI*, p. 58.
[21] Brady, *op. cit.*, p. 14.
[22] See Griffiths' comment on Greene, *op. cit.*, p. 358. See also the Maritains' account of their conversion, in Raïssa Maritain, *op. cit.*, vol. II, p. 40.
[23] Quoted in Fumet, *op. cit.*, p. 64.
[24] *Le Désespéré*, p. 37. Hereafter referred to as *LD*.

who clearly represents himself in *Le Désespéré*, spends long periods
on his knees. His experiences are described in this way: "his religious
soul took wing . . . an hypertrophy of joy swelled his heart until it
seemed his chest would burst."[25] His prayers often brought him
what he termed superhuman transports.[26] Accordingly, he liked religious ritual very little for its programming of the spiritual life and
disallowing "every natural and spontaneous impulsion."[27]

More than one observer has doubted whether the extremes to
which Bloy went during this period were orthodox or even Christian. Seillière sees in such supernatural bursts only a tonic for the
very human will to power.[28] Griffiths asserts of Bloy: "In the mystical
sphere above all, many of his exaggerations were to bring the
revival dangerously near to heresy."[29] Yet we cannot doubt that
there was a deep and genuine core to Bloy's spiritual life. Bloy
himself recognized his excesses when he confessed in 1914: "I have
not done what God willed for me, that is certain. I have dreamed,
on the contrary, what I wanted of God."[30]

Extreme or not, this passion was the ground for Bloy's belief in
his vocation as a prophetic calling. It was his duty to decry materialism, mediocrity or spiritual formalism, and he never hesitated to
use his office. Bloy's faith, in this context, was revolutionary. "If
Beauty persecutes and devours us," he said, "in return let us perse-
cute the whole creation."[31] The rich were a special object of his
fury. Since they obviously enjoy wealth at the expense of the poor,
they are certain to receive eternal punishment.[32] As a result of
the revolution which Bloy proclaims, all rich are to consider themselves "the attendants and domestics of the poor." For the poor
man, on the other hand, "his need is the measure of what is due
him."[33] Here his revolutionary spirit became reactionary. Poverty,
a sign of sanctity, is to be sought and not shunned. And Bloy
practiced what he preached. He so frequently sought material help
from his friends, studiously avoiding any sign of gratitude that
would indicate it was not his due, that he was called the "ungrate-

---

[25] *Ibid.*, p. 375.

[26] *Ibid.*, pp. 378, 380.

[27] *Ibid.*, p. 220. Marchenoir goes on to blast the church in an almost
Kierkegaardian fashion, ending with the final condemnation: that it is
mediocre. Pp. 225ff.

[28] Seillière, *op. cit.*, pp. 239, 204. He calls such adventures: "erotic
amoralisms."

[29] *Op. cit.*, p. 12.

[30] Quoted in Seillière, *op. cit.*, p. 253.

[31] *Ibid.*, p. 25.

[32] Cf. Brady, *op. cit.*, pp. 40-41. Here the United States receives a special
portion of his wrath.

[33] *LD*, p. 426, and Fumet, *op. cit.*, p. 271.

ful beggar," and his friends accused him of bringing poverty into dishonor.[34]

Suffering, as well as poverty, is the lot of man. Bloy's notion of the value of suffering brings to mind Saint Thérèse (1515-1582) and Saint Jean de la Croix (1542-1591).[35] The all-consuming, exquisitely painful nature of faith for Bloy reflects the medieval concept of *blessures d'amour* (wounds of love). The latter were described as very strong impressions of the presence of God, sudden shining sensations that leave the soul thirsting for a full possession of God with a thirst that is at once painful and sweet beyond all expression. The result is printed on the soul in indelible characters: "the resolve to suffer for God; the desire to have many crosses to bear."[36]

Bloy connects this concept with the mystical view of Christ's passion referred to above. For Bloy, human suffering is not only supplemental to the agony of Christ but, symbolically, that very agony itself.[37] Man must bear "the face of Christ in order to receive the slap of any hand at all." So certainly is this the case that the Image of God is almost defined in man's capacity to suffer.[38] Bloy believes that before the death of Christ suffering had no divine sanction. Christ at his death made possible the perfect penitence. At Calvary "suffering crossed the infinite abyss which separates the Accident from the Substance, and became NECESSARY."[39]

Why, in Bloy's view, is suffering inevitable? There are apparently two distinct reasons. At times Bloy calls suffering man's vocation as a proof of his love for God.[40] Thus Veronique (actually Anne-Marie), the prostitute in *Le Désespéré*, soon found it impossible to separate Marchenoir from Christ, even in prayer: ". . . both agonizing because of their love for me."[41] In this sense suffering is man's only link with the supernatural.[42] But suffering is also indispensable because of man's evil nature. Man is prey to an insatiable concupiscence and must purge himself through suffering. Bloy steered carefully

---

[34] Robert Baldick. *The Life of J.-K. Huysmans* (Oxford: Clarendon Press, 1955), p. 125.

[35] Raïssa Maritain in acknowledging the impact of these mystics on her early Christian life calls them "the doctors *par excellence* of the spiritual life." *Op. cit.,* vol. II, p. 42. It would be unusual indeed if this impression were not conveyed to her at least in part by Bloy.

[36] C. Baumgartner, *op. cit.,* p. 1725.

[37] Griffiths, *op. cit.,* pp. 175-181. Though at the core, Griffiths notes, lies the perfectly orthodox view of vicarious suffering.

[38] Fumet, *op. cit.,* pp. 242 and 261. Men are "beings made in the image of the God that suffers. . . ."

[39] *LD,* p. 184.

[40] Brady, *op. cit.,* p. 246.

[41] *LD,* p. 387.

[42] Griffiths, *op. cit.,* p. 176.

clear of any moralism that would render this kind of suffering less necessary. Indeed, war and fighting were for him opportunities for sanctity.[43]

From suffering are born loneliness and unhappiness, two other characteristics of Bloy's "earthly paradise." For Bloy—and here one is reminded forcefully of Rouault—"God is the great Lonely One who speaks only to the lonely."[44] God shares his glory only with those who are solitary; the more one approaches God, the more lonely one will be. But unhappiness is woven into the fabric of life as well. Bloy confides in a letter to his fiancée, Jeanne Molbech: "I am sad by nature, as one is small or blond."[45] Maritain saw this boundless melancholy, founded upon the agony in which the world lives, as the one true, abiding reality for Bloy. All else was a phantom.[46]

A word more is in order about Bloy's apocalyptic expectations. The ecstatic nature of Bloy's faith and his view of his own vocation made him grasp eagerly at the revelations received by Anne Roulet. If he thought himself capable of denouncing the filth of the world, he was as quick to announce the imminent destruction of all things. Although we have seen that the exegetical writings of Tardiff de Moidrey served as a starting point for his mystical interpretation of history, his views soon defied any systematization.[47] His horror at the human situation only quickened the anticipation of some unimaginable event. Dates were set as to when the event would occur, and when the dates passed harmlessly, Seillière informs us that Bloy would curse God for his forbearance.[48] Bloy persisted in his calculations and was certain even at the start of World War I that the end was near.[49]

To conclude this brief look at the major themes of Bloy's thought, it would be well to make some observations about the man. Bloy describes himself accurately when he says of Marchenoir in *Le Désespéré* that "... his heart had been the evangelist to his rea-

---

[43] Brady, *op. cit.,* p. 17. So necessary were these things that Bloy even regrets the lack of suffering in Paradise. *Ibid.,* p. 221.

[44] *LD,* p. 105.

[45] Fumet, *op. cit.,* p. 39. In 1890 Bloy married Miss Molbech and lived rather happily with her for the remainder of his life.

[46] Jacques Maritain. "Quelques pages sur Léon Bloy." *Cahiers de la Quinzaine* (Paris, 1927).

[47] Cf. Griffiths, *op. cit.,* p. 175. It is true as well that his conceptions betrayed the impact of Joachim de Flore, but Seillière is certainly mistaken in likening Bloy's views to the expectations of the Early Church, which were much more definitive and ethically motivating.

[48] Seillière, *op. cit.,* p. 50.

[49] Fumet, *op. cit.,* p. 330. Fumet dismisses Bloy's ideas as trying to give quite simply a definite shape to his wishes. P. 331.

son."[50] Just so. Léon Bloy was a man more given to tortuous experience than to sober reflection. And it was just this lived-through quality that gave his writing a lively, if at times aoristic, quality. Yet faith shone through all he did—spontaneous, paroxysmal, emotional and yet heartfelt faith with a constant awareness of a living and transcendent God.

We should be careful not to see Bloy as an unfeeling cynic, for he certainly was not. Vicious and violent he was, but throughout his work runs a thread of what Colleye has called "this tenderness and this optimism of his soul."[51] His writings reveal charity, but as Marchenoir muses, "Justice and mercy are identical and consubstantial in their absolute state."[52] Love abides; but love, too, must shout anathemas.

It is difficult to make any summary of Bloy's thought, for he escapes classification. This much is certain: Bloy was a man who, as a Christian, could not adhere to the form of the world. "The angel that defends the closed Garden does not allow flesh and blood to enter the holy place."[53] Bloy so stressed the transcendence of God that he had no real sense of his immanence. The incarnation was a mystical, timeless, epic-like event rather than a physical, historical presence of God identifying with his creation.[54] Moreover, in interpreting history mystically and reality symbolically, he had lost the sense of God as creator and sustainer of the physical world. Thus a good part of his ranting against the world was theologically improper. Finitude is no more a moral defect than created reality is essentially ugly.

Naturally, these ideas determined how he worked as a creator and viewed the nature of art. Mysticism had invaded here as well. Art to him was a kind of superhuman activity, almost diabolic in essence. But through transubstantiation art can return to an alliance with God, and the artist can then grow in love until he learns the very secrets of God himself.[55] As there is no "path" to sainthood, there is none to genius. Sanctity is an *octroi surnaturel* (supernatural grant).[56] Nor is there a road to greatness in art; it must be infused. Just as man's nature in no way changes for the better at conversion —indeed, we have seen that suffering and unhappiness may actually increase—so achievement in art is due more to illumination than

[50] *LD,* p. 59.
[51] Colleye, *op. cit.,* p. 238.
[52] *LD,* p. 294.
[53] Fumet, *op. cit.,* p. 245.
[54] Bloy's attempts at a kind of mystical immanence were at times simply vulgar: "if you need my Son, look for him in the garbage." *LD,* p. 244.
[55] Seillière, *op. cit.,* pp. 168, 181.
[56] *Ibid.,* p. 185.

to diligence. The Christian experiences no deepening of human qualities, nor can he live in hope. Hope, Marchenoir admits, is one quality he would never have.[57] Moreover, since faith is vision from God's absolute perspective, Christian art must be undertaken from the same viewpoint. It must inevitably show human suffering and imperfection, for the Christian and the artist can only curse himself and the world. Bloy's diary for Easter, 1904, both illustrates this self-judgment and displays the depth of feeling such art can reach:

> April 4, 1904. Monday of Easter. When the glories of Easter come to mind, my soul is seized with a particular sadness that might be translated thus: I am with Jesus in his Resurrection even though I have not been with him in his death. I have not suffered with him, my fasting has been a mockery. Therefore, I have no right to rejoice with the Saints. And I would die of shame if it were not for the incomprehensible Divine pity.[58]

Despite such self-judgment, Bloy was often tempted to great self-confidence and artistic pride,[59] as was clearly manifested in his judgment of Rouault's painting, which we will discuss below. An absolute perspective eliminated any variation or doubt, and his was an uncompromising vocation. Later in life, nevertheless, he was to admit: "Art has not the least word to say as soon as God manifests himself."[60]

What were Rouault's contacts with Bloy? The first certain contact seems to have been when Rouault came across some books of Bloy's. It was 1903, the year the Gustave Moreau Museum had officially opened (on January 14) in the house where Moreau had lived. Rouault had been designated by his teacher to be the curator. On one occasion Rouault, looking through the books in the section of the museum where Moreau had lived, came across Le Désespéré and La Femme pauvre. He read them and liked their simple directness, a sharp contrast with the symbolism that was current. Courthion tells us that Rouault was so enthralled with some parts that he began talking to all his friends about the passages Bloy had devoted to the middle ages, to Byzantium and to 'Holy Poverty.'[61] Bloy's medieval interest clearly stimulated Rouault's own fascination with that period.

Needless to say, Rouault was anxious to meet Bloy. On March

---

[57] LD, p. 177.
[58] Léon Bloy. Quatre ans de captivité à Cochons-sur-Marne (Paris: Mercure de France, 1959), vol. II, pp. 250, 251.
[59] Seillière, op. cit., pp. 160ff.
[60] Ibid., p. 163.
[61] Courthion, p. 97.

16, 1904, we read this entry in Bloy's journal, written in his characteristic blunt fashion:

> I learn that the painter Georges Rouault, a student of Gustave Moreau, is enthusiastic about me. He found at Moreau's my book *La Femme pauvre* . . . this book struck his heart, wounded him incurably. I shudder to think of the punishment in store for this unhappy wretch.[62]

Through a mutual friend, Auguste Marguillier, secretary of the *Gazette des Beaux-Arts,* they met at a luncheon in April. For Rouault, 25 years younger than Bloy, it was doubtless a coveted opportunity. Bloy recounted the occasion:

> Lunch, Marguillier. He went to fetch Rouault who was still impatient to meet me. A nice face. Apparently he has a lot of talent, too much, in fact, not to remain poor. He is the devoted type who naively expresses his enthusiasm for me.[63]

Rouault had his own impressions of the "Ungrateful Beggar": ". . . a man dressed like a carpenter in a corduroy suit which, at that time, cost about two louis . . . with heavy worker's shoes, sometimes holding onto a pilgrim's staff with his strong hand."[64] In another place he reminisces: "I can still see him, with his white forelock on his forehead, and large eyes that so easily became threatening, and, as easily, compassionate."[65]

Rouault was at a very impressionable time of life. Though he was 33, he had just passed through his most difficult period and was still finding his way as a painter. The friendship with Bloy, which was to be quite close, made a profound impact on Rouault. We will have occasion throughout this study to reflect upon their striking similarity of thought. This is especially clear in Rouault's feeling for the outcast and the suffering, and his view of the Passion may have been affected as well. There can be little doubt that the reading of Bloy's books played a major part in Rouault's thinking at that time, if only to confirm him in a direction already taken. In any case, an understanding of Bloy and his part in the revival is an essential backdrop against which to view the work of Rouault. The artistic sensitivities of both were inspired by the same horrors prominent in the *fin de siècle* mentality, and motivated by a common hope in the power and justice of God.

On the other hand, we cannot always trace specific inspirations. Since most of Rouault's "tableaux noirs" date from 1905 and later, it might be tempting to see here the influence of Bloy. This would

---

[62] *Quatre ans . . .* , p. 248.
[63] Unpublished diary quoted by Courthion, p. 97
[64] *SI*, p. 56.
[65] Quoted in Courthion, p. 97.

be a mistake, as Courthion shows, for Rouault first painted prostitutes in 1903, perhaps as early as 1902.[66] In this instance, Rouault's tendency was fixed before any contact with Bloy.

Jacques and Raïssa Maritain met Rouault for the first time in November of 1905, and Raïssa recalls evenings when she and her husband would sit and listen to Rouault and Bloy discuss "every important question about art."[67] Although Bloy's horrible vision seemed so like that exhibited in the early period of Rouault's work, Bloy found it impossible to accept such pictorial darkness. On returning from the Salon d'Automne, November 5, 1904, Bloy wrote in his diary:

> A sermon on death would have been just as suitable an opening for the Salon d'Automne that I visited with anguish. I had the grief to understand nothing of the *sketches* of my friend Rouault, who probably had as great a future as any modern painter, but who has been pulled down by some weird vertigo. The miserable man began with Rembrandt, only to throw himself into outer darkness.[68]

In the fall of 1905, the differences between Rouault and Bloy began to reach appalling extremes. Earlier that year Bloy had dedicated to Rouault the first chapter of the book *Belluaires et porchers* entitled "Les Chants de Maldoror." Strangely, in the dedication he lauded Rouault's "chants" as the "Good News of damnation."[69] Later in the same year, during a visit to the Gustave Moreau Museum, Bloy had seen one of Rouault's earlier works, "The Child Jesus Among the Doctors," whose classical style, we have noted, recalls Rembrandt. Of this he says:

> A twelve-year-old God and three hypocrites who are, together, a hundred and eighty years old. Jesus is telling them the truth, that is himself, and as he speaks, we seem to see coming out of these murderous men the horrible beast that possesses him and that will one day devour him. I did not know that Rouault had such talent. I know it now and told him so with enthusiasm.[70]

Rarely had Rouault such a sympathetic and understanding viewer.

Then Rouault displayed a triptych in the Salon d'Automne of 1905, one panel of which was entitled: "Monsieur et Madame

---

[66] Courthion, p. 99. These paintings were not shown until the Salon d'Automne, 1904.

[67] *Op. cit.,* vol. I, p. 220. The Maritains were baptized in the summer of 1906. One wonders how greatly these discussions might have impressed Jacques' own thinking, who was then only 24. Raïssa Maritain states of Rouault: "It is in thinking of him especially that Jacques wrote *Art and Scholasticism.*" P. 223.

[68] Bloy. *L'Invendable* (Paris: Mercure de France, 1919), p. 43. Italics his.

[69] Raïssa Maritain, *op. cit.,* vol. II, p. 43.

[70] *L'Invendable,* p. 71.

Poulot. Léon Bloy. *La Femme pauvre.*" It portrayed a bourgeois couple, meant to be the two hypocritical dandies from Bloy's book. This was the final blow for Bloy. On returning from a second visit to that Salon on October 31, 1905,[71] he wrote:

> This artist that I thought was capable of painting seraphim seems only able to imagine the most atrocious and avenging caricatures. The meanness of the bourgeois works in him such a violent reaction of horror that his art seems to be a mortally wounded creature. He wanted to make my *Poulot*. Not for all the money in the world would I accept this *illustration*. Something very tragic was needed: Two bourgeois characters, male and female, guileless, peaceable, merciful; good enough to make the horses of the constellations foam at the mouth. He has made two assassins from the poor district.[72]

Eventually Bloy's feeling reached such a pitch that on May 1, 1907, he vented the following blast:

> To Georges Rouault, my dear friend (!), I saw the Salon des Indé-pendants yesterday. Independent of what? These slaves of stupidity and absolute ignorance! Naturally I saw your unique and sempiternal canvases: always the same slut and the same clown, with the single and lamentable difference that each time the worthlessness appears greater. You say: "Oh yes, Léon Bloy does not like what I do. Bloy is a writer, a poet, who has his needs and acts freely. He does not understand. That is all there is to it." Alas!! My poor friend, how can I make you understand that so far from being a mere dilettante, I am a true *judge* (by divine commission we believe), *your judge, especially sent.* At your present stage it is no longer a question of painting or some art, but of your dignity as a man, of your soul which is so precious, and you are foolish not to believe me. Today I have two things to say to you, only two, the last! After which you will be no more to me than a *mere acquaintance!* First, you are attracted exclusively by the ugly; you seem to be enthralled by the hideous. Secondly, if you were a man of prayer, a *eucharistic*, you would not be able to paint such terrible canvases. A reflective man would feel a little fearful at this point. I have told or written you several times that your obsession grieves me. That has not seemed very serious to you, has it? You have thought of it as a rather amusing whim without suspecting for one minute that it is a question of a very real grief, of a man of the *absolute*, and that is a serious thing. It is time to stop![73]

These remarks, of course, reveal more about Bloy than they do of Rouault's work. A man of the absolute, Bloy could not compromise.

Despite his protesting, Bloy was inevitably being associated with Rouault. One has only to see Rouault's paintings during this period

---

[71] If we are correct in our chronology, this would be the day before a *soirée* in which the Maritains, Bloy and Rouault were together. An interesting evening that!

[72] *L'Invendable*, p. 132. Italics his.

[73] *Ibid.*, pp. 289, 290.

and read but a few pages from Bloy to see how natural is the association. On this Rouault was to comment later, revealing his own calm throughout the debate. "I have become the Léon Bloy of painting without having wanted it or sought it. But Léon Bloy himself would protest violently even though he had a sincere and genuine affection for me."[74] And through it all Rouault was a loyal friend. Courthion tells us that even until the last year of Bloy's life Rouault would take his family on Sundays to visit the "Ungrateful Beggar."[75]

Rouault's words quoted above show that he never consciously sought to transfer Bloy's thinking onto his canvases. In the section on Bloy in *Souvenirs Intimes*, one senses that Rouault felt a deep affection and respect and yet also an independence. Of their affinity he reflects: "*It is the character of the spirit* that binds certain artists together throughout the centuries, and in widely different arts, by *their means of expression.*"[76] But he cautions: "It is too simple a game that is often false to compare artists who practice different arts."[77] Between the two there was more a spiritual liaison than a unity of thought.

Rouault's side of the debate was low-keyed, partially because of Rouault's temperament. He did not have the fiery perversity of Bloy. But there was another reason, which we shall only mention here and discuss further on. Rouault's paintings grew out of much more than mere artistic experimentation. They flowed from an internal necessity, as Maritain observes: "Prostitutes, clowns . . . he was searching for himself, I mean his own inner harmony, in the world of form and color."[78] Raïssa Maritain sees Rouault's quiet before Bloy's invectives as a means to find and test the obstacles which the painter felt within himself. Perhaps he wanted to prove the strength of his painterly instinct, an instinct "that drew him toward the unknown and that had to triumph over every obstacle."[79]

How can we account for Bloy's vehemence toward a vision so much like his own? One reason, often discussed, is Bloy's complete lack of discernment in the plastic arts. Rouault told Courthion that "in artistic matters, Bloy followed his own sentimental impulses. You must understand, I am sure, that there are things that remain

---

[74] *SI,* p. 58.
[75] Courthion, p. 104. June 11, 1917, was Rouault's last visit; Bloy died that same year.
[76] *SI,* p. 58. Italics his.
[77] *Ibid.*
[78] Jacques Maritain. "Georges Rouault." *La Revue Universelle,* 1924, no. 2, p. 508.
[79] *Op. cit.,* vol. II, p. 221.

a closed book to people who see very clearly in another domain."[80] This is doubtless a sound judgment. Bloy could not understand Rouault because he felt his young friend, like Cézanne, lacked the academic finish that he liked. But such a finish, as Venturi astutely points out, was precisely that which Bloy himself was never able to achieve in his own work.[81]

Lack of discernment was involved, but it was not the whole reason. Nor is Rouzet's contention, that portraying the horrors of man in painting may have been for Bloy a sort of sacrilege against the image of God in man, entirely convincing. We have seen that Bloy's view of the *imago* would offer no such hindrance.[82] But it is possible that Bloy could not abide the shock of seeing his own vision translated into painting. Perhaps, as James Soby hypothesizes, "Bloy could not accept the projection in visual terms of a feverish conviction which so *startlingly* paralleled his own."[83]

But a more satisfying explanation may be found in Bloy's creed as an artist and a Christian, which Rouault quotes:

> To tell the truth to all the world, on all subjects, whatever may be the consequences. I declare my firm intention to exhibit an essential want of moderation, to be always brazen and replace all sense of proportion by a perpetual excess.[84]

The audacity of such a confession impresses us more than its artistic sensitivity. As Fumet frankly admits, in Bloy the Christian had "summarily mastered the artist."[85] Bloy is bound to tell the truth, his truth, stripped of the countless nuances and ironies in which it necessarily clothes itself. But no single man is able to see things perfectly, and he who sees only in absolutes risks making the 'truth' into a personal aberration. And here perhaps we have found Bloy's basic difference from Rouault. For Rouault, by contrast, always remained a sensitive artist as well as a man of faith.

---

[80] Courthion, p. 104.

[81] Venturi, 1959, p. 40. Of such comments Raïssa Maritain objects that Venturi failed to recognize in Bloy "the greatness of the writer." *Op. cit.*, vol. II, p. 42n.

[82] George Rouzet. "Courrier de Paris: Georges Rouault." *Le Thyrse*. 1938, no. 40, p. 172. He goes on to speculate that this may be the reason behind the Second Commandment.

[83] *Op. cit.*, p. 10. Italics mine.

[84] *SI*, p. 57. "Program," says Rouault wryly, "that was always scrupulously fulfilled."

[85] *Op. cit.*, p. 381. Seillière makes a similar criticism, claiming that Bloy often simply did his own will in God's name. *Op. cit.*, p. 101.

4. Rouault's Artist Contemporaries

Gustave Moreau had predicted for Rouault a future of sober, religious art. "I hope," he had said, "that the amateurs and dealers may be intelligent enough not to ask anything else from you but to accept it as it is." That path would be a lonely one, he prophesied. To this Rouault responded:

> Solitude is not always what certain exhibitionists think it is: address, ability, or choice. Once a leper, always a leper, they say. So with being solitary: one is born alone, it is better that one dies the same.[1]

In this way Rouault explained what was to become more and more evident throughout his life: his artistic and spiritual loneliness. Critics have often noted his disengagement from his artistic contemporaries. He was no permanent member of any school, nor did he leave behind him a significant following.[2]

Yet Rouault sustained a vital relationship with the art world of his day. Not only did he attend the prestigious *Ecole des Beaux-Arts*, but he counted among his friends many of the leaders of twentieth-century art. He was active with Desvallières, Matisse, Marquet, Piot, Lehmann, Baignères, and the critic Y. Rambosson in founding the Salon d'Automne in 1903,[3] which proved an artistic event of capital importance in the early years of this century. Rouault's writings and conversations would be almost opaque to anyone not familiar with the art world of that day, so replete are they with allusions to art

---

[1] *SI*, p. 30.

[2] Alexander Watt. "Paris Commentary." *The Studio*, July-December, 1952, p. 188; Zervos, 1952, *op. cit.*, p. 102; and Paul Fierens. "Georges Rouault." *L'Amour de L'Art*, 1933, no. 1933, p. 139. These have been among those making this observation, though Fierens sees Rouault's influence in Gromaire and Georg. Janson believes the only one following Rouault's lead in Paris was Chaim Soutine (1894-1943), an immigrant from Eastern Europe. *History of Art* (New York: Abrams, 1962), p. 514.

[3] Courthion, p. 389.

and artists. Rouault often spoke of the impossibility of total isolation. He could not help breathing the air of his day.[4]

Faced with such apparent contradictions, we will attempt in this chapter to discern what sort of rapport Rouault in fact felt with his contemporaries. Though technical interests are not our primary concern, it will be necessary to call attention to what critics have claimed about his artistic parentage. Our concentration on his artistic involvement will help us understand more fully the personal questions to be raised further along.

No artist develops in isolation, and Rouault, like every artist, was influenced by the artistic currents of his time. One of these was the conflict between impressionism, taken in its most general sense as the depiction of sensations, and expressionism, which refers to the expression of inner emotions. This conflict is a perpetual one, as André de Ridder observes,[5] sometimes fought within one artist's mind. Of course, many critics have seen expressionistic tendencies in Rouault,[6] and, since French art has generally leaned toward impressionism, he is often grouped with northern and Germanic expressionists. Descargues claims that Rouault is the only recent French artist who remained expressionist throughout his life.[7]

Michel Hoog has suggested that the impact of Norwegian expressionist Edvard Munch (1863-1944) is evident in Rouault's works.[8] There was a great deal of contact between Munch and the artists of Paris, especially between the years 1890 and 1900,[9] and Rouault must have been exposed to and impressed by Munch's painting. But I have not been able to find a single reference to Munch in Rouault's writings, nor do Courthion or Venturi (1959) mention Munch at all. Certainly Rouault's expression of dramatic states is similar to that of Munch. However, an examination of Munch's work reveals that intense emotions are treated, in contrast to Rouault's practice, more as personal experiences than as profound, religious statements of the human situation.

---

[4] *SI,* p. 30.

[5] André de Ridder. "Naissance de l'expressionisme." *L'Amour de l'Art,* 1934, no. 15, pp. 376, 387. It is perhaps an oversimplification to say as he does that in expressionism what dominates is "the desire to become primitive and strong again."

[6] Cf. Georges Charensol. *Georges Rouault: l'homme et l'oeuvre* (Paris: Editions des Quatre Chemins, 1926), p. 16.

[7] Pierre Descargues. "Les Chefs de file de l'expressionisme français." *La Connaissance des Arts,* July, 1961, no. 113, p. 69.

[8] In a personal interview with the author.

[9] Ragna Stang described this in some detail noting the lively debate being carried on at the time by the Parisian critics over Munch. Exposition catalogue (Strasbourg: Cabinet des Estampes, 1969), no pagination.

Others have likened Rouault to Van Gogh. For both, comments Descargues, "the vision of the painters' world . . . is troubled by the sense of death, affected by a profound disgust of existence and its pleasures."[10] But we do not find in Rouault the violent and troubled spirit, manifested in a mania for writing and self-analysis, that characterized Van Gogh. Rouault's vision of sorrow and violence did not entail a violent and troubled spirit such as Van Gogh's. Courthion sees Rouault as a religious artist in the same sense that Van Gogh was. But Van Gogh, he continues, tried to converse directly with God while Rouault relied on his grace. "The result," Courthion concludes, "was that the Dutchman's vision became confused and frightened, whereas the Bréton Rouault's faith grew constantly firmer."[11]

In all events, the alliance of Rouault with expressionism is a relative one.[12] Rouault was expressionistic more as a need of his personality than a description of his work. Besides, as we have noted, the expressionist school at the beginning of this century was not fundamentally French. There was at that time quite a different sort of artistic investigation going on, called Fauvism after 1905, which much more faithfully reflected the French scene.[13] As Descargues observes, "For the Germans expressionism was a manner of being. For the French, Fauvism was a search for self."[14]

As Puy, among others, has noted, Rouault shares with Fauvism a strong sense of decoration and a special interest in color (dating perhaps to Rouault's time as a stained-glass window apprentice). There is little doubt that Rouault participated in the experimentation with technique for which the Fauves have become well known. But unless the movement is very broadly understood, we cannot call Rouault a Fauve.[15]

---

[10] Descargues, op. cit., p. 70.

[11] Courthion, p. 346. In our chapter on nature, we shall discuss in more detail the affinities of these painters.

[12] It is well known that Rouault disliked classifications. Once when a critic called him an expressionist, he replied: "How can you classify artists like dead butterflies, that are pinned on cork, numbered and placed under glass? It's ridiculous!" Quoted in Marquette Bouvier. "Georges Rouault: expresionista y místico." Goya, 1958-60, no. 25-30, pp. 18, 19.

[13] On this movement see René Huyghe. "Histoire de l'art contemporain: le fauvisme: les coloristes." L'Amour de l'Art, 1933, no. 14, pp. 97-102, 129-132. And John Rewald. Post-Impressionism (New York: Museum of Modern Art, 1956).

[14] Descargues, op. cit., p. 69.

[15] Huyghe, op. cit., is one who tries to broaden Fauvism into three groups: (1) Those concerned with purely plastic problems, e.g., Matisse; (1) those with a strong temperament and expressionist tendencies, e.g., Rouault, Vlaminck; and (3) those longing to return to a nostalgic classicism such as

What distinguished him from this group? In exploring the plastic media Rouault was very much a part of the exciting artistic atmosphere at the turn of the century. He agreed with the Fauves, as Zervos shows, in their championing of the essential freedom of the creative act.[16] What characterized Rouault, in addition to this concern for lines and colors, was the overflow of his interior life into his paintings. Rouault believed that much of modern art, in its exclusive interest in technique, was going down a blind alley. By endless plastic research and emphasis on creative freedom, artists had divorced themselves from the concrete. In one place he called for an end to "this monster *individualism,* cause of all our troubles," which makes artists into "monsters of pride who claim discontentment with the visible world and then proceed to create a world in their image!"[17] Thus, humanly speaking, they are doomed to irrelevancy. But painting, to Rouault, was more than experimentation. Commenting once on Monet, he said: "To search on a more complicated and varied piano for exotic scales and novel harmonies that are as rare as they are subtle is not the be-all and end-all of art."[18]

Christian Zervos, in two noteworthy articles on Rouault, maintains that Rouault's unique genius lay in finding a proper balance between authority and freedom in his work. The authority to which he submitted was not only his faith but also the entire human condition in his time, and it included also the means of artistic expression and the continuity of tradition. Without this kind of conviction, Zervos goes on, one must "remain on the level of the incomplete, doomed to meet nothing but your own echo. . . . (Here) freedom finds itself perverted to such a degree that it is turned against itself and becomes formalism."[19] One cannot turn against the world and remain free. Rouault, always taking the real world into account, successfully resisted any rupture between the subject and the object. "With him, spirit and sensitivity penetrate the real and act on his work in a lively way."[20]

As we will see, Rouault's work underwent an artistic revolution after 1903 which can be viewed in the context of Fauvism. But

Derain. P. 99. Courthion is more blunt: "Rouault was never a real Fauve," p. 294. Cf. Michel Hoog. "La Donation Rouault au Louvre." *Etudes,* September, 1964, p. 217.

[16] Christian Zervos. "Approches de l'oeuvre de Rouault." *Les Cahiers d'Art,* 1952, p. 102.

[17] *Soliloques,* p. 91. Italics his.

[18] Rouault. "Claude Monet." *L'Amour de l'Art,* 1927, no. 8, p. 200.

[19] Zervos, 1952, *op. cit.,* p. 106.

[20] Christian Zervos. "Les Dernières oeuvres de Rouault." *Cahiers d'Art,* 1960, p. 175.

another equally momentous and related revolution, a moral and spiritual one, occurred at the same time.[21] As a result of these transformations, Rouault was his own guide and dictated the terms of his relationships with his artist contemporaries. Let us look at the most important among these in their rapport with Rouault, in order to evaluate Rouault's uniqueness. Questions we raise in discussing these contacts will often occupy our attention in the remainder of our study.

Paul Cézanne (1839-1906). Much in this quiet and serious craftsman from Aix-en-Provence personally attracted Rouault. Yet there remained deep dissimilarities. Influenced by impressionism, Cézanne wanted to make that kind of art something solid and durable. He sought to represent the object painted in all its pictorial depth and "to reproduce, not the finished object, but the fundamental movement that gives it its form."[22] Moreover, he strove to involve the objects in their interconnection on the canvas, introducing an organizing unity to the picture. In this way contours became less fixed and were introduced less to isolate the objects than to establish a liaison between neighboring colors.

Cézanne deeply affected all of his artistic contemporaries, Rouault among them. Cézanne taught them, as Venturi explains it, "the need for a coherence between the elements of the picture apart from all reference to external reality."[23] This discovery brought Rouault, as we have seen, into the kind of study the Fauves were conducting.

But Rouault could not follow Cézanne to the extremes that he took the theory. Cézanne's work is characterized by the complete absence of all organic life. Cézanne worked far from life and from men (his landscapes had no figures), producing an art that left aside all states of soul, all *Stimmung*.[24] But the example of Cézanne impressed young Rouault in a personal and intimate way, although the two never met. Moreover, Cézanne was like Rouault very solitary.[25] Having suffered so often at the hands of critics, Cézanne

---

[21] Venturi, 1959, p. 14, emphasizes the parallel importance of the two revolutions.

[22] Fritz Novotny. *Cézanne* (Paris: Editions du Phaidon, 1948), pp. 5-9.

[23] Venturi, 1959, p. 31. Cf. also Roger Fry. "La Peinture moderne en France." *L'Amour de l'Art*, 1924, no. 4, pp. 141ff.

[24] Novotny, *op. cit.*, p. 7.

[25] The impression this made on Rouault is revealed in a soliloquy that Rouault put into the mouth of Cézanne *(Mercure de France*, November 16, 1910) entitled: "Noli Me Tangere." In it "Cézanne" urges those who wish to come to see him to look at his work, which is his purest testimony.

was chary of public exposition. But he loved his materials and he loved painting.

Renoir tells a charming story that well displays Cézanne's love of his work. One day Renoir saw Cézanne walking down the street with a large canvas trailing behind him that reached clear to the ground. "There is no more money in the house!" Cézanne told him. "I am going to try and sell this canvas. It is a study that is quite well realized, wouldn't you say?" Renoir admired the famous "Baigneurs" (of the Caillebotte collection) which Cézanne showed him.

Several days later Renoir met Cézanne again. Smiling radiantly, the latter said to him: "My good Renoir, I am very happy! My picture has had the greatest success. It is with someone who loves it." Renoir of course thought the lucky artist had found an admiring amateur. The "amateur" turned out to be a Cabaner, a poor musician, who worked a long day for 45 old francs a day. They had met on the street, and the musician was so struck with the painting that Cézanne gave it to him.[26]

Venturi quotes a statement which Cézanne had made into a law. "I have always worked not to achieve the finish that imbeciles admire. . . . I ought not try to complete a work except to give the most genuine and profound pleasure."[27] This was the direction Cézanne took throughout his life, and here Rouault is his follower: not to "finish" but to realize perfectly. Venturi calls this discovery "one of the greatest conquests of modern taste, and just here is the limitation to which Rouault submitted himself."[28] As Rouault expresses it in his section on Cézanne in *Souvenirs Intimes:* "It is less a question of being strong than of singing well your little song." He comments, about Cézanne, "How often the example of his life and his researches has illuminated my way, and relaxed my mind and heart." And what was this example? "Your lesson," Rouault says to Cézanne in the closing poem of that chapter, "is to be yourself."[29]

Henri Matisse (1869-1954). Matisse and Rouault were closer in age, and not only were they fellow-students under Moreau, but they remained good friends throughout their lives. Matisse respected Rouault's painting. Courthion tells of seeing a reproduction of "The Old King" hanging in an honored place in Matisse's apartment. Matisse appreciated especially the density and force of Rouault's work.[30]

---

[26] Michel Drucker. *Renoir* (Paris: Editions Pierre Tisné, 1944), p. 126.
[27] Venturi, 1959, p. 82.
[28] *Ibid.*
[29] *SI,* pp. 71, 72.
[30] Courthion, p. 252.

Yet Matisse's own idea of painting was quite different from Rouault's. He viewed himself as a plastic technician. His confession as an artist is now famous:

> What I dream of is an art of equilibrium, of purity, of tranquility; with nothing alarming or disquieting . . . a sedative, a calmative . . . something like a good easy chair.[31]

Though Rouault makes no direct allusion to Matisse in his *Souvenirs Intimes,* in an article appearing in 1931 he does refer to him. He begins by recalling his own status as an outcast early in the century. He was "the undesirable," he recalls, because he could not perjure himself and speak another pictorial language than his own. What then does he think of purely decorative art which was the alternative in those days? "They have broken our eardrums," he muses, "with these discussions about Decorative Art. There is an art that is neither decorative nor sacred, to the extent that we can express ourselves pictorially."[32] Rouault goes on to say that Matisse would understand this kind of effort. Whether he appreciates this kind of art is another question and one Rouault did not raise. He proceeds instead to show that one can do profound religious art without really setting out to do it, as the primitives have done. They knew nothing of so-called religious art nor of decorative art either. "It was their nature, or rather their way of seeing, of feeling, of loving. Religion took the shape of their life, it was their reason for living."[33]

Finally at the end of the article, entitled "Evocations sur Matisse," he brings himself to speak of his friend, Matisse. Not wanting to express the condemnation that, if we are to believe other things he had said, he must have felt, Rouault admits a rebuke only in the third person. Some, he admits, would reproach Matisse for his prodigality and his ease in covering a flat surface with happy colors. Happiness was not so easy for Rouault. Nor was art. Creation for him was no game; it was a deadly serious pursuit.[34]

---

[31] Quoted in Huyghe, *op. cit.,* p. 99, who goes on to point out that here as with Cézanne there is no intimate allusion to himself, and so, in one sense, no real revolution but only a new art of the establishment, a new academicism.

[32] Rouault. "Evocations sur Matisse." *Les Chroniques du Jour,* April, 1931, no. 9, p. 8. Part of Rouault's hesitation to answer openly is due to his dissatisfaction with vague terms such as "decorative art," which can be commonplace or stunning. Here Matisse agreed with him (Courthion, p. 242). But there can be little doubt that Rouault understood and disliked Matisse's own program for decorative art, the confession of which we have quoted.

[33] *Ibid.*

[34] *Ibid.* Waldemar George concludes this article with a summary concern-

Courthion records an interesting interview that summarizes these differences. He asked both Rouault and Matisse the same question: If you were alone on a desert island where no one would see your work, would you continue to create? Matisse's answer was an emphatic "no." "There are no artists without a public," he explained. "An artist wants to be understood, a painter to be looked it." But Rouault acknowledged he would continue to paint "even without a single viewer, even with no hope of one."[35]

Pierre Auguste Renoir (1841-1919). Just after the death of Moreau (1898), Rouault moved to the Rue de la Rochefoucauld, where he lived for a year just across the landing from Renoir, an established and highly esteemed impressionist. Rouault was young, alone, and trying to find his way. Renoir was a meticulous worker, often redoing a hand or a back more than a hundred times. Even on Sunday he would come to work. Young Rouault, timid as he was, hardly addressed a word to the master, not wanting in the least to disturb his efforts.[36]

Renoir was the "painter of joy," enthralled with his vision of beauty. He sought to transmute nature to a higher, lyrical plane. Nudes and intimate feminine scenes especially suited his vision, but he was never vulgar. Maurice Denis once reflected on why Renoir's nudes were never shocking. "First of all because they are sane. The lyricism, the plastic sense of Renoir, has transfigured them. They are not idealized, thank God! They have become form and color."[37]

But Renoir had discovered that there could be no transfiguration apart from a living ideal. This he felt was missing among many of his contemporaries. Near the end of his life he deplored the loss of such an ideal and saw therein the principal cause of the decadence of modern art. He praised the religious sentiment which in former, sunnier days had provided art with an ideal.[38]

But what was Renoir's own ideal? Michel Drucker described Renoir's efforts in this way: "Renoir was impelled to search in a certain kind of plastic figures for a symbol common to all the sights of nature, with the unity of which he seemed to be more

---

ing Matisse that seems worth quoting in full: "The tendency of Matisse to mark out and localize colors within their borders (which are not the normal shape of objects nor related to the expected colors), represents the drama of the new man isolated in time and space. He is incapable of understanding the unity of the past, present and future, and the continuity of all dimensions, including the fourth, that is, duration." P. 8.

[35] Courthion, p. 300.
[36] *SI*, pp. 76, 77.
[37] In Michel Drucker, *op. cit.*, p. 178.
[38] *Ibid.*, p. 173.

and more imbued."[39] Germain Bazin points out the cosmic—if not religious—nature of this search. "He had to create an idea that would signify at once the cadence in the human spirit and the rhythm animating the universe: the *logos* and the *cosmos*."[40] All the world knows what happy results this search brought Renoir in colors and forms.

With the interest Rouault had from the beginning in colors, he was doubtless fascinated by Renoir's mastery in this realm. In his *Souvenirs* he pays homage in these terms:

> Good for you, Renoir, for not being afraid of making a mistake. Though I would be at the opposite extreme of painting and a prisoner of darkness until my death, I am grateful to you for having been at times almost drunk with color.[41]

"Prisoner of the dark" though he was, Rouault always had sympathy for those who loved the light. His commentary on Renoir reveals an almost wistful longing for this penchant for beauty. Yet Rouault hints that there is more to painting—as to life—than light.

> (Renoir) has understood the joy that always comes with painting under a sunny sky, caressing the eyes with running waters, luscious flesh, flowers and savory fruits. I envy those who can do this without regret, like happy children filled with bright fairies.
> Happy are the simple in spirit, the sweet, the loving who keep quiet and go on loving. Those who are not torn or deformed by life, who have forgotten in the brightness of the morning the grief of the night before. Like you, Renoir, with whom I speak here for the first time as an intimate.[42]

Edgar Degas (1834-1917). Degas had at one time traveled in Italy with Moreau, but they soon parted, each to search out his own path. Degas' way led him through impressionism and into analytical study. Rouault had great respect for Degas. He would sometimes see him walking through the twisting streets of Montmartre . . . "half-blind, tapping the ground with his stick . . . his grave and delicate features becoming peaked and mellow with age, taking on little by little the aspect of an ancient bronze statue."[43] Rouault spent many hours with Degas discussing the latter's work. Degas had an incisive nature that easily became biting. When Rouault praised something Moreau had said, Degas returned: "Well, I was at his funeral."[44] And as easily he could be understanding. Courthion

---

[39] *Ibid.*, p. 92.
[40] *Ibid.*, p. 77.
[41] *SI*, pp. 75, 76.
[42] *Ibid.*, p. 77.
[43] *Ibid.*, p. 94.
[44] *Ibid.*, p. 99.

relates that Degas visited the Musée Gustave Moreau shortly after its opening. He found "The Child Jesus Among the Doctors" in a room closed to the public. Because of his poor eyesight, his nose almost touched the canvas as he examined it. "Moreau certainly did not paint that," he said suddenly. Rouault, standing behind him, was trapped and admitted that he had painted it, making excuse for his borrowing of technique from Dürer, Leonardo and Rembrandt. Degas looked at him sternly and said: "Well, you had a father and mother, too, didn't you?"[45]

Degas had known an aristocratic existence which nevertheless always verged on melancholy. As a painter he was primarily interested in design. He had wanted to study with Ingres, and though he was only granted a short interview, he inherited that master's passion for craftsmanship. "Work much at designing. Oh, the lovely design!" he would repeat. In many ways, Lemoisne shows, his evolution as a painter was merely a search for the technique and the subject matter that fitted his structural inclination. Experimentation brought him to pastels and his now famous dancers. Here he admirably hid his analysis of design in a naturalness that highlighted the play of muscles and the lines of movements.[46]

Degas' care and patience made him admire the ancients. Compared with them, he would say, "we all paint like pigs." To return to their success, he believed, "we must become slaves again."[47] Though Rouault admired his diligence, he felt Degas had erred in restricting his field of experience and becoming a slave to a new analytic.[48] Degas' observations of the world were detached and objective (he detested painting in the countryside as he insisted the air made him sick!). Indeed, for him models were merely material for his investigation into light, color, and form. He studied the world with a cold, analytic eye and dismissed any more personal attachment. Throughout his life Degas bemoaned the lack of interest in the kind of research that was so important to him. Rouault summed up his regret in these words:

> The classic lament of painters like Renoir and Degas (here one can class them together) is that the more they have seen of life, the more their longing becomes bitter. Let us admit it, they mourn the School. . . . The Ideal School, that will never exist.[49]

Rouault had a different view of "schools." He did not share the

---

[45] Courthion, p. 82.

[46] P. A. Lemoisne. *Degas et son oeuvre* (Paris: Paul Braume & C. M. De Hauke, 1946), vol. 1, pp. 84-90, 111-116.

[47] *SI*, pp. 96, 99.

[48] *Soliloques*, pp. 81-87.

[49] *SI*, p. 96. Italics his.

dream of Renoir and Degas. "One can only teach certain things. To build the cathedrals you must have the faith and also the gifts."[50] The latter lie necessarily beyond research; it is to the former that we turn our attention in the next chapter.

Maurice Denis (1870-1943). Lastly we come to one of the most celebrated twentieth-century Christian artists and a contemporary of Rouault who merits our careful attention. Denis, known for his oft-quoted phrase "toward a new classical order," sought to apply intellectual canons to art and especially to Christian art. Formed in the school of Puvis de Chavannes, Denis was also influenced by Cézanne and most notably by Gauguin. His researches led him to the Italian primitives, which some say he imitated almost slavishly and others believe he interpreted with sensitivity.[51] His mission was "to restore a spiritual life to painting, which had become no more than a technique."[52] He describes his aspirations toward a renaissance of Christian French art and his plan for a *schola* of Christian art in two important books: *Théories* (1912) and *Nouvelles Théories* (1922).

In spite of Rouault's distrust for all artificial attempts at stimulating Christian art, the two seem to have had a cordial relationship. In a letter written sometime before 1914 Rouault refers to Denis' desire to see two of his paintings. Rouault, characteristically, welcomes Denis' thoughtful criticism:

> Treat me like an artist trying to develop and perfect himself and his art, who can certainly do some very bad work and some that is better. Most importantly, count me as one whom the compliments and opinions of a transient and fickle world neither irritate nor damage; one who prefers the counsel or careful and serious critique of a superior mind.[53]

But despite the fact that both were motivated by faith, the symbolism which Denis called for differs sharply from the kind of direct symbolism that Rouault achieved. Let us examine their distinctive approaches.[54]

---

[50] *Ibid.*

[51] Cf. Courthion, pp. 196, 197n.

[52] André Michel, ed. *L'Histoire de l'art* (Paris: Librairie Armand Colin), vol. VIII, p. 624.

[53] Maurice Denis. *Journal* (Paris: La Colombe, 1959), vol. II, p. 158.

[54] Dr. H. R. Rookmaaker in his book on Gauguin and his circle (including Denis) refers to the kind of symbolism they sought as "synthetism," reserving the term "symbolism" for the more literary movement to which Moreau was attached. Cf. *Synthetist Art Theories: Genesis and Nature of the Ideas on Art of Gauguin and His Circle* (Amsterdam: Swets and Zeitlinger, 1959), pp. 66-70 and passim. We will touch on this again in Chapter 17 below in our discussion of Rouault's symbolism.

Denis deplored the turn art had taken since the Renaissance. Before that so-called "awakening" Fra Angelico, among others, had achieved the expression of worthy sentiment through his treatment of the subject. Denis noted unhappily that, since then, the subject had become more important than the work itself. He saw in this trend the undesirable effects of the Greek passion for representation.[55] The impressionists' disdain for composition, he felt, masked a similar slavery to a purely literary device. They had sought to place their derived *trompe-l'oeil* between the emotion and the work. In sum, he contends: "In every case of decadence, the plastic arts impoverish themselves with literary affectations and naturalistic negations."[56] As he saw it, painting had to be freed from the slavery of impressionist neo-traditionalism and from the open window of the realists.[57]

The antidote, maintained Denis, was to see technique itself as a means of expression. Paul Gauguin had shown that a work of art, apart from any representational qualities, is essentially a flat surface covered with colors arranged in a certain way.[58] Thus he escaped the dilemma posed by David between the ideal and the real and put modern art on its present path.[59]

Yet once having recalled the essential nature of art, one must not fall into the other extreme of making technique an end in itself. Art remains, for Denis, expression rather than decoration, and the true sentiment must come from the soul of the artist.[60] Such a view immediately suggests the possibility of truly religious painting—not the sentimental variety which extolls piety and prayer but a different sort of art which itself moves the viewer.[61] The sentiment coming from the core of the artist's being must be translated into lines and colors on the canvas by means of what Denis calls the symbolist technique.[62] Denis insists that his is essentially a Christian theory which accounts for art's two most important characteristics: beauty and clarity.

Denis claims that "the Catholics understand neither the apolo-

---

[55] Maurice Denis. *Théories: 1890-1910* (Paris: Bibliothèque de l'Occident, 1912), pp. 40-42. Hereafter listed as *T*.

[56] *Ibid.*, p. 8.

[57] Maurice Denis. *Nouvelles Théories: 1914-1921* (Paris: Rouart and Watelin, 1922), pp. 180ff. Hereafter listed as *NT*.

[58] *T.*, p. 41. "That which Manet was for the generation of 1870, Gauguin was for that of 1890."

[59] *NT.*, p. 24.

[60] *T.*, pp. 9, 10.

[61] *Ibid.*, p. 32.

[62] *NT.*, pp. 228ff.

getic nor even the liturgic role of beauty."[63] The Christians of his day, he said, needed to rediscover the beauty of the human life attached again to God through Christ. Art that is truly religious celebrates this beauty and flees any form of ugliness, for only in this way can art serve as a source of reconciliation among men. Denis did not ignore decadence, for he scored Renoir for his lack of a sense of sin; but the hallmark of Christian art, in his view, is beauty.[64]

Reconciliation through art can only be achieved if the second element of art, clarity, is also present. Here is the heart of the symbolist theory. Art is "to translate and arouse states of the soul, by means of arrangements of colors and forms."[65] There is an equivalence, he implies, between the harmony of the forms and the logic of Dogma. The picture must speak, in its own language to be sure, but nonetheless clearly. As he expressed it, "the material has become expressive; the flesh has been made into the word."[66] For Denis it appears that what art expresses is more than simply the reality of faith and of human joy and dependence: it is the very truth of Dogma. He refers in illustration to the Byzantine advance in the use of artistic language that translated the reality of Christian truth into artistic forms. Moreover, Denis intended to have Thomism taught at the *schola* that he envisioned, for "philosophic errors have been at the root of many of modern art's excesses."[67] Art thus founded and conceived can teach and edify in much the same way as do parables, sacraments and liturgy.[68]

How does Denis' view compare with the expressionism of Rouault? The latter, too, enjoyed the freedom from imitation that Cézanne (and Gauguin) had brought to modern art, but this freedom enabled him to put technique in the service of his perception of the world with its beauty and ugliness. What would appear on his canvas was determined by his vision, not by Dogma or by his faith (except in a deeper, more important way that we shall note). Rouault was not nearly as concerned as Denis with systematic errors, either in philosophy or in theology. But though he did not begin with Dogma it does not follow that he was any less true to it. He was simply intent upon painting his view of the human situation.

---

[63] *Ibid.,* p. 206. Here he particularly criticizes Bloy's emphasis on condemnation.

[64] *NT.,* pp. 109, 252. Cf. Rouault's conception of beauty below in Chapter 8.

[65] *Ibid.,* p. 175.

[66] *T.,* pp. 33, 34.

[67] *NT.,* p. 281.

[68] *Ibid.,* pp. 228ff., to which he compared Christian art as to their nature if not their purpose or end. It must be admitted that it is not always clear with Denis whether Christian art is to instruct or move or both.

Rouault reacted instinctively against Denis' idea of a school of religious art. Denis insisted that sacred art was dead not from lack of faith but because the public was indifferent. To remedy this, he felt, a school was needed to create an atmosphere of vital faith. But, Rouault would claim, no school can accomplish this. Only the faith and the gifts suffice, and these are beyond anyone's ability to teach or pass on. How do we understand this faith to which he so often refers? To this question we must now turn.

SECTION B: ROUAULT'S SPIRITUAL DEVELOPMENT

* * *

5. The Faith of the Artist

Having reviewed some causes of Rouault's spiritual development, let us venture a careful examination of the nature of this thinking. This is doubly hazardous because of the elusive nature of man's faith and also because of Rouault's taciturnity about intimate questions. But the examination must be carried out, cautiously and thoughtfully. We mean not so much to make his faith an object of scrutiny as to see its place as a motivating and determining factor in his art. First we will trace the development of his religious faith, and then we will attempt to sketch a tentative outline of that faith. Rouault often said there is no sacred art, only "an art made by artists who have faith." What then did "faith" mean to him?

Rouault had been baptized in the parish of Saint-Leu on June 25, 1871. Though he did not take his first communion at the usual age, he sought out Dominican Father Vallée while working under Moreau to request the necessary instruction and preparation.[1] This formal relation with the Church notwithstanding, it was primarily Moreau's friendship that provided Rouault with spiritual support during this time. Later Rouault was to say of his instructor: "He has been the one to really draw me out."[2] The difficult discovery of himself, however, was brutally interrupted by Moreau's death on April 18, 1898, leaving Rouault without a spiritual footing. Rouault, not yet 27, had completed the formal study of mythology and de-

---

[1] Courthion, p. 78 n. 15.
[2] *SI*, p. 31.

sign and was moving on to a larger classroom.[3] Rouault knew the methods and had some talent, as he later wrote,

> but I had not taken the time to watch people and life. I was acquainted with religious history and had painted the "Dead Christ" and "Jesus Among the Doctors." But I knew nothing of suffering.[4]

For the experience of this larger classroom of suffering he was unprepared.

The darkness of those days can hardly be overemphasized. Rouault was suddenly bereft of the shelter of studio and teacher. His family had gone to Algeria during this period, and he moved into a room where he had to live alone without support.[5] In this dark time a spiritual reorientation took place. Rouault says of this era: "If my art is harsh, it is due no doubt to this period of my life. Then it was that I understood the saying of Cézanne: 'Life, it is terrifying!' "[6]

This was the period when he lived across from Renoir. When he was not working he would wander alone through the streets of Paris. No doubt it was then, without the support of family or well-placed, stimulating friends, that he took profoundly to heart the anguish of the common worker. He describes some of his study in this way:

> Sometimes on beautiful spring days before going to the studio, I would go out at 5 o'clock in the morning and set myself up under the bridges along the Seine. There I would paint where dockers, naked to the waist, were unloading barges.[7]

Moreau had said that a painter should be grateful if he was poor, for it is difficult for a person to sense the wonder and horror where all the world lives if he has never been down with them. Rouault was there.

Meanwhile a profound revolution was going on within Rouault. Courthion sees this represented in the work that Rouault did in this epoque. His Rembrandt-like style seemed unchanged, but glimpses of his future character showed through. The language of form and color that he was to make his own, and his powerful feeling for people, began to take a prominent position.[8]

---

[3] In fact Moreau had already told Rouault when he was defeated the second time for the Prix de Rome that there was no point in staying in the school, it had no more to teach him. Courthion, p. 49.

[4] Quoted in Jacques Guenne. "Georges Rouault." Les Nouvelles Littéraires, November 15, 1924, no. 109, p. 5.

[5] Only in 1903 at the opening of the Musée Gustave Moreau did he earn a regular income (2400 francs a year).

[6] Quoted in Charensol, op. cit., p. 22.

[7] Ibid., p. 23.

[8] Courthion, p. 76.

Rouault once described the kind of change that was going on:

> Without wanting, a priori, to forget all that I had loved in the museums, little by little a more objective vision sustained me.
>
> I underwent at that time a most violent moral crisis. I experienced things that cannot be put into words. And I set about to paint with an outrageous lyricism that upset everyone.
>
> In spite of this I sent some pictures to the Salon. I had, it seems to me, a perfect disregard for what was happening to me. In order for me to realize that an evolution was taking place I had to read an article that said: "There used to be a Rouault who was a serious painter, but now there is another who is a joker." It was my detractors that helped me to understand what I had done. But I wanted to tell them, if they had had less prejudice, that this instinctive movement, this turn of the helm, was not under the influence of Lautrec, or Degas, or the moderns. It was rather by an inner need, and the wish, perhaps unconscious, not to fall into the mold of conventional religious subjects.[9]

By his own testimony we cannot look to Rouault for a precise formulation of this "turn of the helm." We can only say it was an internal, morally oriented spiritual revolution that resulted in a totally different appraisal of reality. As Rouault expressed it:

> When I was about thirty, I felt a stroke of lightning, or of grace, depending on one's perspective. The face of the world changed for me. I saw everything that I had seen before, but in a different form and with a different harmony.[10]

These two passages reveal, for our purposes, the two significant characteristics of the change for the painter, neither of them abstract or even primarily religious. The first was a transformation of his view of nature. It took on a new perspective for him, one we will want to explore further on. It became more wonderfully human and also subject to a depth of suffering he had not imagined.

A second significant effect of this revolution was a transformation of his view of religious art. In a suggestive reference to his earlier work, Rouault points out to Suarès that "when, around 1894, I painted my 'Child Jesus Among the Doctors,' no one spoke much about religious art. . . ." At that time he was engaged, with Moreau's help, in a research that was more direct and objective.[11] Religious art, after his transformation, came to be viewed as much

---

[9] Quoted in Charensol, op. cit., p. 23. A similar statement, though less explicit, is to be found in SI, p. 50.

[10] Quoted in Grenier, 1957, op. cit., p. 33. As to the date, this would imply Rouault was about 30 and suggests the date as 1901, the year Rouault went to Ligugé (see below). Grenier, however, goes on to say that this was in 1903 when Rouault was 32, giving no reason for his assertion.

[11] Rouault and Suarès. "Moreau." L'Art et les Artistes, April, 1926, vol. 66, p. 246.

more than merely the depicting of religious subjects. The objective research was brought to life. In the *Soliloques* he addresses himself to the vigorously debated question of the subject, and sets it in its proper life-context:

> It is not always the subject that inspires the pilgrim, but the accent that he puts there, the tone, the force, the grace, the unction. That is why some so-called "sacred art" can be profane.[12]

It was just this accent and force that Rouault found during his transformation. Whereas before, Dorival believes, subjects were either handy or suggested to him, later they came with a fervor from his very heart.[13]

It is significant that between 1905 and 1912, Rouault attempted only six religious compositions, only two of them before 1910. The explanation is to be found in the confession we have quoted. His interior need had given him a distaste for banality and superficiality in religious painting. His faith, now a deep and vital one, made him temporarily avoid these meaningful motifs that he feared he might cheapen through overuse.[14]

Though the effects of the change manifested themselves in his art, we cannot escape the conclusion that Rouault's experience was fundamentally a religious one. Venturi sees Rouault's quest for God as the primary factor in this period. Dorival further maintains that Rouault's pictorial enfranchisement was a direct result of his conversion to an evangelical Catholicism.[15] Rouault himself later discussed the change, noting what to him had been the essential factor.

> I was only thirty when Moreau died. Then there was a desert to cross, and painting: an oasis or a mirage? Well, knowing that I knew nothing—having certainly learned quite a bit between twenty and thirty, but considering that I perhaps did not know the essential thing which is to *strip oneself,* if that grace is accorded us after having learned so much.[16]

An important factor, then, in his development was a coming to the end of himself, seeing the limitation of his moral and spiritual

---

[12] *Soliloques,* p. 53.

[13] Dorival. *Rouault: oeuvres inachevées* (Paris: Musée du Louvre, 1964), p. 98.

[14] Venturi points out too the great success of religious paintings that abounded with seraphim and brightness. Rouault's reticence may be in part a reaction against that mode. Cf. Venturi, 1959, p. 18.

[15] Cf. especially Dorival. "Rouault, peintre tragique." *L'Education Nationale,* May, 1958, no. 19, p. 16. Courthion avoids the word "conversion" and insists instead on a continuous evolution rather than an abrupt revolution. P. 84.

[16] Quoted in Soby, *op. cit.,* p. 131. Remarks sent by Rouault for the retrospective exposition at the Museum of Modern Art in New York, 1945.

resources and, we may infer, seeking their supply in God. There
is a legitimate sense in which the experience can be termed a
"conversion." In any case, the shape of his future life was fixed after
these years. A formal faith had become a living one. The interior life
that Moreau had stimulated was stumbling upon divine realities. The
faith which was awakened at this time, however, still needed content, and we believe his encounters with Bloy and Huysmans provided it. The will to believe was present; the credo was supplied
by these two friendships.[17] Bloy we have considered earlier, and
now we turn to another of the leaders of the Catholic revival,
J.-K. Huysmans.

Joris-Karl Huysmans (1848-1907) was of Dutch descent, though he
lived most of his life in Paris working as a functionary for one of
the governmental ministries. His life was a curious combination
of sensitive bohemian existence and regimented bureaucratic rou-
tine. There can be little doubt that he was one of the most important figures of the artistic and literary world of Paris during the
1880's.

While he was holding his tedious job in the government, he was
active in his role as art critic defending "modern" art against academicism. One biographer goes so far as to call him an inventor of
impressionism.[18] But his most lasting contribution, and the most
significant for our purposes, came through the leadership he provided for the shift in French thinking that has been called the
"decadent spirit."

During the 1880's the influence of men like Baudelaire and Hello
lived on in the desire to provide an alternative to the strictures of
naturalism. In the graphic arts, Impressionism, though it was an
attempt to achieve a greater naturalism, produced effects that led
to the purely artistic and anti-naturalistic post-impressionist movement. In literature, Huysmans captured the troubled spirit of his
time and set the tone for what was to come in his book *A Rebours*,
published in 1884. Nourished on German Idealism rather carelessly
understood and a persistent strain of Plotinism, *A Rebours*, which
means literally "against the grain," suggested a spiritual retreat from
reality that would capture all the pure joys of art.[19]

---

[17] Maritain believes as well that it was faith that brought Rouault to Bloy
and Huysmans, rather than they who brought him to faith. He describes "a
profound religious sentiment, the stubborn faith of a hermit that brought
him to Bloy and Huysmans and that led him to see the image of the Lamb
in all the outcasts." *La Revue Universelle*, 1924, vol. II, p. 507, no. 2.

[18] Robert Baldick. *The Life of J.-K. Huysmans*, pp. 70-77.

[19] On Huysmans' contacts with and influence on the artists and the development of their thinking see Rookmaaker, *op. cit.*, pp. 77-81, 97. See also

This work more than any other embodied the "decadent spirit," and in so doing it may have served as a crucial link between Baudelaire and such symbolist writers as Mallarmé and Verlaine, on the one hand, and painters such as Moreau and Redon on the other. But this decadence was only a way-station, and Huysmans' continued literary pilgrimage[20] led him around 1890 to a deep involvement with the occult, recorded in the novel *Là-Bas*. He then set out to investigate the other side of the supernatural realm, and describe his research in another book. When *En Route* finally appeared in 1895 it proved to be an account of Huysmans' own conversion to Catholicism.

In his mystical spiritualist quest, as well as in his pessimism about the world around, Huysmans had much in common with Bloy.[21] The two were close friends for many years, though by 1890 they had fallen out: Bloy had accused Huysmans of using in *Là-Bas* ideas that he had provided. But after his conversion Huysmans continued to send Bloy money and was greatly influenced by the uncompromising spirit of the Ungrateful Beggar.[22] This was especially true in his view of vicarous suffering, a problem which was much in the air at that time. Huysmans was impressed by the visionary Boullan, though he avoided the excesses to which the latter took the theory of suffering.[23] Under the influence of Bloy and Hello, Huysmans came to share their emphasis on mysticism, revelations and miracles. His delight in suffering was at times so pronounced that it verged on sadism. A certain humility, however, distinguished him from Bloy in his view of suffering: he gave a much larger place to the mercy of God and man's limitation. He agreed with the Apostle Paul, especially near the end of his life, that he was not worthy to suffer extreme punishment for God.[24]

Another characteristic of Huysmans' that set him apart from Bloy was his insight and influence in matters of painting. Venturi attempts to dismiss his impact on Rouault by asserting that "Huysmans was a trifler in religious art, fastidious, aspiring only to retreat and dream in peace." Moreover, suggests Venturi, his temperament was not such

---

A.-M. Schmidt. *La Littérature symboliste* (Paris: Presses Universitaires, 1942), pp. 36-42.

[20] Griffiths, *op. cit.,* seeks to show that the research that brought Huysmans to faith began as a literary quest, i.e. he sought in what he called "naturalistic spiritualism" an escape from naturalism, avoiding its sterility without losing its concern for accuracy. Pp. 100, 102.

[21] Schmidt, *op. cit.,* p. 42.

[22] Baldick, *op. cit.,* p. 167.

[23] Boullan maintained that in suffering for another there was an actual transference of the sin from one person to another.

[24] Griffiths, *op. cit.,* p. 188.

as to make an impact on the energetic Rouault.[25] But it was precisely his thinking on questions of painting and his embodiment of
the reactionary spirit that appealed to Rouault, and gave him a
parallel role to Bloy's in Rouault's development. Rouault understood this and recalls Huysmans warmly in his *Souvenirs* as a devotée
of art. Indeed, Huysmans' ideal of religious art led him later to
retire to Ligugé, a little Benedictine monastery near Poitiers. It was
here in 1901 that Rouault and Huysmans were to meet.

In 1898 Huysmans had left his job in the ministry to go to Ligugé.
There he bought a piece of ground and began to build a little
place of refuge. Huysmans wanted to establish there a little community of artists and writers who could work out their faith un-
hampered by the temptations and snares of the big city. Descaves
describes the frustration Huysmans felt in working on his project,
"a dream too beautiful to be realized." Around 1900 the project
was almost abandoned, and at the beginning of 1901 it was threat-
ened by a new law that would ban religious communities.[26]

In April Rouault came to Ligugé to join his friend, Antonin Bour-
bon, who had been a fellow student under Moreau. The two lived
rather precariously with peasants and attended religious services
at the monastery. Apparently Huysmans still had enough faith in
his project to urge Rouault to join it, as Rouault describes:

> We were a few friends who formed a little group around Huysmans,
> and we tried to lay the foundations for artistic and intellectual work
> that would be dedicated and selfless. Huysmans wanted to bring
> together men who, having abandoned the farce of Paris, would count
> neither on money nor on influence; no Bachelor's or Doctor's degrees,
> and no specialists; just men who had put behind them all the non-
> essentials in life: degrees, medals, prerogatives. He wanted to or-
> ganize this with me, Antonin Bourbon, and a few others.[27]

Doubtless the time of quiet and meditation made an impact on
Rouault, who certainly had ample opportunity to discuss the concepts of Christian art with Huysmans. However, the decision to
spend this time in Ligugé should be viewed as a result of his con-

---

[25] Venturi, 1959, p. 32. Griffiths has shown how important aesthetic questions were to Huysmans both before and after his conversion. *Op. cit.*,
p. 108.
[26] Lucien Descaves. *Les Dernières années de J. -K. Huysmans* (Paris: Albin
Michel, 1941), pp. 66ff. Discussion on the law was begun 15 January 1901
and it was finally passed 2 July 1901 on the pretext that these congregations were political in nature. It in effect outlawed all associations whose
freedom was restricted by a superior, affecting 753 religious congregations.
Cf. Ch. Seignobos. *L'Histoire de la France* (Paris: Hachette, 1921), vol. III,
pp. 220, 222.
[27] Courthion, p. 78.

version rather than a cause of it. That he actually thought of re-
tiring to the monastery he himself tells us:

> I knew Bloy and Huysmans and went to Ligugé thinking seriously of
> retiring there. When the laws of separation were voted, Huysmans
> was proposing that a group of artists should live there together.
> "They will work in peace," he said, "far from the Salons and other com-
> pensations. They will do what they want."[28]

In any case his sojourn at Ligugé was a manifestation and confirmation of the religious direction that his life had already taken.

But the experiment of Huysmans was doomed to be shortlived.
Only two months after Rouault had arrived, the laws banning religious communities were passed. After the last mass on June 27
the priests of the monastery entrained for Belgium. The lay members
of the community stayed for a short time, but by the end of October they were all back, inevitably, to the "farce of Paris."

By 1902 the revolution Rouault had experienced was largely complete. Yet times were still not easy, as he testifies:

> About 1902, we joined together to form the Salon d'Automne. I was
> at the end of myself, morally and physically, not having been away
> from Paris for years. Happily my family came back to France. I fell
> seriously ill; I really thought I was finished. Still all I could think of
> was painting.
> I began to improve, however, and went to Evian to convalesce.
> When I returned I was disgusted with my somber painting. I had
> stayed too long in the "end of the season." The rest over there, the
> sky and the snow, had cleansed my eye. Nevertheless the emotions
> of those long tragic years that had bruised me so were stored up in
> me. A kind of release took place, and I set to paint with a frenzy.[29]

Though indeed the development of Rouault's spiritual values, manifested in his paintings, continued throughout his life, his direction
was set and his faith was firm.

What exactly was the faith of Rouault? Certain characteristics of his
religious life can be sketched, less from his testimony than from
that of his friends and from the evidence of his life and work.
His was a faith unexpressed and yet orthodox, humble and yet
morally intense. Let us consider these aspects in turn.

In the first place, Rouault's faith was largely inexplicit and unexpressed. It was the faith of an artist-layman who saw intuitively

---

[28] Quoted in Charensol, op. cit., p. 24. Cf. Dorival, Oeuvres inachevées,
op. cit., p. 98, who suggests that the ardour of a new convert was tempted
to enter retirement in this way. Cf. also Soby, op. cit., p. 13.

[29] Quoted in Charensol, op. cit., p. 24. Roulet insists the change in Rouault's thinking was complete by 1902, op. cit., p. 164, and Courthion's contention noted above that the prostitutes, the "tableaux noirs," could very
well have begun in 1902 would support this.

rather than that of an articulate student of Christianity who saw
logically. Part of this was perhaps due to a natural reserve. Although
his art was consistently of religious inspiration, in his writings and
conversations he makes only scattered and oblique references to
his faith. Roulet notes that in the twenty years of their acquaintance,
Rouault spoke of religion only three or four times, and that was
when Roulet spoke of it first.[30]

In Rouault's writings and conversations his religious references
come from deep, almost inexpressible feelings. He sees the human
situation profoundly and intuitively, causing him an inner, almost
painful nostalgia.[31]

> I am naked and sad like the truth, watching silently in the night, clack-
> ing and grinding my teeth, my skin covered with goose pimples even
> in mid-summer. My legs shake, my eyes far off in the midst of this
> civilized world: only Jesus who shed his blood deigned to hear me.[32]
>
> Easter, 1942. Perhaps we will live to see the day when, more and
> more, even the cleverest, the wisest, or the most innocent will con-
> fess—in spite of themselves—what they really are. By means of this
> well-beloved art, they will say who they are whether they want to
> or not, because they have found just the right means of expression.
>   It is curious in the light of this for people to say about me: "When
> will he start showing his better side?"
>   Perhaps one far off day when a true and genuine inner peace will
> control the mind . . . of the pilgrim, far from the prostitution of the
> word. When force will be less visible and more intuitive, secret and
> discrete, then perhaps I will show my "better side." For what we
> see with our eyes and think we touch with our diseased hands or
> weigh so precisely, is not all there is in this clever and mechanized
> world.[33]

Deep though these feelings were, they were not confused or uncertain. They shine clearly in all his painting, for he was first of all
a painter. But of this we shall have much more to say presently.

Rouault's faith, though often unexpressed, was, in the second
place, orthodox. This is not to say it was spelled out as in a doctrinal confession; we have just seen it was not thus expressed.
But it was free of distorting aberrations. There was a catholicity to
his faith that eliminated the temptation to follow down personal
fancies or grudges. We may pick out a few elements that he accepted to illustrate his general submission to the teachings of the

---

[30] Roulet, op. cit., p. 45.

[31] Cf. Maritain, "Rouault," La Revue Universelle, p. 506.

[32] Quoted in Marquette Bouvier. "Georges Rouault: expresionista y
místico." Goya, 1958-60, nos. 25-30, pp. 18-24.

[33] Preface by Rouault to Dorival. Georges Rouault (Paris: 1942), p. 1.

Church. These came to him not as a result of formal study but were impressed upon him in the classroom of the world.[34]

Rouault had a vivid sense of his sin and personal inadequacy. This bore fruit in the artistic humility that we have already noted. In the *Cirque de l'étoile filante* (1938), Rouault cries: "My friends, you have always been kind to me. And I have only been an ingrate. *Mea culpa, mea maxima culpa,* it is my fault that I have been thus."[35]

Nor was this merely a false sense of modesty. It came from a genuinely theological root: his recognition of the supreme worth of God. We have already mentioned Rouault's fondness for the motto of the anonymous workmen whose faith and dedication he admired: "Those happy companions whose names we no longer know used to engrave on the ridge-pole of the cathedral: *Non nobis domine sed nomini tuo da gloriam* (Not unto us, Lord, but unto thy name be the glory)."[36] He was preoccupied, too, with the passion of Christ. "As a Christian in such hazardous times, I believe only in Jesus on the cross. I am a Christian of olden times."[37] Here was a simple yet deep-seated faith that put not only his work but his whole life in a proper perspective. We recall the Apostle Paul's saying: "For you have died, and your life is hid with Christ in God."[38] Rouault felt more intuitively than speculatively his unity in Christ with men of faith throughout the ages.

An interesting illumination of Rouault's faith is found in a letter to his friend André Suarès on the subject of their collaboration on Suarès' *Passion*.[39] This was to be a religious volume, yet it is no secret that Suarès was not a believer in the sense that Rouault was.

> If he did not believe as I did, I was not proud of the fact. I thought we would be able to treat together one of the great themes that had always occupied me, the sufferings and death of Christ. And I felt that we could work together without either one having to sacrifice to the other his personal convictions or his interpretation of certain words or facts reported in the Gospels. I did not know if Suarès believed in the resurrection of Jesus or not, a fact which I never

---

[34] Roulet suggests this in his introduction to the *Soliloques*: "I believe that Rouault found in the accounts of the Old and New Testaments and, in a more general way in the affirmations of the Catholic Church, confirmation of his experience as a man and as a painter." P. 53. Life, in the Providence of God, sometimes provides its own Confirmation. Such was the case with Rouault.

[35] P. 32.

[36] *Sl,* p. 51.

[37] Quoted in Charensol, *op. cit.,* p. 8.

[38] Colossians 3:3. Revised Standard Version.

[39] Vollard, 1939. Intended as a companion volume to *Cirque,* illustrated by Rouault with 17 etchings in color and 82 wood-engravings.

doubted. In any case he did not make any allusion to it in the work, while I celebrated the event in one of the last plates.[40]

The passage is revealing not only of Rouault's faith, assumed rather than debated, but also of his view of the relationship between faith and art. Living faith informs an art, Rouault suggests, but does not thereby seek to proselytize. Faith expresses rather than defends itself in art.

A third aspect characterized Rouault's faith. In 1945, writing for the exposition of his work in New York, he summarized his spiritual life in this way: "I have respected a certain internal order and laws which I hope are traditional; removed from passing fashions and contemporaries—critics, artists, or dealers—I believe I have kept my spiritual liberty."[41] Here that northern obstinacy had become a feature of his spiritual life. Rouault exhibited the most strict moral austerity, a moral intransigence approaching the spirit of Léon Bloy. Perhaps we should avoid the word "moral," encumbered as it is with codes and specific moralities.[42] Rouault pointedly denied any desire to "moralize." "I do not wish to moralize," he would say. "Art is infinitely above the ethical." But his entire work, like his faith, is informed by an intense moral strength. This was evident in Rouault's refusal to resign himself to mediocrity or hypocrisy. Maritain says of Rouault, "He hides a soul that knows neither indifference nor disdain."[43] It is in this light that his blasts against society are to be understood. What he decried above all was the lack of moral fortitude, or strength of purpose. He said of Europe during the Second World War: "It is the spiritual or moral meaning that is wanting everywhere. The lack of any spiritual directive ruins everything." By contrast, he testified of himself that ". . . the only force I have had is to resist spiritually."[44]

This gave to his faith a stern character that led Venturi to say: "It is a pure faith that is rigorous, jansenist, and sometimes cruel. It is closely tied to the most scrupulous moral austerity."[45] But this severity was not an end in itself but a means to achieve the glory that belonged to the world from creation, lost through moral sloppiness. Rouault clung to a crucified Savior as the only way to find

---

[40] Letter from Rouault printed in L'Art Sacré, March-April, 1965, p. 25.

[41] In Soby, op. cit., p. 129.

[42] At least this is the case in the English language, where every definition given by the dictionary save one (moral as in "moral victory") is related to standards of conduct. The French language has preserved a distinction between standards on the one hand and intellectual or spiritual character on the other.

[43] La Revue Universelle, op. cit., p. 506.

[44] Quoted in Roulet, Souvenirs, pp. 258, 259.

[45] Venturi, 1959, p. 18.

again the meaning that had been lost. Because of this, he saw in the homeless and destitute a pathetic vestige of the honor that belongs to man. "The religious inspiration is constant in his work," writes Raïssa Maritain. "One feels he is perpetually watching over the evangelical values of human life."[46]

---

[46] *Amitiés*, vol. I, p. 227.

6. Rouault's View of His Work

What is as important for our purposes as the faith of Rouault is the way he practiced that faith in relation to his work. Here we must search out the reasons for the vague way he verbally expressed his faith. He was not primarily a thinker or writer, he was an artist; better, an artisan. This seemingly obvious fact demands careful consideration, for it illuminates a portion of the mysterious question of Christian creativity. To accomplish this we will first examine the primacy of the means and the artifact for Rouault, then proceed to discuss the way in which he viewed his vocation as an artist, and finish this section by drawing attention to the impelling, intuitive nature of this vocation.

Rouault's silence on the questions of his faith or his art does not stem simply from mere taciturnity or the difficulty of referring to deeply meaningful subjects. As he says in one place: "If I have always been reluctant to discuss these questions, it is because our language is form, color and harmony."[1] In fact, these artistic means of expression are more than a language. They are the very embodiment of his personality, the means of making himself present to the world. Again he confesses: "Images and colors, for a painter, are his means of being, of living, of thinking, and of feeling."[2] Here we have gone far beyond the kind of translation of faith into painting that Denis envisioned. Rouault repudiated this kind of enterprise. "More and more I am reluctant to make a declaration of faith in pictures. . . . I refuse to be called in to judge in my own case."[3]

Rouault, an artisan, is in the long line of craftsmen who demonstrate their reflections by their hands. Maurice Morel in his sensi-

---

[1] Quoted in Charensol, *op. cit.,* p. 7.
[2] *Soliloques,* p. 66.
[3] Letter published in *Cahiers d'Art,* 1928, no. 3, p. 102.

tive introduction to Rouault's *Miserere* points out the paradox that Rouault, one of the real "spiritualist" painters of this time, "thought with his hands and in the material, pondering with his eyes. . . ."[4] Deeply thoughtful and reflective though he was, he felt no frustration or disaffection with the plastic means of expression that were his sphere. It is not by accident that Rouault in his preface to *Miserere* speaks only of the material processes necessary to bring the work to completion and makes no pretense at a commentary. Only a poem (another piece of art) garnishes the preface with insight.

Not that there were no struggles in his work. In 1911 he described to Suarès the kind of battles he went through to create as he did. But he qualified the nature of the difficulties. "I am not referring to mental or interior struggles, but simply to battles of technique and material means. . . ."[5] This was the sort of problem that Degas illustrated in his search for the proper means for expressing his vision and that brought him to pastels. Near the end of 1913, as a result of this kind of struggle, Rouault came to see that the medium of oil best suited his needs. The practical, physical nature of an artist's anguish was the cause of Rouault's frustration in communicating with others the nature of his work. The critics and doctors listened too often with "theoretical" ears. Gilson has put his finger on this problem:

> One of the main reasons painters find it so hard to make themselves understood when they speak of their art is that their hearers listen with their minds only, not with their hands. If it is a question of painting, the artist himself can form no clear notion of his own art without including in it manual skill.[6]

Rouault reiterates this in a letter to Suarès: "It is not enough to apply your will, you must possess the pictorial *means* to reach the result you aim at."[7]

The reference to the result aimed at reminds us that art is primarily a physical process but also transcends that process. Says Rouault of the place of the skill: "the hand is only the docile servant of the watchful spirit, of the alert mind."[8] The skill is the servant, or better, the partner of the spirit. Both are necessary to the work of art, and Rouault often connects them:

> To attempt to paint with success an epic or heroic work, one must

---

[4] *Miserere*, 1948, p. 2. Cf. Dorival. *La Table Ronde,* October, 1952, no. 58, p. 179.

[5] *Correspondance,* December 27, 1911, p. 10.

[6] Gilson, *op. cit.,* p. 54.

[7] *Correspondance,* p. 86. Italics his.

[8] *Stella Vespertina,* no pagination.

have not only the mind and heart highly placed, but also the means to express oneself properly in a style that adapts itself completely to the conception.[9]

To think, for a painter, is it not to have a sensitive and creative vision of form and color, and the faculty of expressing oneself with more or less success pictorially?[10]

This is to say much more than that an artist takes his vision and translates it into a painting, just as the model in his studio becomes an image on the canvas. One could say rather that the vision incarnates itself in the work and completes its existence therein. Maritain engages in a helpful discussion of means as *habitus* in *Art and Scholasticism*.[11] *Habitus,* unlike habit which resides in the nerve centers, "resides principally in an immaterial faculty, in the intelligence or the will."[12] It functions within the spirit with reference to the object in view, a work of art. This conception is helpful not only in avoiding the mechanical connotation of "means" but also in designating the relationship of the physical activity to the vision. The "means" are the "condition" of the vision. Moreover, this conception accents the activity of the spirit in the material. The *habitus,* explains Maritain, sharpens the point of its activity with reference to a definite object "to a certain maximum of perfection and thus of operative efficiency."[13]

We will consider Professor Maritain's views more fully below. But let it be noted here that his view of art as a virtue (in some ways inhuman, as he puts it) threatens to reduce the physical activity to the negative activity of "removing the impediments." Rouault, by contrast, at times seems to speak of the plastic expression itself as determinative of the vision. He once wrote to Suarès: "I tell you that to the degree the form refines itself, even in my horrible pieces, the vision becomes more beautiful."[14]

An instructive object lesson on this question comes from the life of Rouault. After the sudden death in a 1939 auto accident of Ambroise Vollard, Rouault's dealer, a debate arose over which paintings belonged to the dealer's heirs and which to the painter. The contract between Vollard and Rouault had specified that all of the artist's work belonged to the dealer. But what was "work"— all that was in Rouault's studio at the time of Vollard's death, or only what the artist considered finished and had signed? In 1947

---

[9] *Soliloques,* p. 109.
[10] Quoted in Michel Puy. *Rouault, op. cit.,* p. 16.
[11] Pp. 12ff.
[12] *Ibid.,* pp. 12, 13.
[13] *Ibid.*
[14] *Correspondance,* p. 134.

the court decided for Rouault against the heirs of Vollard and in so doing recognized an important aesthetic principle. A work of art consists neither in the vision of the artist alone nor in the physical results seen on the canvas alone, *but in both together.* That is to say, only when the intention of the artist is fulfilled on the canvas can the work be considered "completed," and until then it is the sole property of the artist.[15]

If the work is primary for the artist, then his writings must be of secondary worth. Rouault knew this very well and wondered out loud to Roulet one night: "My writings are not worth as much as my painting. . . . " He admitted that sometimes he felt like burning them all to avoid any interest that would be purely literary.[16] Of what value then are the titles of his pictures? Though they are ordinarily affixed after the work is completed, Dorival acknowledges that they are not to be disdained.[17] Salmon claims that one would advance a great step in understanding Rouault if his inscriptions are studied and understood, especially in the *Miserere.*[18] Perhaps it is safe to say that while their value is small in itself, as a part of the work with which they are identified they are useful.

In any case, the titles ought not to be taken as explanations. For a work of art is a sufficient explanation in and of itself. It needs no commentary. In fact, it often illuminates factors that can be "understood" in no other way. It is often said that one needs to know something of the life of the artist to understand his work. But the reverse is more proper: works of art help to illuminate the life of an artist. Rouault himself warns against trying to apply the facts of a person's life to an understanding of his art. Sometimes, he observes, the two are in harmony and sometimes they are not.[19] But more than that there is a mysterious connection between art and life. Rouault notes: "My life and my art make a single whole."[20] There are contradictions in Rouault's life that Venturi thinks have no justification outside of his work. In fact ". . . the life of Rouault is a function of his art."[21] Pichard probably overstates

---

[15] The court "decided that a given estate cannot claim rights belonging essentially to the person. And in particular it has no claim on intellectual and moral rights which guarantee the freedom of artistic creation." Georges Izard. "Le Droit moral de l'artiste dans les procès de Rouault et Bonnard." *L'Art de France,* 1961, no. 1, p. 210.

[16] *Soliloques,* p. 13.

[17] "Autoportraits et portraits de Rouault." *La Revue des Arts,* December, 1953, p. 237.

[18] André Salmon. "Le *Miserere* de Georges Rouault." *L'Amour de l'Art,* 1925, no. 6, p. 186.

[19] *Soliloques,* p. 93.

[20] Quoted in Roulet, *op. cit.,* p. 71.

[21] Venturi, 1948, p. 44.

the case: "The life of Rouault has no 'history', it does not interest us, except to convince us that his life is nothing else than his work."[22] In all events, the work is the unique and primary witness to the artist's identity as an artist, as a man, and, in the present case, as a Christian.

Rouault was keenly cognizant of this explicative nature of his work. He alludes to it often:

> Such a very few things suffice for us to know a living man and an artist, one word, a characteristic, an attitude. But afterwards, for us mortals, all that remains as testimony is our poor work.[23]

> I mean the poor fragment of canvas or paper before which our contemporaries and those to follow will sing "Hallelujah" or else "Miserere," sometimes without any idea of the conditions under which the creator may have been constrained to work.[24]

> In principle the artist ought to disappear behind his work. O artist, it should defend itself alone.[25]

Further, the work is a revelation—personally if not objectively—of the spirit and the being of the artist.

> The work of art remains a vow and a confession of what we really are, without our suspecting it.[26]

> The work of art moreover is a touching confession, more true than could ever be put into words.[27]

The life and the person of the artist are identified with the work. The two can be distinguished but they cannot be separated. Maritain compares the work of the artist with the work of the divine Word of God. Nothing that God accomplished was done independently of the Word. Similarly, it is *through his art* that the human artist must attain, rule, and bring into being all his work."[28] We will want to argue below that this analogy of synergism is not merely a gratuitous observation but is a result of the image of God in man.

To say that the work of art is sufficient unto itself is to say also that it carries its own "clarity" within itself. Inasmuch as an artisan or an artist thinks with his hands, one could almost say that the artist gives to the work its own perspicuity—not verbally translatable but expressed in its own pictorial language. Rouault spoke often of the special ingredients of form, color, harmony, that compose this

---

[22] "L'Oeuvre de Georges Rouault." *L'Art d'Eglise,* 1953, no. 1, p. 181.
[23] "Souvenirs du jeune âge," p. 20.
[24] In Soby, *op. cit.,* p. 130.
[25] *Soliloques,* p. 107.
[26] "Souvenirs du jeune âge," p. 32.
[27] Quoted in Puy, *op. cit.,* p. 16.
[28] *Art and Scholasticism,* p. 93. Italics his.

other "language."[29] Before this kind of presentation even those
wisest in the verbal wisdom of this world have nothing more to say.
The simplest piece of art, Rouault says expansively, can derail the
wisest doctors for a hundred years.[30] If the "gest" is the verb of
silence, what can be the "word" fit to judge art? In disparaging
attempts at explanation and commentary, Rouault once commented:

> Form, color, harmony, one more often discusses them stupidly than
> well. But tomorrow only the poor work of art remains to defend
> itself, completely apart from the subtle and delicate eloquences of
> the partisans of the moment. Farewell press, dealers, critics, friends
> or followers.[31]

He warned young painters to stay away from critics:

> For these gentlemen deform everything while they think they are
> explaining it. Especially an epic or legendary art escapes such an
> exercise in intelligent "dissection" that wishes to leave nothing in the
> shadows.[32]

Can art be explained?

> It is hardly the function of the artist, certainly not of a workman at
> his best. These are the things one feels without being able to explain:
> in fact they lie in the area of prescience.[33]

> "We make a mute art". The end of art is delight.[34]

The perspicuity of art cannot be explained nor its syntax precisely described. But a general sort of explanation must be sketched
if we are to proceed at all in the discussion of faith and art. For
having established the primacy of the work in our considerations,
if we further conclude that it is thereby inviolable and utterly im-
pregnable the relation of faith and art is a purely academic question. Rouault has spoken of his art as "mute," but he qualifies its
aphonia by stating that the end of art is delight. Something is com-
municable. Rouault, in another place, implies that the "language"
of art can be learned, at least in part.

> The language of forms and colors . . . must be seriously learned, ab-
> sorbed during a whole lifetime of love and, in addition, of authentic

---

[29] This word should be used cautiously. Artistic language lacks the regu-
larity and flexibility of verbal expression, but it is not thereby purely emotional nor strictly anti-verbal. Susanne K. Langer has attempted to describe
the kind of symbolism employed in art as presentational form. Cf. *Philosophy in a New Key* (New York: The New American Library, 1951), chapter 4.
[30] *Soliloques*, p. 66.
[31] *Cahiers d'Art*, 1928, *op. cit.*, p. 102.
[32] *Soliloques*, p. 93.
[33] Rouault. "Enquête." *Cahiers d'Art*, 1935, p. 14.
[34] *Ibid.*, p. 11.

gifts. One spends his life, in a spirit of love and humility, decipher-
ing imperfectly Nature and Humanity.[35]

It is crucial to recall here two facts. First, Rouault never has divorced himself from the human situation or from nature. In fact, he
suggested that in his mind his paintings were subordinated to the
human condition he felt so deeply. Do not give me so much importance, he would say:

> A cry in the night. A stifled sob. A suppressed laugh. In this world,
> every day, a thousand unknown persons that are worth more than I
> labor on and die at the task.[36]

Yet, secondly, Rouault belongs to the artistic movement that has
removed all external reference points from the picture itself. This
we considered in Chapter 3 and need not belabor. Critics have
not failed to point out this fact. Rouault has maintained the full
importance of his subject while at the same time liberating his own
powerful aesthetic emotions through the subject.[37] Space is not
that given in reality but comes from the imagination.[38] His forms
also emphasize impression rather than simple anatomical resemblance.[39]

In other words, painting, for Rouault as for most modern artists,
is more than simple representation. But never having isolated himself from humanity, tirelessly tracking down the glory that is in
man, he is not any less "true" to reality. Though one cannot point
out exactly what real subjects Rouault is painting,[40] all the world
can identify with the human situation that emerges from his canvases. Leon-Martin expresses the same thought:

> No one has made a work at once less *exact* and more *true,* and just
> here lay the initial misunderstanding of the artist with his public. He
> imported such justice of relations! Few artists have known how to
> capture the truth to this degree.[41]

The point is crucial: exactitude is not the measure of truthfulness

---

[35] Quoted in Louis Leon-Martin. "Georges Rouault." *Art & Décoration,*
1930, vol. 57, p. 111.

[36] Quoted in Charensol, *op. cit.,* p. 7.

[37] Jewell, *op. cit.,* p. 11.

[38] Venturi, 1948, pp. 34, 35. See Brian O'Doherty's fine discussion of
Rouault's use of space in *Studies,* Spring, 1956, p. 71.

[39] Robert Rey. "Rouault et Vuillard." *Bulletin des Musées de France,* June,
1929, p. 126.

[40] It is doubtful that in fact Rouault used models for his prostitutes, for
example; he seldom painted portraits. Dorival concludes his article on this
subject by noting that for Rouault "the individual cannot be the object of
art." *Op. cit., La Revue des Arts,* 1953, p. 237.

[41] *Art & Décoration, op. cit.,* 1930, p. 112. We shall return to this point
in our discussion of nature in Chapter 15 below.

in art. A work can be less exact and more true-to-life; no contradiction is expressed or implied.

We can perhaps draw these reflections together by looking at religious art in Rouault's work. Among those trying to track down Rouault as a religious artist, René Baucher makes some interesting comments in an article appearing in 1951. Beginning with the assertion that art is not a document, he seeks to show that it is really a catalyst to achieve integration of the inner man. The actual "contents" of a work are then viewed negatively. Baucher believes "their only possible function is to efface themselves while preparing the way for something else. . . ."[42] This "something else" for him is a prayer of meditation.

But the fact that art is not a document or a representative likeness does not mean that it cannot be "truthful," as we have noted. It can be true in and of itself; its value need not consist in what it does to or for the viewer. Analogously, the fact that art is not a confession of faith does not imply that it cannot be true to those confessions. It may say the same "truth" in a different manner. If we deny this we risk separating faith from life in a way that many modern artists have separated art from life. For the Christian after all it is the truth and not art that should move us to prayer. This unity Rouault felt and strove after, commenting, "All my work is religious for those who know how to look at it."[43]

The fact that art was paramount though not unrelated to life suggests the way in which Rouault viewed his vocation as an artist. That he was an artist defined all other aspects of life. He did not view himself as an artist only in a professional sense. Being an artist was for him what it meant to be a person. We can illustrate this by considering two metaphors which he employed for his view of art: that of a promised land and that of salvation.

Art for Rouault was a "promised land" in the dual sense of a refuge and an envisioned goal. The love he had for his vocation ("I love my art as much as I ever loved my father," he told Suarès after the death of his father[44]), and the boundless satisfaction he found therein made him look upon it as a refuge and an oasis in the midst of black and troubled times. His studio was for him a world apart. For art had for him, above all, spiritual value; it was a fountain from which his soul could take deep draughts.[45]

---

[42] "Rouault et la peinture religieuse." *Synthèses,* January, 1951, pp. 224, 225.

[43] Quoted in exposition catalogue, Musée de Dieppe, 1963, Introduction by Jean Lapeyre, p. ix.

[44] *Correspondance,* p. 19.

[45] Cf. "Enquête," *op. cit.,* pp. 12, 14; also Roulet, *op. cit.,* p. 304.

Beyond a present satisfaction as a "homeland," art held for Rouault a future hope. There was a prospect of fulfillment in art that transcended human capabilities, an infinite quality the way to which was barred to finitude. He admits to Suarès in 1925: "I am unhappy and lonely, like Moses searching for the promised land."[46] In a sensitive article written in 1913 he notes how this sense awakened early in his life:

> When art was for me the Promised Land, so far away (it will be so until I die), Forain awakened in the child that I was, with a black and white sketch, a glimmer, the inner intuition of a rare thing.... This, after the task of *well made* designs of the evening classes, made me hold on to a hope.... If I was joyous it was because I felt a distant echo in myself by a phrase overheard, a word, a gesture, as though I was just passing by. I did not have *the means* to say it. I had much to learn, but I had a secret instinct that made me feel here was a truly living source.[47]

To attempt a commentary on this ineffable sense would be vain. Let us simply note again the duality of this metaphor: art is at once a present refuge and a future promise. Indeed, the abiding satisfaction points beyond itself, calling for an infinite context. Rouault sensed this.

> The bad side of my character is that I am never *content with myself*. I do not fully enjoy *my successes*, and I have always progress to make, in the eye and in the mind.[48]

Art then presents us with a parable, and perhaps an instance, of the eschatological character of human spiritual capacities. As for the Christian, salvation is both a present possession and a future fulfillment, so for the artist the present reaches beyond itself.

At first blush such a comparison with salvation appears as an overstatement. But the second metaphor Rouault used shows that it is not: At times he refers to his art as a kind of "salvation." We observed earlier that in an artist who has faith one cannot separate the realms of Christian creativity and religious experience. They can be distinguished but not isolated. Rouault attempts to express the quasi-redemptive quality of art in this way.

> Beloved art, you are not always so guileless as they like to say and explain. Would it be too much to claim that you were for some ancients or moderns, in a sense, our security, I almost dare to say

---

[46] Letter of August 24. *Correspondance, in loc.*
[47] "A Propos de Forain." *La Vie*, 25 January 1913, no. 3, pp. 410, 411. Italics his.
[48] *Correspondance*, pp. 81, 82. Italics his.

our redemption. For these good companions and for me especially, this is the meaning of our tenacious effort.[49]

In another place he calls art a "deliverance" for him, as when a mother brings a child into the world.[50] To Suarès he confesses: "My resurrection and my only function is to paint."[51]

Painting for Rouault was a deadly serious pursuit. In his *Soliloques* he decries those lovers of pleasure for whom the function of art is merely to pass the time. "For this poor wretch," he professed, "art is the sole *raison d'être*."[52] It takes none of the joy and excitement out of art to admit that, for the artist, to create is serious and deeply meaningful. The happiest hours that children spend playing are when they are most serious about the rules of their games. For in such experiences a person discovers more about himself and his world. Here the Socratic rational knowledge of oneself is enlarged to include self-discovery in the active adventure of doing, making, and forming. Rouault urges this upon Suarès in 1913.

> *To know yourself,* not by discussion, analysis, and verbiage, but to know yourself by suffering and in suffering. To know yourself by living and in living, far from snobbism and the contrived, but in the truth and in *the effort* of all our being.[53]

This means the artist, as the rich young ruler of the Gospels, must "leave all."[54]

The artist's pursuit is of course primarily aesthetic, but for the Christian artist it is not wholly secular. Like all of life, it has a religious dimension. If art points to the eternal future, it is God who provides the surety. If art blossoms in dark anguished nights of creative struggle, it is God who has so endowed the human spirit. Again Rouault notes in a letter to Suarès:

> If God gives us the "inner humility" we are saved, for the "language of God" and his Spirit come to the aid of him who retires sincerely within himself, following *the gifts* he possesses.[55]

---

[49] "Le Pêcheur de perles." *Op. cit.,* p. 32.

[50] *Soliloques,* p. 52.

[51] *Correspondance,* p. 137.

[52] P. 46.

[53] *Correspondance,* p. 43. Italics his.

[54] *Ibid.,* p. 126.

[55] *Ibid.,* p. 11, 1911. Italics his. It is this acknowledgment of the Divine Presence that sets Rouault clearly apart from a Sartrian view of creativity. Jean-Paul Sartre too says: "By writing I was existing . . . and if I said 'I,' that meant 'I who write.'" *The Words* (New York: Geo. Braziller, 1964), p. 153. But his universe is closed to any divine activity, and in denying any future fulfillment, the creative tension noted in Rouault is missing. Cf. especially his "François Mauriac." *Literary and Philosophical Essays* (New York: Collier Books, 1962).

We would stop short of saying that creating for Rouault and truly Christian artists is the means of salvation, for this is clearly provided by a sovereign and loving God. But creating is clearly their Christian vocation. It is perhaps involved with what Paul urges upon all believers in Philippians 2:12 and 13: "...work out your own salvation with fear and trembling, for God is at work in you, both to will and to work for his good pleasure." But this possibility must be more a point of departure than a conclusion, and it will lead us to consider further questions: What does man experience in the state of grace? Should we not see in salvation a healthy aesthetic enrichment and responsibility as well as an ethical rebirth?

In the section dealing with Rouault's contemporaries, the painter's individuality became readily visible. Now we come to discuss a different sort of loneliness that was a part of the fabric of Rouault's view of his vocation. This is the essential privacy of Rouault's vision, a world the artist can share with no one. "Creators... are and ought to be solitary,"[56] he proclaimed. "One is born alone.... Solitude is the natural dwelling place of all thought."[57] One does not seek such retreat; it follows from the liberty of spirit that is the artist's prized possession. When an artist creates, only his personal vista is relevant.

> What does it matter then what you say, or what you do, or what you think, the moment I am not forced to see reality and men's works on the same horizon as you.[58]

If what others thought made little difference to Rouault's work, he was just as willing to admit that his opinion was irrelevant to the work of other artists. An artist ultimately must be silent as he stands among his peers and cannot be their critic. When questioned once about his views on A. Derain, Rouault refused to answer either for or against, excusing himself by saying: "It is enough to be *very much in love with your own art* in order sometimes to render a very false critical judgment about another."[59]

This independence of spirit must immediately be balanced by noting Rouault's deeply felt community with others. His solitude was *artistic*, essentially asocial rather than anti-social. True, he kept his address from all but Suarès,[60] but this was for professional rather than personal reasons. He was afraid that the people would not

---

[56] Quoted in Henri Perruchot. "Georges Rouault: l'insatisfait." *Le Jardin des Arts,* June, 1967, no. 151, p. 10.

[57] Quoted in Dorival. *Rouault* (Geneva: René Kister, 1956), p. 10.

[58] *Soliloques,* p. 68.

[59] Rouault. "Pour ou contre." *Les Chroniques du Jour,* January, 1931, no. 9, p. 3. Italics his.

[60] *Correspondance,* p. 161.

understand what he did; thus he exhibited what must have seemed an extreme artistic shyness. He confessed this to Suarès:

> I always have the impression of being nude and trembling when I show my work even to those who understand me infinitely better than most people. This can become physically painful. You might say I am sick. It is possible.[61]

He knew well the fickle nature of the approbation of the crowd. He sought a beauty and dignity that was more secret than they would understand. He believed that one cannot

> ... ask the crowd to support, understand and love that which is not always lovable, but is sometimes painful and hard to penetrate. It 'is possible that they understand one minute, but that they will detest tomorrow what they adored yesterday.[62]

Artistically, then, he could not but live in isolation. To those who felt him proud he responded that they would never know "the dread of birth pangs that a man isolated from the world can feel. . . . No one will ever be his judge, in spite of all the pawns, the critics and the people of good sense and reason."[63] Nevertheless, personally he felt himself one with the people. "I am of the people," he would repeat. Rouault consistently displayed a deep feeling for others. How can one be detached in art, Rouault often wondered, and little concerned with the happy or unhappy events of the next person? How can an artist remain a stranger to humanity?

By way of illustration and explication we will conclude these comments on Rouault's view of his vocation with a reference to his relationship to Ambroise Vollard, his dealer. Through the 22 years of their cooperation, Rouault's vocation was severely tested and became clearly evident. When Vollard became Rouault's dealer in 1917, he was already recognized as an astute, well-established dealer who had previously championed Cézanne, Renoir, Pisarro and Degas. The last once called Vollard the "slave trader"—and indeed, Vollard was known to have a piratical side to his nature. This somehow made him fit uneasily into Paris life.[64]

Though he was a well-established figure in 1917, an unfulfilled urge led him to produce books. He had soon persuaded Rouault to do a series of etchings for a book Vollard envisioned, Les Réincarnations du Père Ubu, a task both Forain and Derain had previously refused. Rouault agreed and set to work with such vigor that he virtually disappeared from sight for the fourteen years it took to com-

---

[61] Ibid., p. 169.
[62] "Enquête," op. cit., p. 11.
[63] Correspondance, p. 57.
[64] In fact he was born on the Reunion Island.

plete the task.[65] Of Rouault's fate Louis Vauxcelles commented: "M. Vollard has done with him what he did with Cézanne, he has stored him away in the cellar."[66]

What was Rouault's own reaction to the "bondage"? The case is often overstated, for their relationship was quite cordial. Vollard left Rouault completely free to do as he liked with his illustrations for *Père Ubu,* and the theme Rouault developed suited the painter well: exposing the stupidity and dishonesty of the rich. He sought an analogue to the text rather than an "illustration." In all, Rouault admits, Vollard, under his rude aspect, was generous with him.[67]

Still, those were demanding days. Rouault was pressed both by an impatient editor and by his own inner needs. Rouault at times admitted to Suarès that he had taken on too much. "I have a horror of continuous and useless little struggles. . . . You use up your energy, often without much result."[68] Often Suarès, who also had occasion to work with Vollard, decried to Rouault the dealer's lack of sensitivity. Once he wrote to Rouault: "He does not take our lives into account. There is the error."[69] Yet through it all Rouault never once lost the sense of his calling. In 1935 he told Suarès: "I have an inner peace—not always—but infinitely more often than the likes of those who imagine painting is done with the end of your tongue rather than with brushes and color."[70]

Two years later he emphasized: "I have an infinite patience when it is a question of spiritual matters. But patience can still be used up and human energy sometimes has a limit."[71] Art for Rouault, intensely personal and serious an affair of the spirit though it was, was determined from within and blossomed even in the most adverse circumstances. The nature of this interior drive will occupy our attention in the final section of this chapter.

In considering Rouault's own view of his vocation we have discussed the primacy of the artistic process and the intensely personal nature of his calling. Both of these facets resulted in a third characteristic: the impelling and intuitive nature of his art. An artist *works,* for he must. An artist *creates,* for he is impelled. He neither

---

[65] The prodigious output of these years became apparent only much later. Among the books alone that he worked on then, in addition to the *Ré-incarnations,* which appeared in 1932, were *Miserere,* 1948; *Legendary Landscapes,* 1929; *Depressed Suburbs,* 1929; and his own *Souvenirs Intimes,* 1926.

[66] *L'Ere Nouvelle,* April 24, 1924, quoted in Courthion, p. 186.

[67] Cf. "Georges Rouault et Ambroise Vollard." *Beaux-Arts,* June 16, 1933, p. 6.

[68] *Correspondance,* p. 287. Cf. also pp. 289, 291.

[69] *Ibid.,* p. 290.

[70] *Ibid.,* p. 294.

[71] *Ibid.,* p. 307.

analyzes nor debates. The reason, we repeat—for it bears repetition
—is that in his activity as an artist he finds his meaning in life.

It is one of the strangest aspects of the life of Rouault that this
somewhat timid, solitary figure should create an art that ran contrary
to all contemporary taste, frightful to himself and those around him.
His deep-seated sensitivity toward all tragedy and darkness stands in
sharp contrast to the peaceful and more or less happy character of
his life. He suffered through three wars, though he never was a
combatant. He sorrowed with the homeless though he was himself
never without a home. That his vision was at times horrible even
to himself he admits. In the early years of the century

> When I looked at some of my pictures I said to myself: "Did I paint
> that? Is it possible? It is frightful what I have done."[72]

Something of the ugliness he had created seemed not to suit him.
Yet he could not forbear:

> I had the nostalgic and naive feelings of a little apprentice from the
> poor neighborhood.... I was not made to be as terrible as they said
> I was.[73]

Vision for the artist is not expendable, no matter what the hin-
drances. And obstacles abounded for Rouault. We have noted already his immutability before the withering blasts of Bloy. Two additional situations serve to illustrate the profound sort of opposition
Rouault faced.

During the early days of his sojourn at Versailles[74] the Maritains,
his neighbors, tell of the debate Rouault was having with himself.
He had to support his family, and his style was so far from the
contemporary mode that his pictures were selling badly. It would
have been easy to paint pictures that would sell. He had but to
return to the style of "Child Jesus Among the Doctors." Some
friends advised him to do so. But for Rouault the purity of his
artistic conscience was more important than a large income. It
could not be renounced even to follow such a one as Rembrandt.
Still, the daily needs of a growing family made his decision exceed-
ingly difficult. "The dream of Rouault," he confessed once to Suarès,
"is to meet by himself the needs of his little family without sur-
rendering an atom of his ideas."[75]

In 1911 Rouault met a writer who was to be a great source of
strength and encouragement to him, André Suarès (1868-1948). Their
long and sensitive friendship lasted until the death of Suarès. In

---

[72] Quoted in Charensol, op. cit., p. 24.
[73] SI, p. 13.
[74] Rouault moved to Versailles with his family in 1911.
[75] Correspondance, p. 52, 1913. Cf. R. Maritain, op. cit., vol. 1, pp. 222, 223.

many ways their correspondence reveals a deep mutual understanding. Yet even Suarès began to tire of Rouault's constant emphasis on the negative. Don't stay long in hell, he would urge: "it is enough to pass through."[76] "The artist ought," Suarès explained in one letter, "to deliver the world from pain, even if he does not deliver himself from his own suffering." Rouault answered: "I know my weakness: although I have a quick critical sense, I still ask too much of men."[77] Perhaps, Rouault implies, this accounted for his personal dissatisfaction. Then in 1913 Suarès rejoined, in the spirit of modern psychology, that since you had this in you it had to come out. But now make an end of it, Suarès advised. "Live in love with nature from now on." Above all, do not deny. "We are artists in order to affirm, that is, to create a beautiful form. . . . Our business is to be and not to deny."[78] Soon Suarès began to show a slight irritation with Rouault's persistence.[79]

Clearly Suarès was much more a man of classical culture: he was the Erasmus, Rouault the Luther. He despised anger ("One cannot despise himself enough for the times he has gotten angry."[80]). He laid great stress on the love of God ("It is the love of God that unites us."[81]). He took great pains with the clothes he wore and with his appearance. It is little wonder that he should find the melancholy side of Rouault difficult to understand. Yet fifteen years later, in 1929, Suarès began to speak much more of tragedy. He dedicated Variables "To my dear Rouault, who has a deep understanding of our mystery and of our tragedy."[82]

As an artist Rouault remained totally unmoved by all such pressures. He too felt the need to affirm, and put it this way in an article he wrote together with Suarès in 1926: "Artists should create and not always criticize and deny. The one who creates has need of a great faith in the midst of indifference and hostility."[83] But what is to be affirmed is not always pretty. Besides, affirmation is not suggested from without; it must spring from within.

Critics have not failed to note this constraining nature of Rouault's vision. Puy describes this vision as one that seizes him and creates exciting beings through him.[84] Lhote calls it his urgent message: "The conviction that a work of art has a mission greater

---

[76] Correspondance, pp. 38, 63; 1911, 1912.
[77] Ibid., p. 41.
[78] Ibid., p. 62.
[79] Cf. especially ibid., p. 65.
[80] Ibid., p. 85.
[81] Ibid., p. 225.
[82] Ibid., p. 253. On Suarès' refinement see pp. 84, 85.
[83] "Moreau." Op. cit., p. 242.
[84] Puy, op. cit., p. 7.

than entertainment to fulfill."[85] Indeed Rouault confessed that his themes were not chosen but imposed upon him from within.[86] J. Maritain asserted that Rouault could not reply to the blasts of Bloy because "he is obedient to a living necessity stronger than himself."[87]

This impulsion, then, came from an inner necessity that was founded on his faith. R. Maritain describes him as struggling

> ... toward a personal form of art, adequate to his deepest need, that which was uniquely true for him, uniquely authentic.... He was penetrated by the absolute demands and postulates of his faith. It was a faith that was simple and profound, perhaps like that of the builders of the cathedrals.[88]

From this position we are able to see a bit more clearly how his faith worked itself out in his work and determined his vocation. Faith was not sought after, nor was it a religiously motivating guide. It had taken root in the artist and sprung up flowering after its kind. Here again we will venture a Biblical analogy. Perhaps we can see in Rouault's spiritual motivation and impellent the kind of impulsion St. Paul felt to preach the Gospel.[89] Especially when it is guided by the Spirit of God, truth demands expression.

So we have come the full circle. Art was not a declaration of faith, for art as a medium was primary. Art must be its own end; it is not conditioned nor directed from outside itself. Yet for the truly Christian artist there comes a deeply felt impulsion to create a world after the image of the creator-believer. Art becomes after all an ardent confession: not a recitation of faith by pictures but a cry of faith in the dark night of unbelief.

---

[85] *La Nouvelle Revue Française.* 1934, vol. II, no. 43, p. 304.
[86] Georges Charensol. "Rouault." *L'Art Vivant,* 1926, no. 28, p. 128.
[87] *La Revue Universelle, op. cit.,* 1924, p. 508.
[88] *Op. cit.,* vol. II, pp. 44, 45.
[89] I Corinthians 9:16.

7. Phases of Development in the Work of Rouault

Around the turn of the century, we have observed, a radical change in the work of Rouault coincided with a spiritual revolution. This change was seminal to all that followed. From that point, though his painting did not remain static, the evolution of his style —which is so obvious even to the casual observer—was formally determined. The subsequent path should be seen as a flowering rather than a quest, a material growth rather than a formal revolution. To ascertain this we must not only study Rouault's unfolding work, but also what critics and students of his work may have noted about its development. A brief study of this kind may not only throw light on the question of chronological development but also serve as a helpful introduction to the thematic study of Rouault's work which follows.

We will make use of the catalogue of works prepared with the cooperation of Isabelle Rouault, reproduced in Courthion's book.[1] The tentative nature of all questions of date is underlined in the case of Rouault by his practice of finishing a work only after long periods of time and by many sessions often years apart. Thus the

---

[1] Courthion's listing of Rouault's work although not exhaustive is comprehensive enough to be informative for our purposes. In the following discussion we shall use the following abbreviations: C., followed by two sets of figures = Courthion, page number and date; cc., followed by two sets of figures = classified catalogue number and date; M., followed by one set of figures = *Miserere*, 1963 edition, and plate number. Page numbers alone refer to reproductions in this book. The tentative nature of our figures ought to emphasize from the start that there is no unanimity as to which paintings belong in which category. For example, are Biblical or Christian names such as "Marie" cc. 383 or "Veronica" cc. 386 always to have a religious connotation or are they simply, as Courthion's list implies, studies of women? The counts in every case are the present author's, whose responsibility must be the errors in categorization.

date on the painting does not always accurately represent chronological development. Nevertheless, certain broad periods can be
defined as follows, with the fundamental agreement of the critics:
(1) 1902-1912, (2) 1913-1932, (3) 1933-1940, (4) 1941-1958. Let us
look at each briefly in an attempt to discover the key aspects of
each and their unfolding.

(1) 1902-1912. This is the period of Rouault's *tableaux noirs*. Not
until 1902 was the "turn of the helm" fully accomplished, and then
Rouault began the black drawings for which this period is known.
Courthion lists 167 works in this epoque, among them not more
than 17 of the notorious prostitute motif. An additional 20 are of
bathers and nudes, often done in the same dark style (though no
less than 14 of the nudes and prostitutes date from 1906). Some 34
are of clowns and circus themes. Eight deal directly with fugitives
and social ills (all in 1911 and 1912), while nine deal with courts
and accused men. Only six are occupied with religious themes (only
two prior to 1910). The balance consists of landscapes and studies
of men and women. Though an emphasis on somber colors and
dark, heavy outlines predominates, even here there are instances
of the rich color that was to become evident later.[2] While his work
during this period was not exclusively occupied with these tragic
aspects as has often been assumed, nevertheless human degradation seems to have been a primary theme.

Venturi claims this period was for Rouault the voyage into hell
(of which 1906 marked the extremity), from which he returned with
fresh resolve. In the "Nude with Raised Arms" of 1907, C. 85, Venturi
sees already a fresh current of grace. After this, Venturi claims, "he
forgets the violence and detaches himself from the world with which
he was irritated, and grace seems to fall on him, spontaneously, from
the sky."[3] But he is quick to qualify the detachment of the later
Rouault. The painter finds his serenity not by forgetting hell but by
finding an answer to it in grace. Gustave Kahn had asked in the
Mercure de France, 16 January 1912: "Is this violent and satiric art

---

[2] Not only Courthion but also Roger-Marx had early seen the parts color
and tone were to play in Rouault's drama. Marx wrote in 1896 regarding
"The dead Christ mourned by the Holy Women": "The trace can still be
seen there of his fervent study of the masters. But a gift shines through in
the severe ordering of the composition and in the choice of this greenish
tonality that is sumptuously spread over the whole surface and that adds
so much to the horror of the drama." "Salon des Champs Elysées," *La Revue
Encyclopédique*, 1896, p. 299. Recently Albert Boime has studied Rouault's
offerings for the competitions of sketch compositions held four times a
year at the school. The freedom and stimulus of these sketches provided
occasions for Rouault to demonstrate signs of his future style. Cf. *Art Journal*,
Fall, 1969, vol. 29, no. 1, pp. 36-39.

[3] Venturi, 1948, p. 60.

the last word of M. Rouault?" Perhaps, he goes on to wonder, after having crossed hell he will return to Eden.[4] But that, as Venturi notes, is just what Rouault could never do. Once he had seen hell, the world would never look the same again.

It is well to remind ourselves that only the year before Kahn's comments, Rouault had confessed in a letter to Suarès: "... To this day my conscience as an artist has remained pure.... But the struggle seems to me so arduous and so wearisome that I would not advise anyone to follow me."[5] Certainly we would do well never to separate the work of this period from the anguish Rouault was suffering. All traces of hypocrisy were absent; his conscience was pure.[6]

If Rouault could never see the world except in its damned perspective, neither could he help but see damnation in relation to grace and salvation. The enumeration of paintings done in this phase has shown that the blackness in the early years is often overstated. Moreover, even in the most tragic of the themes, that of the prostitutes, the subject is not unmitigated depravity. Rouault's *filles* are not merely coarse but horrible, for though they have lost hope they are not painted without reference to hope. Even in the worst, Cocagnac notes, there is a kind of luminosity that seems to reflect the love of God.[7]

It is tempting to see in this period only depravity, so that the change in the later years shines more brightly by contrast. Michel Hoog, though he is careful to avoid making these characterizations overly narrow, believes this period represents "fallen humanity," and in the period after 1912 he perceives a clear religious evolution.[8] The discontinuity before and after 1912 is abundantly obvious; as Hoog rightly insists, one cannot equate a clown in this period with one done later. The blackness before leaves a bitter taste. But the continuity must also be pointed out. Grace does not miraculously enter the work of Rouault after 1912. Rather, the grace which during the early years made the darkness profound glowed even brighter in the years following.

(2) 1913-1932. Jacques Rivière, after Rouault's first one-man show at the Gallery Druet in 1910, discussed the fierce strength of his

---

[4] Vol. 85, p. 409. Kahn sees in the blackness of the early period a vengeance due to a lost happiness and abandonment of its search.

[5] *Correspondance,* August, 1911, p. 6.

[6] Cf. Pierre Berthelot. "Rouault." *Beaux-Arts,* 1931, A. 25, p. 24. How much more fallacious in the light of this is the insidious suggestion of Berthelot that Rouault was continuing in his excesses for reasons of financial gain!

[7] *Op. cit., L'Art Sacré,* January-February, 1964, 5-6, p. 6. Cf. chapter 12, below.

[8] *Op. cit., Etudes,* September, 1964, p. 218.

forms and concluded: "However, we will ask that from now on Rouault show us a more controlled manner." So many studies, he supposed, ought to end in a more definite realization.[9] And the change he looked for was not long in coming. By 1913 or a little later (Courthion sets the date 1915, Venturi not until 1917) a distinct evolution had occurred. In the period from 1913 to 1932 there are 163 works listed by Courthion. Only one takes the prostitute theme and six others depict nudes and bathers. No less than 32 studies are of clowns and the circus. Four times he returned to the courtroom motif. The sins of pride exhibited by high society concerned him four times, other social and spiritual ills of poverty and hopelessness eleven times. Seventeen works deal with religious subjects. Most of the rest of his work consisted of gouache and etchings for Vollard's books. So there is no clear transformation in Rouault's subject matter, except in the relative frequency of different subjects.

Courthion sees the change largely in the importance given to the subject portrayed. After 1910, he felt, the image on the canvas became increasingly less prominent. What mattered henceforth was what Courthion calls the genuinely transcendent emotion expressed through line and pigment.[10] Venturi concurs in the judgment that style overtook subject matter. In this stage (especially after World War I), he says, color constituted a catharsis for passion. Rouault's work was less architectonic and more spontaneous; his colors were more phosphorescent.[11] He achieved more of the autonomy modern art has championed. It is the synthesis of planes and colored areas which builds the image in a manner that is autonomous with respect to nature.[12] Venturi believes Rouault at this stage was less interested in revolt than in composition. From the ferocious attack of the early period, Rouault moved to create a technique "which is the very style of the message itself, without, however, having to resort to that message."[13]

E. A. Jewell, who accuses Rouault of a primitive obscurity during the earlier period, claims that around 1916 the terror began to give way to more tenderness. The fire burned still, he stresses in an apt metaphor, but softly and radiantly. Then, in what is perhaps an overstatement, he summarizes that "the violence gives place to an almost angelic splendor."[14]

---

[9] "Exposition Georges Rouault." *La Nouvelle Revue Française,* 1910, 3:538.
[10] P. 154.
[11] Venturi, 1948, p. 80.
[12] Venturi, 1959, p. 62.
[13] Venturi, 1948, p. 65. Cf. also p. 66.
[14] Jewell, *op. cit.,* p. 9.

For Michel Hoog, while the first period was "fallen humanity," the second has as its theme "Christ suffering." Humanity is thus inevitably changed.

> It is a humanity still fallen, but it struggles in its degradation which it has come to recognize. Above all, hope now appears: "He who believes in me, though he dies, yet shall live."[15]

Hope is indeed more prominent in this period, beginning with the first "Christ on the Cross" in 1913 and increasing in the following years. But we ought not to conclude that hope was an entirely new element, completely alien to Rouault's earlier work. For that is not the case. Withal, the change that brought Rouault out of his darkness was primarily one of style and not one of subject matter. The latter was inevitably affected, but we cannot call the change a religious evolution.

(3) 1933-1940. That Rouault's work had not essentially changed by 1930 is evident by the blasts that continued in his direction. In 1931 Roger-Marx asserted that so far Rouault had only shown his somber face. "Tomorrow, no doubt, liberated, redeemed, he will open to us his paradise."[16] Certainly it is in the third epoch that Rouault reached the full expression of his ability. Rouault's works during these eight years number 224.[17] Prostitutes and nudes disappear as a theme and do not reappear in the rest of Rouault's life. But the circus motif is treated 61 times, courts and judges five times. Above all this is the flowering of purely religious themes, which receive attention in some 58 pictures. The satanic theme also becomes more prominent, appearing 5 times. Rouault's world is a more peaceful one, yet the tragic is by no means absent (the sorrow and loneliness of the poor appear on 11 occasions). Marcel Arland said of Rouault's 1937 retrospective in the Petit Palace that while this exhibition marked the high point of the painter's work, his world was still the most tragic a painter had ever created.[18] Other than a ripening of the painter's ability, what were Rouault's achievements during these years?

The critics agree that this time marked the triumph of Rouault's compositions and the culmination of his researches therein. In fact, Venturi goes so far as to claim that Rouault's search for chromatic and structural perfection "distracts Rouault from his original vio-

---

[15] Hoog, op. cit., Etudes, September, 1964, p. 218.

[16] "L'Oeuvre gravée de Georges Rouault." Byblis, 1931, p. 100.

[17] Although in 1938 Rouault signed together a large number that he had worked on over a period of many years.

[18] "Premier regard sur l'exposition des maîtres de l'art indépendant." La Nouvelle Revue Française, 1937, 25 année, p. 352.

lence, whether religious or social."[19] In the "Crucifixion" C. 274, 1939, "the drama is no longer expressed by the faces and the gestures but by a harmony of the forms themselves."[20] The elements of the picture themselves had become expressive.

Dorival, in a similar vein, notes that the expression and plastic elements unite with Rouault, and the whole becomes filled with spiritual life and human signification. Even the subject serves the meaning thus imported and is raised to a kind of type. Dorival lists "The Old King," p. 111, 1937, as a prime example.[21] That work also marks a stage in the gradual reduction of the human figure to just the head, a process which was finished after 1940. The emphasis is on the person, not as an individual but as an expression of human and spiritual significance.

Soby feels that this process so softened Rouault's vision that it belied his prediction that he would be a prisoner of darkness until his death. Even the "Wounded Clown" C. 258, says Soby, "is treated fairly dispassionately, and depends for its impact upon more traditional esthetic qualities."[22] Venturi, too, notes the importance of this work—which he dates around 1933—but supremely as a plastic event. It is an example of the image being taken up into the composition. He adds quickly that the drama remains, though now expressed by the pictorial elements themselves. In a happy phrase he notes that the figures hereafter live in a melancholic meditation upon the theme.[23] The drama here is a logical extension of the darkness of Rouault's early period. The same message which was earlier depicted is now incarnated in human figures.

(4) 1941-1958. In the final period serenity reigns. Rouault worked continuously almost until his death, producing many of his *chef-d'oeuvres* in these later years. His works here number 205, of which 42 present the circus theme, 5 judges and court pieces. Religious subjects make up an even greater percentage: 47 canvases, including the important Biblical landscapes. He is still occupied with the subject of death—4 times—and paints a number of twilight and late autumn landscapes (4 of these in 1952 alone). Certainly the keynote is a luxurious depth that enabled Christian Zervos to say of the 1952 retrospective in Paris: "It is no longer a question of bruised hopes but of an almost mystical serenity."[24] This, too, stimu-

---

[19] Venturi, 1959, p. 82.

[20] Courthion, p. 96.

[21] *Cinq études . . .*, p. 22. Soby sees this painting as also the culmination of Rouault's increasing interest in sensuous qualities of pigment. *Op. cit.,* p. 17.

[22] Soby, *op. cit.,* p. 28.

[23] Venturi, 1959, pp. 95-96.

[24] Zervos, "Approches . . .," *op. cit.,* p. 101.

lated Agnès Humbert to claim that a peace had transfigured his art by the end.[25]

If the previous period marked the triumph of composition, this final one hails the victory of color. Venturi claims that after 1940 the image was more and more absorbed by sumptuous, hot colors. Until 1948 blues predominated, after this date greens, yellows, and reds. Forms themselves display the vitalities of color.[26] This gives what Venturi calls a religious sense to everything.[27]

Claude Roger-Marx, whose father, Roger-Marx, was one of the first to notice Rouault's gifts, sees also a culmination of the contemplative but feels this resulted in a *less* religious art. Even religious scenes such as " 'The Flight into Egypt' are more traditional than mystical, more profane than supernatural. Here hope is missing." Rouault, he concludes, was a religious painter by aspiration only. "His feet are still mired in the mud."[28] Even in the final years Rouault, according to Roger-Marx, failed as a religious painter through lack of purity. We are tempted to suggest that Roger-Marx is revealing as much of his view of religion as of his critical judgment.

Dorival, by contrast, believes these final years produced the finest of truly sacred art. The landscapes which became more prominent towards the end tended toward the abstract. Along with color, Rouault emphasized ellipses and semi-circles, giving to the whole the movement of the cosmos. Dorival concludes: "It is surely a sacred jubilation that is set loose in this series."[29]

Michel Hoog also finds a great religious importance in the last period. Believing Rouault's art has followed the history of mankind, he sees the key in "Veronica" C. 249, 1945, and cc. 386, 1938, and correctly notes the importance of the face for Rouault. In the first period Rouault's art stressed human depravity; in the second, Christ on the cross—that is, Christ bearing on his visage the sin of man. The final era Hoog describes in this way: "The face of sinful man, which Rouault took to give to Christ, has been given back to man by the Savior, but redeemed and appeased. 'Veronica' is the one who by a gesture of pity has transmitted to man the face of Christ."[30] Though Hoog insists this is not a neat pattern, it nevertheless intimates that there was no hopelessness in the last. Here the evidence suggests caution. The *Stella Vespertina* published in 1947, for exam-

---

[25] *Scottish Art Review,* vol. VI, 1958, no. 4, p. 6.
[26] Venturi, 1959, p. 107.
[27] Venturi, 1948, p. 94.
[28] "Rouault le pathétique." *Spectateur,* 18 February 1947, no. 90, p. 5.
[29] *Cinq études . . . ,* p. 84. Especially in the landscapes, Dorival sees an evolution toward peace. P. 81.
[30] Hoog, *Etudes,* p. 219.

ple, contains many peaceful pastoral scenes and sunsets but also includes the fugitives and the hopeless citizens of the "vieux faubourg." Redemption is present but not everywhere victorious, as indeed is the case among mankind. So clearly is this true that Father Morel claims in the preface that Rouault here presents overwhelming evidence for original sin.

What conclusions can we draw concerning Rouault's development? Evolution there was: from the predominance of line and somber colors, he came to a unified sense of composition that involved—rather than enclosed—rich and luminous colors. Violence subsided, and peace became more and more evident. But there is a unity running through his work as well. There is little evidence of a radical, far-reaching change that cannot be accounted for by maturation of the man and the artist. We see no religious evolution. As Courthion puts it, Rouault was wholly present in all he did and sought a single meaning in a few typical figures to which he was faithful throughout his life.[31] If this meaning is missed all is lost. In Dorival's words it is better to refuse to see his work than to fail to see in it "an imposing, majestic, organic whole."[32]

This was the way Rouault himself saw his work. In fact, all his life he would refer back to what he did in the early years as being no less important than what came later. As Cogniat explains it: "For him it is only an evolution, the affirmation of a technique and a temperament."[33] Charensol notes one cannot avoid the relationship uniting

> the faces of the prostitutes that he painted at Montmartre at 20 years of age and those of the Virgins brought to life under the brush of the 80-year-old master.[34]

It is the persistent tension, in a constantly changing complexion, between degradation and grace that became a creative force for Rouault and gave his work its dynamic. This lost, his art would probably have become either coarse or sentimental and certainly unreal. It never did. For in this world there is a constant tension, but no contradiction, between the hell of a man-made city and the beauty of a world made and remade in God's image.

---

[31] Courthion, pp. 352-354.
[32] Cinq études . . . , p. 8.
[33] Raymond Cogniat. "Rouault." Le Point, 1937, p. 116.
[34] George Charensol. "Rouault." La Revue des Deux Mondes, 1958, no. II, p. 153.

PART TWO:

The Artist's Work

SECTION A: THE THEME OF DEGRADATION

* * *

8. The Place of the Beautiful and the Ugly

Human discussions of the nature of beauty are discouraging under-takings. Responses to the question, "What is Beauty?," as to Pilate's question about truth, have betrayed a persistent uncertainty. Opin-ions range from the naturalist view of George Santayana, who counts beauty as a critical or appreciative perception, to neo-thomism such as Maritain's, who describes beauty as the intellect delighting in matter intelligibly arranged. To the former, value is merely an in-explicable reaction of the vital impulse, while to the latter it is given to all created beings by the one who is value itself, namely God.[1]

Ernest Hello, whom we have mentioned as a spiritual ancestor of Rouault, seems to second Maritain: "Art is the sensitive expres-sion of the beautiful. It is the manifestation of the ideal in the natural order."[2] Beauty for him was always associated with a God-given order. As mathematics is the basis of music, so order is the foundation of beauty. He who would seize beauty detached from order finds it eternally fleeing from reach. In a statement not without relevance for modern ethics as well as modern art, he summarizes: "Error always believes that order and love are contradictory."[3]

With these preliminary witnesses on record, where, we must ask, does the intuitive Rouault find his place? What was beauty for him, or rather, what was the goal of his art? It becomes immedi-ately obvious that conceptions of beauty are all in some manner strange and unimportant to this child of the suburbs. Painting, he confesses, is not always "a happy arabesque, a harmonious rhythm

---

[1] George Santayana. *The Sense of Beauty* (New York: Dover, 1955), chapter I, especially pp. 25ff. Maritain, *Art and Scholasticism,* pp. 23, 25.

[2] *L'Homme, op. cit.,* p. 281.

[3] *Ibid.,* pp. 20, 202.

under a serene sky."[4] But beauty, his friend Jacques Maritain insists, is just that. It preserves the savor of terrestrial paradise, because it restores, for a moment, the peace and the simultaneous delight of the intellect and the senses.[5] Rouault, however, is clearly suspicious of those who make this beauty their goal. Writing in 1947 from the maturity of his thought, he warns:

> Under the pretext of beauty, one comes very soon to the trivial when he no longer looks at nature, life, or human behavior.... In this way the eye comes gradually, not to find the horrible beautiful as the romantics wished, but to draw forms out of the day by day sights that provide all the variety of life, and at the same time release in themselves their power of emotion.[6]

Art for Rouault was to penetrate the banal to the rich sources of meaning and emotion of life. If one pole of his work is the play of plastic elements, the other is its human orientation. There was never a conflict between its humanity and its plasticity; rather they were blended, each reinforcing the other. Beauty, therefore, for him always had a human as well as a plastic component.[7]

Because of this, Rouault felt the search for order had often been a blind alley. In 1932, when interviewed about the nature of beauty, he spoke of a false sense of order. It is easy enough to put things in order, "but if this is empty how do we arrive?"

> Form, color, harmony
> Mark not so simply their borders.
> Beauty is not always
> So easy to distinguish.
> But how the blind
> Love to speak of colors
> In the light!
> And the deaf
> Of subtle sonority
> As each one knows how.
>
> Where language
> No longer is prostituted
> Neither beauty trapped
> In worn out formulae
> Or monopolized.[8]

It may well be that in broadening the ideal of beauty Rouault has actually changed his purpose. He admitted to Courthion once:

[4] Quoted in Benoist. "Rouault." *Les Tendances,* 1965, no. 37, pp. 446, 447.

[5] *Op. cit.,* p. 25.

[6] Quoted in Benoist, *op. cit.,* p. 446.

[7] Cf. Dorival's comment that Rouault sought "through plastic tonality to attain the totality of the human and even of the sacred." *Cinq études . . . ,* p. 92.

[8] Georges Rouault. "Art et beauté." *L'Intransigeant,* 8 February 1932, p. 5.

"I am not pursuing beauty but expressiveness."[9] He elaborated in another place: "For me, it is only a matter of trying to transcribe plastically my emotions."[10] But it would be a mistake to separate beauty from expression altogether. Rouault sought to record what was primarily moving in reality. Form became a mirror held up to the world that was meant to show its profound depths. His vision was stimulated in every case by a deeply emotional—one could almost say spiritual—reaction to reality. It is this reaction that informs the plastic elements of his work and is conveyed both by the subject and its treatment.[11]

The emotional component, important in all art, is of capital importance in the work of Rouault. The identification of the viewer with the human situation on the canvas is an emotional one. This is successful largely because Rouault was able to incorporate the plastic elements in the expression of sentiment. In his landscapes, for example, the sun, though shining, often appears cold in keeping with the loneliness of the subject. Its light does not warm (see p. 172). Suarès recognized this aspect of Rouault's work, writing to him in 1923 that he had the desire to realize a religious sentiment in a durable kind of beauty. "You are looking not so much for the form as for the expression, and you do not cultivate lovely material so much except to make of it the handmaiden of sentiment *ancilla Domini.*"[12]

Rouault's emotional priority is the more striking by contrast with modern art's emotional sterility. Contemporary art is at times deformed and ugly, morally and plastically; but more importantly, it is an absurd deformity before which anger or sorrow is irrelevant. Picasso, especially in his later works, has displayed this genre of ugliness. In the world of Picasso, man is defenseless and pursued. The act of creation is as desperate as life. Hatred, however, is irrelevant; anger is superfluous. All that is left for the artist and for man is to play in the ruins. For Rouault, by contrast, emotion is unavoidable because hope and wonder are only perverted and not lost.[13]

Paul Klee's search for beauty and harmony of form has similarly discounted human emotion. Art, for him, has its goal in the sphere

---

[9] Quoted in Courthion, p. 240.
[10] Quoted in Huyghe. "Le Fauvisme." *L'Amour de l'Art,* 1933, no. 14, p. 131.
[11] Courthion, p. 86, claims Rouault achieves "a genuinely transcendent emotion." What this could be he fails to make precise, since he does not make the transcendent or supernatural realm a vital and consistent part of Rouault's work.
[12] *Correspondance,* p. 184, 5 December 1923.
[13] Cf. Baucher, *op. cit.,* p. 218, where these characteristics of Picasso are discussed in relation to Rouault.

of the cosmos. In transcending the visible world, art tracks down the original laws of reality. These laws it makes visible in the act of creation. "Art penetrates things. It goes beyond the real just as it goes beyond the imagination."[14] The artist seeks universal laws, which are in a sense the spiritual base of human reality. But in the end human values and emotions have no home in this rarefied atmosphere. André Chastel commented on a 1969 exhibition of Klee's in Paris: "The human element for the artist is only something to link him to the earth; and the laws of design and color are to join the earth to something universal."[15]

Rouault, too, relates his work to a "universal," but it is one that insures the validity of human values and thus of emotional reality. Significantly, when Rouault refers to beauty it is in the context of the human-divine presence of Christ. For man beauty is a fugitive that he seeks constantly to track down.

> Jesus can always resurrect in any well-born heart, if he is lucky, . . . the hope of seeing a certain beauty born in this world that perspires tedium and smells of death. . . . Everything has a price, force, beauty, grace and the faith in you, Jesus, a great price. And for all that is valuable, I would prefer, if you feel I am worthy of it, to pay with my flesh.[16]

Thus in one sense Rouault agrees with Maritain that God is the source of beauty. But apart from the touch of this master-creator what is striking in this world is not the beautiful but the ugly. Such has been the consistent burden of Rouault's vision, much to the dismay of critics and public alike. We cannot conclude that Rouault was predisposed to see the evil wherever he looked. We have touched on this above, in Part I, and it is worth recalling here. Often he would plead: "I have not wanted to create a scandal. I have never sought out debates, neither have I desired to shock or wound anyone."[17] One would have a difficult time explaining the blackness of his vision as a psychological malevolence. The painter himself has claimed that those insisting on seeing sadism in his work "have never understood the core of my feeling toward this humanity that I seem to ridicule."

> Poor mariner
> Upon the limitless ocean
> I am indigent dust
> That is swept by the wind
> I love the Divine Peace

---

[14] Paul Klee. *Théorie de l'art moderne* (Geneva: Gonthier, 1964), pp. 30-39.
[15] "Paul Klee: Doctor Angelicus." *Le Monde,* 27 November 1969.
[16] *Le Cirque de l'étoile filante* (Paris: Ambroise Vollard, 1938), pp. 36, 37.
[17] *Soliloques,* p. 56.

> And the light
> Even in the blackest nights.
> At war for a spiritual good
> That I would never betray.[18]

Even in the midst of his blackness, Rouault felt a joy and peace that we have noted before. His security existed in spite of the darkness he saw and not because of it.

> I have always been happy painting, crazy over it, forgetting everything else even in the darkest affliction. The critics have not been aware of this because my subjects were tragic. But joy, is it always in the subject you paint?[19]

His vision was determined by no prejudice but was captive to the human situation and its imaginative richness. He confesses:

> I have never laid down a program for myself. My art rests on no single combination. I dread more than anything the burden that it must carry. I grant that the grotesque and the tragic are juxtaposed in my work, but are they not at times together in life?[20]

But neither love for the light nor divine perspective can erase the *fact* of human darkness. Rouault's paintings, faithfully reflecting the human situation he saw, were derided for their melancholy depths. This burden, which Rouault often referred to as his "medieval vision," could not be renounced even for so high an end as the beauty of forms. Raïssa Maritain has understood this better than most. In Rouault's situation, she notes, it was impossible to have beauty of form, poetry, and spiritual renewal all at once. This Léon Bloy could not understand. He had complained to Rouault that if only he were a man of prayer he would not paint such ugliness. But, the poetess responded, it would take more than prayer to reconcile beauty with freedom. For that, one would need another epoch of faith such as the middle ages. Then beauty, in the sense again of terrestrial paradise, would blossom and Rouault's deformation would be unnecessary.[21]

But must we explain away the ugly to do justice to Rouault? Must not the ugly be a part of all art that seeks truly to portray humanity, whether in the Renaissance or in the twentieth century? Are we forced to conclude that Rouault's views were psychologically or cul-

---

[18] *Ibid.* Cf. Adolphe Basler. "Le Problème de la forme depuis Cézanne." *L'Amour de l'Art,* 1930, no. 11, p. 366, who tries to claim for Rouault a taste of deformation.

[19] Quoted in Perruchot, 1967, *op. cit.,* p. 8.

[20] Quoted in Jacques Guenne. "Georges Rouault." *Les Nouvelles Littéraires,* 15 November 1924, no. 109, p. 5.

[21] R. Maritain. *Amitiés, op. cit.,* vol. II, pp. 225-227.

turally determined? To answer these questions we must inquire into the part which the "ugly" played in Rouault's art.

Here students of Rouault's work have given varying analyses. In a fascinating article in 1960, Jean-François Revel distinguished "miserable-ism" from "naturalism" or "realism." The "miserable" consists of projecting sadness or ugliness upon subjects which are not necessarily either sad or ugly in their natural state. The purpose of such projection is emotional, not one of design. Thus Daumier is a "miserable-ist" but Degas is not, though both painted the ugly. More recently, Revel argues, Buffet has in effect killed "miserable-ism" by making the misery lie only in the distortion of forms and not in anything miserable in the subject. Buffet lacked the profundity of Rouault, for whom the "miserable" was an emotional as well as plastic expression.[22]

The ugly was more than a plastic solution for Rouault. And it was not a *parti pris,* as Rouault himself stresses. He refused to take sides, choosing his heroes and then calling (and making) everything else ugly.[23] Critics have recognized Rouault's success in this regard. Venturi claims a complete absence of pride and condemnation in Rouault's ugliness.[24] Neither, Charensol notes, is any satire to be found, as there is in the work of Bosch, Callot, Daumier, and Lautrec. There is no hidden smile; the vice is real and ugly.[25]

Others have tried to see in Rouault's ugliness a kind of social criticism. Jewell, who believes the whole matter has been over-analyzed, thinks he has found a very simple explanation. Rouault looked around him and saw the violation of a sacred cause: the unjust treatment of the weak and feeble. This he protested against violently with the help of symbols which we have called the "ugly."[26] But this view only explains certain themes. How can we understand the rich, the prostitutes and the clowns as the persecuted weak? Roger-Marx denies that Rouault's criticism was of the same type as that of, say, Daumier. "With Rouault the allusion is more vague. It is less a particular epoch he flouts than a kind of universal tare."[27]

The "universal tare" suggests something of the depths Rouault meant to plumb. The painter himself detested all superficial explanations of his "blackness." He sought universal realities, like Klee, but of humanity rather than of the cosmos. He complained

[22] "Le Misérabilisme tué par Buffet." *La Connaissance des Arts,* 1960, no. 100, pp. 53ff.

[23] "Enquête," *op. cit.,* p. 12.

[24] Venturi, 1959, p. 21. He sees passion and understanding throughout. Cf. 1948, p. 40.

[25] "Georges Rouault." *L'Art Vivant,* 1926, no. 28, p. 128.

[26] *Op. cit.,* pp. 8ff.

[27] 1931, *op. cit.,* p. 98.

that while these impersonal analyses of his darkness were posed and clarified, everyone overlooked

> ...the real ugliness, the absolute ugliness. And this is the mediocrity of spirit, shortsightedness that is enamoured with the vulgar.... The stupid anecdote, baseness of spirit or heart, there is the truly ugly.[28]

Art for Rouault was less a quest for a terrestrial paradise than the celebration of a paradise lost. The profundity of Rouault's "ugliness" can only be grasped against the background of the glory that is man's birthright, a grandeur of vision and a largeness of spirit which have been lost through moral default. Rouault is concerned with the ugliness of a world fallen from grace, of mediocrity of spirit.

The modern temperament finds such a viewpoint particularly unpalatable. Contemporary tastes are better reflected by a school of modern art that has excluded Rouault. The modern vision is perhaps somewhat parallel to the mentality of the middle ages. According to Johann Huizinga, French citizens of the fifteenth century suffered from a mental atrophy due to the violent and pessimistic tenor of their life. They craved exotic and exciting entertainment, the more spectacular the better, and the crowds enjoyed watching torture and executions. Correspondingly, the sense of beauty was limited to grand sensations of light, pomp and splendor.[29]

If the medieval mentality resulted from under-exposure, that of the twentieth century stems from over-exposure. Contemporary man is barraged with such a variety of stimuli—newspapers, radio, all sorts of publicity, and more recently television and cinema—that he no longer has the capacity to evaluate and react appropriately. The result for many is a state of mental stupefaction. If fifteenth-century man was too easily moved to tears, contemporary man is seldom moved by anything. So, now as then, only the most spectacular happenings draw attention and awaken the mind from its torpor. Beauty now as then is reduced to sensations of light, pomp and splendor.[30]

"The grandeur of man comes in that he knows himself to be miserable," wrote Pascal, and his words apply to the work of Rouault. For modern man, who either no longer knows that he is miserable or tries to hide it by a hundred distractions, the grandeur is replaced by an all-consuming apathy of spirit. Here lies the focus of Rouault's revolt. It was precisely this hebetude that his "ugli-

---

[28] "Enquête," p. 12.

[29] Cf. Huizinga, op. cit., chapter 1 and p. 257.

[30] Many modern commentators have decried this modern stupor; most notably perhaps has been David Reisman, The Lonely Crowd. Morel has also noted this in connection with Rouault's work, decrying the century's replacing quality with quantity, so that it can no longer support the intensity of a Rouault. Cf. Art & Industrie, April, 1946, p. 63.

ness" was to protest. Rouault once said: "This old anguished world, so little civilized, is quite peacefully dancing its way back to chaos."[31]

Ernest Hello could have been writing specifically of Rouault's work when he said one hundred years ago: "Art ought to be one of the forces that heals the imagination; it must say that evil is ugly."[32] Rouault stands virtually alone in recognizing, in the first place, that evil actually exists. As we shall note in the next chapter, his view of evil is centered on his view of man. It is human evil he is concerned with, rather than a cosmic surd.[33] Moreover, this spiritual-human reality is associated with moral default.

But not only does evil exist, it manifests itself in a visible, plastic, and of course human ugliness. Rouault the painter, we repeat, sees as a painter and reflects with his hands. In his work the spiritual reality is seen not in a cosmic and theoretical perspective but in a concrete, creatural setting. He reminds us that Biblical evil was a human reality before it was a doctrinal formulation.

Yet the extremes of Rouault's darkness must be understood in their relation to supernatural truths. Just as the greatest art of the middle ages soared to hieratic heights, so Rouault's work often rose far above contemporary taste to supra-mundane realities. His horror has been compared to that of Nebuchadnezzar in the medieval north transept window at Chartres.[34]

Here Blaise Pascal touched on a point that is illuminating. Just after what has been called his second conversion in 1654, in his meditations at the Jansenist center of Port-Royal, he came to the profound realization of two truths: the grandeur of man as created, and the corruption of his state by sin to that of beasts. In this way fear is perfectly balanced with hope

> ... by this double capacity resident in everyone, of grace and of sin, which lowers far more than reason alone can do, yet without despair; and which raises infinitely more than natural pride can do, yet without being puffed up.[35]

Grace lowers further than reason. Reason alone in art makes distortion a merely plastic element, reducing art to a game. Reason and pride see only that we are better than another and make another

---

[31] *Paysages légendaires* (Paris: Editions Porteret, 1929), no pagination.

[32] *Op. cit.,* p. 19. Modern art, he said, suffers from a logic of delirium: "The beautiful," it insists, "is the ugly!" Pp. 37, 369.

[33] Though his depiction of Satan (cf. "The Prince of Darkness" cc. 250) indicates that evil also transcends its human dimensions. Anne Bettems sees here a subject that goes beyond the confines of painting. Cf. "Rouault." *Pour l'Art,* 1950, no. 14, p. 24.

[34] "Rouault and the Middle Age Spirit." *The Studio,* 1938, no. 116, p. 167.

[35] *Pensées II* (Paris: Ed. Léon Brunschvicq, 1904), Fr. 435, p. 354. Cf. also Emile Cailliet. *The Clue to Pascal* (Philadelphia: Westminster, 1943), pp. 68ff.

the "ugly." Reason loves to dwell on social criticism and find its
raison d'être as a crusader fighting for the terrestrial paradise. This
is the ethical mistake which corresponds to the artistic mistake of
seeing the purpose of art as the creation of an earthly paradise.

Yet grace does not bring despair. We shall note in all our themes
of degradation that hope is never lost. But such hope is not provided by reason or human effort; it is an alien hope sent from
above. This foreign element makes Rouault's work so discomfort-
ing. From a natural point of view, nothing could be made of his
blackness, for there is no human beauty untainted with this persistent and devilish ugliness. But if one cannot accept the hope
Rouault imported, then he cannot accept the ugliness. And just here
is the rock on which so many well-meaning analyses of Rouault run
afoul: they either perceive the light and ignore the darkness or see
the absurd darkness without the divine light.[36]

If ugliness must be placed in this theological context, so must
beauty. Like ugliness, beauty for Rouault is not an abstract concept
but a personal insight and an expression of real human emotion.
A mother's love, divine companionship, brotherly concern form
the nucleus of a world of human beauty that Rouault sensed. As
we have observed earlier, he is less eager to elaborate the theological
context that we have noted than simply to record the warmth of
human values and the fact of divine presence.

Beauty is not a matter of perception alone. Rather, in Rouault's
hands it has become a plastic and emotional intuition into divine
and human realities. It is the reaction of the artist's total sensitivity
to human degradation and divine grace.

---

[36] Cf. Charensol, *op. cit.,* pp. 36, 37, where he says of the work of Rouault: ". . . If we treat him as exceptional it is because we would rather not
accept his hopeless conclusions."

9. Rouault's View of Man

If the question of beauty for Rouault has a human as well as plastic dimension, it is worth inquiring into his idea of man. Who is this creature of Rouault's paradise lost? He is surely seen in the context of the melancholy and mediocrity that plague his existence. In fact, Rouault bases his view on the belief that when one looks at man apart from God there is only evil to be seen. Léon Bloy's dictum suits Rouault: sainthood is "a grant" somehow alien to man —alien and yet precious. Man for Rouault is a fit object of grace, while more visibly born in and for suffering.

Human reflection upon the nature of man that avoids cynicism is invariably tempted to make man into a quasi-divine being. Such humanism wears many disguises. And it is in the name of a humanistic "faith" that Rouault's blackness has often been called a kind of blasphemy. A shocked bourgeois audience reacted at times with a pious rage. At the same time, Rouault's obvious religious intentions have motivated some critics to make astounding statements. Marcel Brion announced in 1950, for example, that there had never been a painter who gave so clearly the feeling that "God" is a man and that "many are the secret, captive, and wounded gods who exist, suffering within man's heart."[1] Such a diversity of reaction speaks something of the subtlety of Rouault's thought, and the caution befitting our investigation.

What can be said without reading either too much or too little into this painter's intention? First, Rouault felt a deep-seated love for and identification with man. He rarely painted a work that did not contain human qualities. In a passage about clowns that we will examine later in more detail, he admitted: "Be he king or emperor, what I want to see in the man standing before me is his soul. And

---

[1] Marcel Brion. *Georges Rouault* (Paris: Braun, 1950), p. 5.

the more exalted he is and glorified by man, the more I fear for his soul."[2]

So great was Rouault's identification with man that he hesitated at times to speak at all about himself, fearing to place himself above his fellows. In one article he describes his loyalty to France, but afterwards he rebukes himself. Why do I speak so much about myself, of my petty individuality, he wonders, when there is so much misery in the world? He adds: "If I speak of myself, fellow sufferer, I am thinking of you; and perhaps even more I am thinking of my faith that so many stuffed-shirts discuss in the forum."[3]

Furthermore he sensed a grandeur in man, struggling to create and build in spite of his infirmities. Man is like a chained lion, he once wrote, like a captive eagle—aspiring on earth, an exile from eternity. "The more of a man he is, the more his genius is composed of hopelessness and hope, of revolt and acquiescence, of pain and joy, of melancholy and serenity."[4]

But he did not underestimate the effects of man's infirmities. He watched with a mixture of mirth and sorrow the elaborate plans of the self-appointed builders of the future. They never say "larghetto," he observed wryly, but always "allegro." As a wizened man who has outgrown the simple idealism of youth, he contemplated the futurists' dreams. "The apostle keeps his eye fixed on the future, his mind sharp and his finger pointing toward the distant horizon. And the dark clouds everywhere? He does not bother noticing them, nor does he remark about man's infirmity."[5] Rouault preferred to identify himself with a wide-eyed child. "Sometimes at the market, when he has lost his way, the wan child stops his ears against the abusive sneers. Between the dream and the reality, what gulfs!" Or he appeals to Don Quixote:

> In these sad and gray times
> Don Quixote de la Mancha
> Stranger to this breed that believes itself progressive
> Adorable and dear fool, help us.

Rouault feared that man, far from improving his lot, was making for himself a life he could no longer control.

> By all the most practical means,
> Man destroys himself so well.
> Chemistry and mechanics, sad idols,
> Chemistry and mechanics, sinister idols.

---

[2] Letter to Edouard Schuré, written in 1905. Cf. also Bouvier, op. cit., p. 19.
[3] Rouault. "Le Visage de la France." Verve, 1940, vol. 2, no. 7, p. 18.
[4] Rouault. "Trois artistes." Op. cit., p. 654.
[5] Cirque, op. cit., pp. 16, 18.
[6] Ibid., p. 19.

People so learned will be no more master
Of their fatal inventions: will that which
Should serve to succour humanity
Serve to destroy it?[7]

The lines sound as if they were written after the carnage of World War II and the growing nuclear threat. But these words were published in 1938 and perhaps written even earlier. For it was not history which Rouault feared but man's nature. As Baucher points out, Rouault never mocked the image of God in man but sharply attacked what man was able to do with it.[8]

Such is the state of man ignorant of God. For Rouault worked always with reference to a living God. He noted in one place, sensing realities that were beyond understanding, that all of his efforts centered on expressing "nostalgia for the infinite."[9] Morel, the painter's close friend, said of Rouault: "He who has once apprehended the absolute, can see its evidences throughout the relative, and of all things make a sign."[10] Rouault himself emphasized: "I have known the joy of a complete effort toward the absolute of my soul. It is a small thing. My art was a means, not an end."[11]

Toward what end was Rouault's art a means? It was neither aesthetic experience alone nor emotion, though it involved both of these. The end of Rouault's work was to inspire in the viewer the same religious effort toward God, the absolute, that the painter himself felt. This absolute, he felt, was reflected in God's highest creation, man.

That man somehow reflected the glory of God tempered Rouault's anguish. For he always insisted on man's dignity, as some of his greatest works reveal. Among them is the "Old King," p. 111, where age and wisdom unite to fill the canvas with a profound depth whose dignity is garnished (or is it mocked?) by the small flowers in the wizened king's hands. Here one feels deep respect—mixed with pity—and a sense of the greatness with which man is endowed. "The Workman's Apprentice" C. 199, a self-portrait painted in 1925, captures the innocence and melancholic ideals of one beginning to wonder and hope (see book jacket and frontispiece).

Throughout his work the second part of Pascal's dictum comes to mind: Grace is so mixed with hope that it can not only reveal new depths where despair is unknown but can exult infinitely more than does the pride of nature, yet without arrogance.

---

[7] *Ibid.,* p. 167.
[8] *Op. cit.,* p. 218.
[9] "Trois artistes," p. 658.
[10] *Stella Vespertina,* preface.
[11] "Trois artistes," p. 654.

Le vieux roi — 1937
The Old King — 1937

But in spite of his dignity, man finds suffering his lot. Rouault's view here must be seen in relation to the thought of Bloy and other Catholic writers. So dark was the world to these writers, so necessary was suffering, that Christian hope at times was eclipsed. Sainthood was no escape from the common lot of suffering, bringing as it did the added responsibility of suffering for others.[12]

On this point Rouault was the heir of Bloy.[13] He declared once to Suarès: "I believe in suffering, it is not feigned with me. That is my only merit."[14] But Rouault saw suffering less as an article of faith, as did Bloy, than as a tragic part of man's condition. Nor did the painter proclaim the need to seek out suffering as a sign of divine attention. In fact, Rouault may have been thinking of Bloy when he wrote:

> Do not deny suffering, but do not make it your duty to cherish and cultivate it every minute.
> One must endure with patience
> The storm winds, Son.
> Without sighing too much, or whimpering.[15]

Suffering is the constant but not essential lot of man. Like its theological counterpart, evil, it is a surd. "Doesn't he [man] always want to believe in happiness, even in the midst of suffering?"[16]

For man senses that happiness is more a part of his being than is suffering. In examining Rouault's view, one must not confuse animality with depravity. We do not agree with the writer who said of Rouault: "The agony and sometimes the horror of the human visage and the human figure are qualities in his strong and brooding paintings which recall us to as humble a sense of our origin as the theory of evolution."[17] For Rouault, agony reminds man of the heights for which he was created, not the depths from which he has come. Rouault shows that man's dignity is the very basis of his anguished suffering when he says, significantly in the form

---

[12] Cf. Griffiths, op. cit., p. 153. This author believed vicarious suffering became disproportionately important by reason of the small number of believers and the ghetto mentality that developed as a result. P. 159.

[13] Griffiths says on this point: "The harshness of the particular approach to suffering of the writers of the revival is vividly reflected in the work of a man closely connected with them, Georges Rouault." P. 156.

[14] SI, p. 14. Cf. "O suffering, flower of desire! Sometimes it is necessary to pick it just on the edge of the abyss." Quoted in Speaight. "Hommage to Rouault." The Dublin Review, July, 1941, vol. 209, p. 64.

[15] Cirque, p. 135.

[16] Ibid., p. 18.

[17] Anonymous critic. "Contemporary Painting." Studio, Autumn, 1939, p. 53.

of a prayer: "Lord, when one is poor and born with a certain dignity, he is put to the test of suffering, even if he curses it."[18]

Already we are speaking of grace, which will occupy our attention further on. From here we proceed to discuss the themes where suffering is made visible. It should be said at the outset that there is no contradiction, either in reality or in the work of Rouault, between degradation and grace. For where sin is plentiful, God has made grace that much more plentiful.[19]

It would be tempting to see in Rouault's view of suffering an expiation for human sin. We will note in our discussion of the prostitutes how popular this point of view has been among the critics. But Rouault's view of the human situation was more personal and concrete. He approached it as a sensitive friend rather than a commentator. He certainly saw the reality of sin, but he viewed it less as the breaking of laws than as man's loss of part of his human treasure. He sympathized without excusing; he denounced without condemning. His attitude toward human infirmity reminds us of Tolstoy's insight that all men are guilty and all men are innocent. Man is at once sinner and sinned against.

This leads us to a restatement of a principle that has become increasingly clear in our study: Rouault's realm is sensitive observation of nature, not speculative extrapolation from it. His sphere is empirical rather than theoretical. All that we have discussed of Rouault's work, therefore, results in an illumination of the *condition* of man rather than of his nature. Such a pictorial statement can be appropriate to a religious doctrine of man, but it cannot be read as a precise formulation of such a doctrine.

But although commentary is muddied, Rouault's work is clear. Let us therefore discuss the themes where suffering is made visible. Any attempt to abstract elements for study must be somewhat artificial, for an artist's work is never subject to neat divisions. As we consider four major areas, let us remember that each motif and each work must be considered as a complement of all the rest of Rouault's works.

---

[18] *Cirque*, p. 36.
[19] Romans 5:20b.

10. Judges and Relative Justice

Although the courtroom motif comprises a scant 23 canvases of Rouault's work,[1] it forms an important part of the painter's iconography. Its obvious social and religious implications have made it a favorite subject for commentators.

The theme seems not to have been attempted before 1906 or 1907.[2] Around that time a friend of the painter, Deputy Prosecutor Granier, invited Rouault to visit a courtroom of the tribunal of the Seine. On many occasions, it appears, the impressionable artist endured the dehumanized drama of legal proceedings. One particular case was to achieve immortality under the painter's brush: that of the condemnation to death of a man named Vacher. This event was recorded in the "Condemned Man," p. 115, first shown in the Salon d'Automne in 1908. Courthion comments of this painting: "In this canvas, with a dark purplish-red-russet background made warmer through the addition of reds and blues, the man who paid the price is put before us with terrifying effectiveness."[3]

The circumstances which gave birth to the theme suggest the way in which it is to be understood. Rouault did not set out to depict the nature of justice, though there are suggestions in this regard in each treatment of the theme. He wanted rather to draw attention to the fate of the particular case of Vacher. He was not interested so much in Vacher alone as in all the poor (and perhaps guilty) folk who stand where he stood. Rouault's canvases are always human without being particular or anecdotal. The sentencing of Vacher awakened in Rouault a horror of the terrible gap that

---

[1] Courthion lists a total of 759.

[2] Courthion lists two other subjects as men of law painted prior to this date, viz. cc. 91 and cc. 92, but it is not clear that these are personages of the courts.

[3] Courthion, p. 145.

Le condamné — vers 1907
Condemned Man — about 1907

may exist between the relativity of human justice and the finality of its judgment. His comments were motivated not by an objective appraisal of the legal situation of Parisian courts but by his complete identification with both judges and condemned—people of real life. Cailliet tells us that the *Pensées* of Pascal grew against a backdrop of judges and people in court silhouetted in his memory. Similarly, Rouault's work has its roots deep in the actual world of human law, of which Cailliet comments: "Justice is a minimum of goodness and is only this world's conception of true charity."[4]

Consistently, Rouault's focus is human rather than social. It is this that sets him clearly apart from Daumier, with whom the theme of justice is so often associated. As Roulet recalls, Rouault never concerned himself with politics or social reform programs. He looked on such official activity as a spectator "amused or distressed, but never as a censor of laws and morals."[5] It was not the *cause* but the *person* that intrigued Rouault, and as a result, Venturi believes, his work is more a statement in its own right than an illustration as are those of Daumier.[6] With Daumier, Dorival stresses, the lawyer is emphasized more than the judges. But with Rouault the judges and accused are the center of attention and the object of a parallel interest.[7]

This final point brings us to one of the most unusual characteristics of Rouault's court theme: the virtual identification of the face of the judge and the accused. Rouault stresses neither the background nor the context of the proceedings but concentrates the drama in two protagonists: the judge and the accused. And these two appear almost to be the same person in different habits.[8] Rouault has acknowledged this doubling and explains: "If I have happened to confuse the head of the judge with that of the accused, this error only betrays my perplexity. . . . The judges themselves I cannot condemn."[9] It is the men that interest Rouault, and their differing functions are not essential to their humanity. If their roles were reversed the central truth of the painter's focus would remain unchanged: the frightening relativity of man's judgment.

This is all highlighted by yet another plastic element, the immobility of the figures in the composition. Note, for example, "Men

---

[4] Cailliet, *op. cit.,* p. 122.

[5] Quoted in Roulet, *op. cit.,* p. 196.

[6] Venturi, 1948, p. 61.

[7] Bernard Dorival. *Cinq études . . . ,* pp. 43, 44.

[8] This technique of Rouault's of identifying faces to increase the symbolic quality deserves to be studied in more detail. Michel Hoog, *op. cit.,* points out that the face of "Veronica" C. 249 is almost identical to that of Rouault's "The Holy Countenance" C. 293; see chapter 16 below.

[9] Quoted in Jacques Guenne. *Op. cit.,* p. 5.

Hommes de justice — vers 1913
Men of Justice — about 1913

of Justice," p. 117, 1913, a watercolor in which the composition seems to catch and hold the figures in their learned and legal reflection. Behind them is a Christ on the cross, to which we shall refer further along. Or consider the famous "Three Judges" C. 187, 1924, where one judge in the middle contemplates the legal outline before him, deciding with a divine finality the fate of some person, while the two others sit beside unconcernedly. In this almost inhuman immobility there is pity mixed with fear. For the protagonists, despite their shared humanity, are irreparably fixed in their roles. The immobility seems also to make the figures into types disparaging their humanity.[10] They *must* judge and be judged. Confesses Rouault:

> If I have made of the judges lamentable figures, it is no doubt because I was betraying the anguish that I feel at the sight of one human being having to judge another. I would not be a judge for all the wealth and happiness in the world.[11]

To describe the pain Rouault felt that one human had to judge another is not to say that he felt it was wrong to so judge. To say he could never be a judge is not to say no one should judge. Some critics, Grenier among them, have said that Rouault believes the judges are violating Christ's command not to judge.[12] No, Rouault cries out against the roles which trap them and thus destroy human compassion. Their impassibility is a function of their immobility.

In the end Rouault achieves more a cry of commiseration than of protest. For the painter was setting human judgment not against a finite standard of justice but against the judgment of God. It was not the innocence of the condemned that bothered him nearly so much as the guilt of both judge and accused before God. He does not excuse everyone so much as remove excuses from all alike. We see this in a sensitive plate drawn for *The Miserere:* "Are we not all convicts?" p. 119. No one is exempt from human fallibility. At its best, therefore, human justice is a parody. True justice is a divine affair.

This caricature of justice was most clear for Rouault in the trial of Christ. "Christ Mocked" was an appealing theme to which he returned often,[13] and which, along with "Behold the Man,"[14] serves to illustrate the folly of human judgment. The final irony for Rouault was that the one in whose hands all judgment has been placed

---

[10] Cf. Dorival who says the figures become symbols "which incarnate all the vices and mechanization of man in his social function." *Op. cit.,* p. 47.
[11] Quoted in Guenne, *op. cit.,* p. 5.
[12] "Idées de Georges Rouault." *Op. cit.,* p. 36.
[13] Painted twice in 1912, once in 1913, 1930, 1932, 1937, 1938, 1939, 1942.
[14] Painted in 1948 and 1952.

Ne sommes-nous pas forçats?
Are We Not All Convicts?
(Miserere, Plate 6)

should be submitted to the farce of human justice, even to mockery, which is the antipode of honest judgment.[15]

In a poem published in 1929 Rouault evokes the juxtaposition of human law and the God-man in lyrical terms.

> The condemned man went away
> Indifferent and weary.
> His lawyer in hollow
> Pompous phrases
> Had proclaimed his innocence.
> A red robed prosecutor
> Held society blameless
> And indicted the accused man
> Under a Jesus on the cross
> Forgotten there.[16]

Illuminated by this divine dimension justice is seen in its truly tentative character. But love is the end of the law. Miscarriages in human judgment point not to a day of social justice but beyond, to a day when love becomes lived in truth. Short of this, human justice, tainted as it is by pride, can only appear as a travesty. For Rouault the cross is the point where injustice finds its solution; this theme will occupy us in a later chapter.

As always we must avoid the temptation of reading more into the paintings than is there. Rouault's statements are simple and yet artistically profound: since we all share in human weaknesses, what anguish it is for one human being to judge another. Rouault himself constantly stressed the simplicity of his themes. In a letter addressed to James Johnson Sweeney in 1938 about the judges, he said:

> I dare say the legendary and pictorial aspect of my patient and humble efforts has often gone down badly. I will say again, that which seems to my eyes so simple pictorially has been considered as a curious enigma.[17]

One who sees intently and sensitively the human situation is often accorded by God's grace a glimpse of heaven's finest secrets —which, as even children know, are quite simple, when viewed through the eyes of faith. For of such simplicity is the Kingdom of God.

---

[15] Dorival sees the religious dimension becoming especially important after 1930, as seen in the work "Christ at the Tribunal," which he says was painted that year. Cinq études . . . , p. 50. This work is listed in Charensol, op. cit., plate 34, but not—insofar as I can tell—in Courthion.

[16] Paysages légendaires, 1929, no pagination. "Forgotten there" is probably a double entendre meaning not paid attention to or removed, as crucifixes were taken from courtrooms after the separation of Church and state in France.

[17] Quoted in E. A. Jewell, op. cit., p. 64.

But it is well to remind ourselves that themes often please an artist in a plastic sense before they are profound or moving. This is again the paradox of an artist's intuitive vision. Rouault once said of his courtroom theme: "Black bonnet and red robe make pretty splashes of color, and that is all that is necessary. As far as that goes the good judge can go fly a kite."[18]

[18] Quoted in Michel Puy, *Georges Rouault,* p. 16.

11. The Complacency of the Rich and the Hopelessness of the Poor

> Life is a dream
> And death, tell me,
> Death an assassination.[1]

In verse such as this and consistently on his canvases, Rouault exhibits his cloudy vision of life. Relativity of justice was not limited to the courtroom but woven into the fabric of existence. This conviction stimulated a group of topics throughout his life that at first glance appear to be social comments but upon closer examination emerge as human revelations. As with the judges, his intent is not to condemn so much as to lament. We have somewhat arbitrarily placed these themes together in this chapter, for they all recall in different ways the distress Rouault felt in the world. They are the fugitives, the rich, the poor, and the terrors of war.

These themes are most fully treated in Rouault's masterpiece, the *Miserere* series of engravings.[2] The motifs he treated therein were impressed upon him during the First World War. It was during those dark days that he did a large portion of the work on the 58 plates that were finally published in 1948.[3] No canvases of Rouault exude more intense emotion than these engravings. The impact of each work is enlarged by the captions placed under each drawing, which, often employing understatement or hyperbole, reach almost dramatic proportions.

This series is without doubt the most consistently religious of

---

[1] *Divertissement* (Paris: Tériade, 1943), p. 63.

[2] Rouault originally wanted the title to be *Miserere et guerre* but Suarès convinced him that the mixture of French and Latin was unsuitable. *Correspondance*, May 21, 1922, p. 173.

[3] The 58 drawings were first done with India ink, then transferred onto copper plates from which 500 copies were made. Finally in 1948, 425 were published in an edition by L'Etoile Filante.

Rouault's works. Where the inspiration was not realized in a religious subject, the impact remains rich in theological implications. Rouault tells us in the preface that this work was of great personal and artistic importance. He recounts the black hours following the death of Vollard and during the war, when he despaired of ever living to see the appearance of the work. In the preface he attaches a capital importance to its publication: "I rejoice that I have reached port before leaving the earth."[4]

The impact of the appearance of this work in December, 1948, on aesthetic circles in Paris is recounted by Courthion, who compares it with the greatest graphic series of all times.[5] Georges Borgeaud in 1949 made the obvious comparison of the series with that of Francisco Goya (1746-1828), who depicted the wartime atrocities of Napoleon's 1808 invasion of Spain in drawings which were also published as a series of etchings. But, Borgeaud observed, there is an important difference: "Rouault is a Christian and does not hate."[6] Benoist believes that in this work Rouault succeeded in denouncing without anger. "Rouault places himself above the day by day battle to strike at the basis of human misery."[7] As Abbé Morel reminded the world in the stirring oration delivered at Rouault's funeral, his was the voice of a prophet. And the world, tired of dreams, needed as never before the fire of a prophet "who touches evil with the greatest profundity but also with the clearest purity."[8]

Rouault maintained a purity that did not deny the reality or power of evil, but sought to juxtapose it with the equally powerful reality of justice and righteousness. He displayed the anguish of man, who, yearning for justice, can only do evil. Plate 7 of *Miserere* is a drawing entitled: "Thinking ourselves Kings." In the smiling, self-assured figure Rouault means to show not only delusion but also the awful contradiction that is man: not only that man has fooled himself, but that he was created "kingly" and is no longer so.

Though most of the themes of this chapter find their highest expression in the *Miserere*, they are of course treated elsewhere in Rouault's work as well. The fugitive motif, for example, is interpreted 11 times, all outside the *Miserere*. The poor industrial suburbs occupy his attention in 20 canvases from all periods of his creativity. Let us look then at each theme in turn to discuss its essential content and its theological implications.

---

[4] *Miserere*, 1963, p. 10. This was a mechanically reproduced edition in small format.

[5] Courthion, p. 298.

[6] "Un évènement capital." *La Vie Intellectuelle*, March, 1949, p. 303.

[7] *Op. cit.*, p. 456.

[8] "En Souvenir de Georges Rouault" (1958), p. 65.

La fuite en Égypte — vers 1938
The Flight Into Egypt — about 1938

The fugitive. Rouault first attempted this subject in 1911, and the last one is dated 1952. A comparison of these two interpretations illustrates a typical change and transformation that took place in Rouault's work. The 1911 "Fugitives" (also known as "Exodus"), p. 177, depicts a family group with their belongings, backs bent under the load, the father reaching down to urge the child along. There is movement in the composition, and the rich but somewhat darkened colors dwell on certain details of the cold, barren snowscape. In the 1952 version, "The Flight into Egypt" cc. 538, the realistic details are almost missing and there is little movement. The little family seems to stand with their mule as though trapped. Though the interest in the theme remained, the emphasis shifted from the event to the people embroiled in their fate (see also p. 124).

Once again we must note the absence of social criticism. Although the homeless and displaced persons struck his imagination, Rouault was not concerned with the injustices of wars, which only reflect a deeper sense in which all men are fugitives. Some have seen Rouault's treatment of poor refugees in 1911 and 1912 as prophetic of the desolation of the coming war. Dorival claims the paintings done during this period were astonishing premonitions.[9]

But Rouault was a prophet only in the vague sense in which anyone who understands the nature of man can predict the shape of future activity. Moreover, Rouault intends his exiles to comprehend a much larger segment of humanity than those suffering the devastation of war. Those who see the fugitive motif as prophetic of wars to come overlook the importance this theme held for the nineteenth-century writers of the romantic movement and the Catholic revival. Especially in Léon Bloy, who saw suffering as the instrument of redemption, the role of the outcast took on a capital importance.[10] Though Rouault, we believe, did not accept Bloy's view of vicarious suffering, there is no doubt that this is one of the sources for the figure of the fugitive.

The reality behind the motif was equally apparent in peace or in war. Being an exile does not refer only to physical distance from home. In a universalization that will become familiar, Rouault is asking whether we are not all exiles. Is not life essentially—not accidentally as when that monster war intervenes—a flight? Rouault makes this point in his *Soliloques.* Man flees sickness, boredom, misery and especially death. Flight becomes so much a part of life that he forgets he is running. He knows no other life. The anguish of Rouault's canvases, he admits, is due to the vanity of man's quest.

[9] *Cinq études . . . ,* p. 64 and "Georges Rouault." *La Table Ronde,* October, 1952, no. 58, p. 178.
[10] Cf. Griffiths, *op. cit.,* p. 143.

The object of his search is an illusion; like the fugitive, man really has no place to go, and like the homeless, he would not recognize his home if he could return to it. Rouault comments: "Farther on, there is nothing. Only the sea and the desert."[11]

Rouault found the supreme example of "flight" to be that of the Holy Family fleeing to Egypt to escape the edict of King Herod (Matthew 2:13-21). Their innocent flight was as useless as their pursuit was vain. Their enforced sojourn in Egypt symbolized the exile that man's greed and jealousy forces upon him. In every case, whether of the Holy Family or of a desperate fugitive, Rouault lends these distressed persons a visage of tenderness that avoids making a judgment and seems to reveal a great depth of understanding on the part of the artist. See especially the version of the "Flight" reproduced on p. 124 where the fugitives have paused to rest under a fragile tree that stands over without offering protection. The mother comforts her child while the father resting his hand on her shoulder looks anxiously about for their pursuers. Here consolation and fear are allies.

What is the real goal of man's quest? Rouault implies that the nature of the search is spiritual. What man wants cannot be seen or weighed. The signing of a peace treaty cannot assure it. It is rather to be found "in a certain spiritual realm, far removed from all negation and blasphemy." Human goals short of this only increase the anguish and destroy hope. "This happiness that furnished him with such dreams, he no longer believes in." Without grace man can only flee.

> The road is long
> It twists down and then up
> Then down again,
> Until the end of time.
> Fugitives!
> Spring will come again
> It always comes again
> As suffering comes on the pilgrim.[12]

The complacency of the bourgeois. Here one of the sources for Rouault's emphasis must surely be found in the thought of Bloy. Bloy's hatred for the rich reached extreme proportions. For him the mere possession of wealth was culpable.[13] Yet the bourgeois also came in for their share of criticism by reason of their all-pervading mediocrity. Bloy's famous couple, the *Poulots* of *La Femme*

---

[11] *Soliloques,* p. 196.
[12] *Ibid.,* p. 197.
[13] Cf. Brady, *op. cit.,* pp. 42ff.

pauvre, demonstrate how an odious pride can thrive entirely without material foundation.[14] In short, there was a spiritual smugness attendant with position and riches that the impetuous Bloy could not abide.

Rouault borrowed the attitude but not the uncompromising manner of Bloy. It is well known that Rouault had a streak of violence that manifested itself in his portrayal of this theme.[15] He treated not so much the evil of riches in themselves as the complacency of persons of position. It was not the possession of money or culture that he despised but the privileges assumed to come with such possessions.

This theme is amply interpreted in the *Miserere,* as the captions alone reveal. On p. 128 a finely coiffured woman looks to one side, a satisfied set to her mouth. The title explains: "Woman of the upper class thinks she has a reserved seat in heaven." Plate 39 announces below two well-dressed, wide-eyed men: "We are fools." In another, a woman dressed for an evening out folds her arms in accustomed defiance over the title: "The nails and the beak" (M. 50).

Rouault's bourgeoisie were the very incarnation of pride and self-indulgence. The evil he insists on is not vice so much as pharisaical self-satisfaction. In fact, one is reminded of Christ's words to the Pharisees: "Truly I say to you, the tax collectors and the harlots go into the kingdom before you" (Matthew 21:31). Self-righteousness is the worst of all vices, Rouault saw, for it often covers a multitude of crimes: "What appetites, betrayed beauty, concealed cowardice, hypocrisy, thievery, rapes, and trafficking (it hides) that the law does not cover."[16]

The haughtiness of privilege shows original sin in its worst form, blind to the emptiness of its own existence. However vehemently Bloy rejected Rouault's *Poulots* C. 125 as an illustration of his own characters, one has only to read Bloy's description of them to sense the parentage. Mme Poulot was, Bloy tells the reader: "In her own eyes at least, the most striking princess in the world. It would be impossible to find one who imagined herself to be more exquisite."[17] No other commentary is necessary to some of Rouault's interpretations of this theme. Under a delusion of greatness, man attempts to gain by privilege what is his by divine right.

---

[14] Cf. *La Femme pauvre,* pp. 244-248.

[15] Léon Lehmann wrote of Rouault's treatment of this theme: "Do not try to fathom Rouault. He is violent, savage, hostile . . . and just as much the contrary." "L'art vécu, Georges Rouault." *Op. cit.,* p. 2.

[16] Quoted in Venturi, 1948, p. 28.

[17] *La Femme pauvre,* p. 248.

Dame du haut-quartier croit prendre pour le ciel place réservé
Upper-Class Woman Thinks to Have a Reserved Seat in Heaven
(Miserere, Plate 16)

The loneliness of the poor. At the end of the nineteenth century peasants at work were a common subject of artists. Following the lead of Millet were Van Gogh, Degas, and of course Daumier. Rouault's attraction for the poor—who occupied his attention far more than did the rich or middle classes—was, however, deeper than an attraction for the peasant. For many artists this attraction was basically the yearning of a city-bred person for the simple pastoral life of the country. The image that resulted was idealized and bore little or no resemblance to reality. Rouault's interest was based on a personal affinity for the common person that he felt throughout his life. His pictures of the poor, in fact, were far more accurate than his portrayals of the rich. Dorival admits Rouault believed that "there are more righteous folk among the poor than among the rich."[18] He seemed to share the common person's innate distrust for the highly placed person, which suggests that he never wholly rejected Bloy's assertion that riches are a source of evil.

Often the poor are depicted as the innocent victims of life. Lehmann says of Rouault's style: "He envelops the images of poverty with a delicate tenderness."[19] No matter how awesome their task, they always appear humble and accepting. Rouault's paintings on this theme have an air of inevitability appropriate to the melancholic suspicion with which he faced life.

> Weep my mother night and day.
> Stammering poet, you know his misery;
> Weep for having brought such a lonely soul into the world.[20]

In the *Miserere*, plate 11, a man alone and frightened attempts to cling to a branch in the midst of a storm. The title calls out a song without a melody: "Tomorrow will be nice, said the one lost at sea." Here there is empathy, but hope is uncertain. Venturi observes: "Rouault senses always the weakness of men and the promises of God. But he seems always to be bowing before an inevitable destiny."[21]

Rouault often portrays poverty by means of what have been called the "social landscapes." The poor not only forfeit the privileges of society but also dwell in a hostile environment. Cogniat gives this description of Rouault's industrial suburbs:

> His depictions of outlying areas are sinister in their banality. The distressing buildings stretch along monotonous and rectangular streets. They are hopelessly deserted, and if, by chance, a silhouette ventures

---

[18] *Cinq études . . . ,* p. 62.
[19] *Op. cit.,* p. 2.
[20] *Paysages légendaires,* no pagination.
[21] Venturi, 1948, p. 75.

out, it only adds a human hopelessness to the hopelessness of the setting.[22]

In the *Miserere,* this is admirably illustrated in plate 23, our p. 131, "Street of the lonely." Here the stark white and the brownish-black add to the loneliness of the subject. One commentator has noted that even the blotches of ink seem to be swept along by the tempest, giving the whole the impression of wind, storm, cold, hunger, and fear.[23] This is another example of Rouault's ability to take the plastic elements up into the content of the picture in order to create a single emotional impact.

Treatments of the suburban areas appear not less than 20 times beginning in 1911 and continuing until 1950. Rouault several times employed the title "Vieux faubourg des longues peines" (old faubourg of toil and suffering) to highlight the loneliness by the hostile setting. Man must work alone, a painful and unrewarding drudgery. Often a poor family is pictured huddling together, symbolically straining for a meagre existence. "Motherhood (Run-Down Faubourg)" cc. 117, 1912, tenderly portrays a mother protecting her child against the harshness of the world.

Beginning with "Christ in the suburbs," p. 132, 1920, Rouault occasionally alleviates the blackness by introducing the person of Christ. In this picture two children who would otherwise be alone on a deserted street appear protected by the strong presence of the Lord. Among several others, "Christ and Poor Man" cc. 235, 1937, is striking. Here Christ and the poor man, two equals, stand alone under a darkened sky.

What message can be read from these canvases? Social criticism cannot be the motive in this theme either, for the poor suffer a fate far deeper than material deprivation. Rouault nowhere makes reference to physical poverty alone but has a deeper interest:

> Pearl of such pure water. The tender look of a mother long since passed away continues to stabilize and console me in the desert of Hostility, Indifference, and Negation! In the land of hunger and fear the wan child wanders about.[24]

The vanity of human aspiration is most visible in the poor. It is this vanity as a human condition that Rouault intends to focus upon, whether found in rich or poor. ". . . The rich and the poor bend toward the earth, where they will be sleeping tomorrow."[25] The poor, with all their misfortune, face life with fewer delusions and

---

[22] *Op. cit.,* p. 10.
[23] Bouvier, *op. cit.,* p. 23.
[24] *Cirque,* p. 3.
[25] *Ibid.,* p. 16.

Evau cuime pour Faubourg-de-longue Peine — Premiers essais   *Georges Rouault*

Rue des solitaires
Street of the Lonely
(Miserere, Plate 23)

thus see its conditions in a clearer light. Their life, unlike the wealth of the rich, makes no promises it cannot keep. This insight was shared by another writer of the Catholic revival, Georges Bernanos:

> Rich or poor, look at yourselves in poverty as in a mirror, for it is the image of your fundamental self-deception. Poverty maintains here below the place of paradise lost; it is the emptiness of your hearts and of your hands.[26]

The emptiness, shared by rich and poor alike, is vulnerable to but a single force: Christ on the cross. Here the poor take on special significance for Rouault. In identifying Christ with the poor, as he does later in his work, Rouault identifies their suffering with his. He thereby suggests that, if meaning is to be found in the suffering of the poor, it is to this Person and his Work that one must look to find it. Rouault's faith made him discover the image of the Lamb

---

[26] Bernanos. *Journal d'un curé de campagne* (Paris: Plon, 1936), pp. 79, 80.

Le Christ dans la banlieue — 1920
Christ in the Suburbs — 1920

of God in all the abandoned and miserable on whom he took pity.

It is in this religious dimension that Rouault's view of the poor must be understood. They are not the ransom of a corrupt society but the victims of the sin that corrupts all of society. They display a human emptiness and loneliness that cries out for the presence of God.

War. The subject of war, strangely enough, finds little direct reference in Rouault's work. War for this painter was only an instance of man's inhumanity. Even in the *Miserere,* whose inspiration was largely drawn from World War I, there are very few plates that do not have a more general signification than the war. The message of the entire work, typified in plate 37, "*Homo homini lupus*" (Man is a wolf to man), is the lesson which war teaches.[27] But the unfortunates pictured in the 58 plates include many more than those suffering from war's destructiveness: a high society lady (plate 16; our p. 128), a victim of a shipwreck (plate 11), an army officer (plate 51) and Christ suffering on the cross (plates 20, 31 [our p. 194], 35, and 57) are among the subjects.

Venturi suggests that the disaster of war was simply too immense. The painter could only touch it obliquely, finding comfort throughout in piety.[28] But there is a more important reason that better explains Rouault's emphasis in the *Miserere.* We mentioned in chapter 5 the heart-sickness Rouault felt over the war; his reaction embodied the same horror that gripped the entire world. But it is worth noting that in one of the few direct references to war, Rouault pictures "German William II" in plate 49: "The more noble the heart, the less rigid the collar." To the painter this was the worst atrocity: not that men can kill one another, for that is a symptom and not the disease, but that one is tempted to consider himself superior to another. That is the horror. And this horror exists as often on Fifth Avenue as it did at Ardennes. The latter is but a fruit of the former, and perhaps not its most bitter. It is man, not war, that is the wolf to man.

In the other references that bring to mind the pains of war, Rouault treats death. In some half dozen drawings he pictures persons

---

[27] Also C. 315, a painting dated in 1948. In fact at Vollard's request Rouault made paintings of many of the subjects of the *Miserere.*

[28] Venturi, 1959, p. 68. This touches on the important aesthetic question of whether unmitigated horror can be good art. Rolf Hochhuth in his historical postscripts of *The Deputy* tells how he had to tone down some of his facts to make the horror of war into a semblance of art. He said: "I have endeavored throughout this work to *underplay* the already almost incredible events of Hitler's war and the number of its victims. ... Thus to adjust events to fit the human capacity for imagination." (New York: Grove Press, 1964), p. 293.

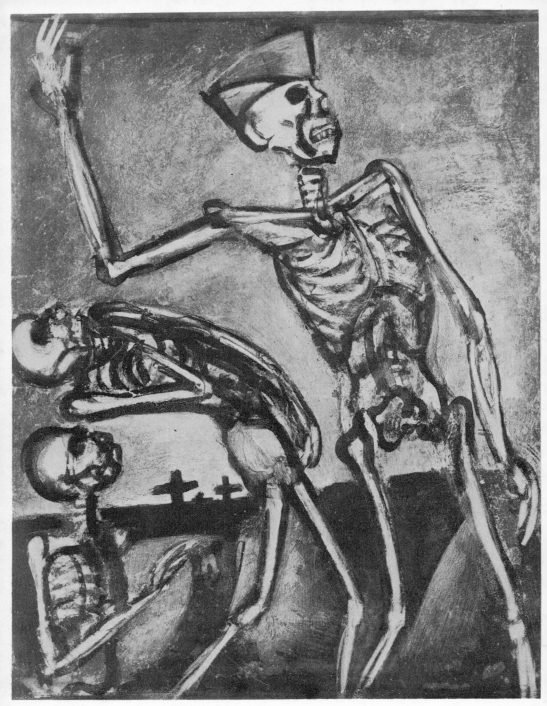

Debout les morts!
Stand Up All the Dead!
(Miserere, Plate 54)

in the grip of death, often alone, under a picture of Christ, as on p. 182; or he creates the actual presence of the power of death by showing skeletons walking. In all there is unmistakable connection with death and the person of Christ. This becomes explicit in plate 28, "He who believes in me, though dead, yet shall live," and in plate 54, our p. 134, "Stand up, all the dead!" But although war serves to remind us more forcibly of death, we never escape its activity among us. With death as with war Rouault treats a part of that single enemy that infects man, vulnerable only to the power of Christ on a cross.

12. The Prostitutes

The impact of Rouault's prostitutes has been as intense as the number of canvases was small. According to our count, less than twenty are of this genre, and all but one of these were done before 1912. Nevertheless, it has been one of the most discussed of Rouault's motifs and deserves a careful consideration. Never has a theme been so rich in extra-pictorial implications.

The appearance of this subject must be viewed against the background of nineteenth-century naturalism. We have noted Léon Bloy's use of the prostitute in Le Désespéré. One could add the names of Zola, the early Huysmans, and Goncourt. These fashioned a kind of literary realism for which the prostitute had a natural attraction. Their iconoclastic temperament led them to reject the Greek ideal of the human body, which had reigned since the Renaissance.[1]

In painting, the names of Guys, Toulouse-Lautrec, and Degas are worthy of attention for their use of the prostitute motif. The first, Constantin Guys who died in Paris in 1892, made much use of filles de joie in their surroundings, painting them complete with their picturesque gests. Dorival in discussing Guys sees no influence on Rouault. The former, diverted by expressions, treats prostitutes with anecdotal images full of sympathy, with a feeling of liberalized modernity.[2] Any such atmosphere was foreign to Georges Rouault.

Toulouse-Lautrec painted several prostitutes around 1890. Claude

---

[1] Their burden was to present reality, sordid or not, as an object of admiration. Huysmans in his book En Ménage describes the Gare du Nord as just as worthy of admiration as the Parthenon. Of course, they viewed the prostitute the same way. Cf. Baldick, op. cit., pp. 72, 73. On the rejection of the nude ideal in painting see Kenneth Clark, Le Nu (Paris: Livre de Poche, 1969), vol. II, chapter 8.

[2] Cinq études . . . , p. 29.

Fille au miroir — 1906
Prostitute at Her Mirror — 1906

Roger-Marx describes the attachment that Lautrec felt for these
"femmes de maison." There was nothing unwholesome about his
interest, this critic insists, "but feeling as he did a brotherly affection
for these models, perhaps also a solidarity with other reprobates, he
gave to them a warm and even poetic intensity that is missing in
the works of Degas."[3] But his influence on Rouault was limited. In
the first place, the "fraternal" interest Lautrec took in these subjects
resulted in a kind of transfiguration and idealization. If he saw in
them, as many believe he did, a reflection of a societal rejection
he himself felt due to his physical deformities, he was certainly
anxious to champion the difficult role the world had forced upon
them. They, like him, were the unfortunates of a hypocritical society, less to be pitied than to be admired. Secondly, Dorival points
out how occupied Lautrec was with the trimmings of such an
occupation: the outline, shapes, accessories such as clothes.[4] This
was no doubt due to his naturalistic interest and its concomitant
documentary style. All this resulted in a third characteristic that
could aptly be termed curiosity, verging at times on a taste for the
vice he portrayed. Soby comments that ". . . few of Rouault's early
paintings show the sensual relish of decadence for its own satanic
sake which characterized Lautrec's work. To Lautrec's cynicism
Rouault opposed tears and rage."[5] Though Rouault must have seen
and studied the older artist's work, these elements show that Lautrec took an approach entirely different from that of Rouault.

A similar gulf separates Rouault's prostitutes from Edgar Degas'
filles.[6] Degas, too, was convinced of the primacy of the plastic concerns. Human feeling, such as there was, was incidental to the
main impact of his work. The method determined the subjects he
treated more than did any meaning they had to offer. Rouault himself scolded this coldness in his Souvenirs:

> You are seldom tender with your models. . . . You have set them
> amidst the fireworks of stage-lights, often in very subtle harmonies
> or in carefully contoured designs of a more lofty stroke. You seemed
> desirous of making the naturalism of which you were prisoner, say
> what it never was able to say.[7]

---

[3] Toulouse-Lautrec (Paris: Hachette, 1962), p. 136.

[4] Cinq études . . . , pp. 31ff.

[5] Op. cit., p. 12. Cf. Benoist, op. cit., who says of Rouault's attitude toward
vice: "He suffers because of it, cries about it and invites us to condemn it
with him." P. 447.

[6] There are some prostitutes Degas painted around 1879 that bear a striking resemblance to those of Rouault, which M. Marcel Giry kindly pointed
out to me and which are to be found in the Rijksmuseum, Amsterdam. Cf.
especially "Trois filles assises de face" and "Trois filles de dos" in Lemoisne,
op. cit., vol. II, p. 308.

[7] SI, p. 98.

Whatever may have been the influence of this milieu in suggesting this theme to Rouault, we must look elsewhere for the immediate source. When did he decide to begin painting the prostitutes? The importance of models for Rouault has been much debated.[8] Benoist claims that while Rouault was renting at Montmartre, just after he had left school, the painters in the area let the prostitutes warm themselves in their *ateliers*. This was a common practice among the artists and Rouault perhaps made use of models in this way. But the inspiration that so fired his imagination must certainly be sought elsewhere than in this casual practice of his contemporaries. Claude Roulet relates that Rouault, while living in Versailles, once was walking the streets and came upon a woman standing in the doorway, offering herself to those who passed by.[9] Then it was that he was gripped by the horrors of prostitution and he went to his studio to paint them. Roulet questioned Rouault on this experience, and the painter explained:

> For me it was the shock, the suggestion. I saw this bluish lady just as anyone else can, though more clearly since I am a painter. When I returned home, this began to work on me.... The spectacle I happened upon was transposed, a transposition or perhaps a call from the inner world. Nothing was premeditated.... Thus the woman seen in the door is not the one I painted. That one and the others corresponded to the state of mind I was in.[10]

While this event may be genuine,[11] it can hardly be counted as the source for his *filles*. For he moved to Versailles in 1911, but he had begun painting his prostitutes as early as 1902. We ought rather to see this event as the manifestation of an abhorrence that had often been awakened by the sight of these girls walking the streets near his studio in Paris. In all events, the sight was enough to suggest to him the whole pregnant and sordid universe of the prostitution of human love.

Here then is the faculty that distinguished him from both Lautrec and Degas: a glance was sufficient to open an entire universe of emotional reality. He had not seen prostitutes so much as felt in his soul the life they lived. Charensol well reminds us at this juncture that Rouault was basically an expressionist rather than a realist.[12]

Why is it that the interest in prostitutes lasted a relatively few

---

[8] Cf. especially Dorival, "Portraits et auto-portraits," *op. cit.*

[9] Roulet, *Souvenirs, op. cit.*, p. 188. Roulet had probably read about this source in G. Chabot, *La Revue d'Art,* 1928, pp. 101ff., where Rouault recounts this adventure.

[10] Quoted in Roulet, *op. cit.*, pp. 188, 189.

[11] Dorival, *Cinq études...*, goes so far as to suggest the experience does not ring true. P. 27.

[12] Charensol, 1958, *op. cit.*, p. 149.

years? In 1904 at the Salon d'Automne Rouault first shocked the art world with 8 oils and 32 watercolors all done in his peculiar monochromatic darkness. It appears that he was in an emotional state at this time that affected all he did; the darkness was not limited to the *filles*. He described, in a passage referred to above, the kind of fury that held him:

> . . . The emotions of those long tragic years that had bruised me so were stored up in me. A kind of release took place, and I set to paint with a frenzy.[13]

Perhaps for this reason he settled on the prostitutes as a theme that fit his emotional experiences at that time. This, too, accounts for the fact that during these years one can hardly distinguish his prostitutes from his nudes.

Later in his work he researched the feminine body in a more plastic way and the interest in the prostitutes weakened (although one is prominent in the *Miserere*, plate 14, "So-called 'Daughter of Joy' "). The researches of Cézanne, whose influence was especially strong in Paris in 1907 and the years immediately following, also affected Rouault. Soby sees the example of Cézanne in Rouault's nudes of 1907.[14]

It is not correct, however, to see Rouault's choice of subject as an attempt to purify his vision. Grenier comments: "The prostitutes, the judges, and the clowns are the dark counterpart of purity and humility." Thus he wished virtue to shine more brightly by contrast.[15] The prostitute is but one facet of a single message that Rouault continued to proclaim throughout his life. If he left behind the prostitute motif, it was because its message was carried adequately in other ways. Contrary to Grenier's claim, Rouault does not arrive at his ideal in the second part of his life by stressing purity. We have tried to show that, like a diamond turning in the light, Rouault's work gives off a single brilliance from its well-honed multiplicity.

The intensity of Rouault's canvases on this motif can hardly be overemphasized; critics have described them in the most extreme language. Gustave Coquiot claimed in 1914: "Rouault takes a woman in order to marinate her in vinegar or in acid, to dry her out like a bat, or to bloat her like a bladder."[16] Some have named misogyny as the cause for his dark palette. Benoist believes ". . . his misogyny was due to a youthful overestimation of women and his pessimism

---

[13] Quoted in Charensol, 1926, *op. cit.*, p. 24.
[14] Soby, *op. cit.*, p. 16. Cf. Dorival, *Oeuvres inachevées, op. cit.*, p. 54.
[15] Grenier, 1957, *op. cit.*, p. 35.
[16] Gustave Coquiot. *Cubistes, futuristes, passéistes* (Paris: Librairie Ollendorff, 1914), p. 159.

constituted a reaction against his lost illusions."[17] Such a statement hardly needs refutation, for Rouault's whole work reveals the contrary, especially in his sensitivity toward motherhood. Hatred and fear, moreover, are conspicuous by their absence in this theme.

Coquiot on the other hand argues that the blackness serves a punitive function: Its fearful aspect served as a motivation for chastity. "If ever a painter has been a cruel torturer, it is surely Georges Rouault."[18] Kenneth Clark makes a similar point in claiming Rouault chose the feminine body because by distorting it he could express the maximum of suffering.[19]

But Rouault disclaims all such artificial aims and ulterior motives:

> No, I never had the intention of being an "avenger," or a moralist. There is such an emphasis in the heads of my *filles* that some thought I wanted to show off the shame of these creatures. This dishonour I did not even notice until after they pointed it out to me. Actually, I could only pity them.[20]

Rouault, innocent of all pamphleteering, simply painted the image that struck him.

But this image consistently was one of exaggerated aspect and gests. Why? In one of the most illuminating studies of Rouault's prostitutes, Puy lists a series of contrasts that Rouault employed to move the viewer. They are worth quoting:

1. Their profession over against their aspect.
2. Their theatrical pose—their filthy bodies.
3. Their divine flirting—their heavy disproportionate bodies.
4. The disenchanted desire of their lovers—their ambition to quench an infinite thirst.[21]

Sensing if not understanding these paradoxes, the viewer becomes uneasy. But what can be the significance behind this emotional impact? E. A. Jewell is certainly not alone in thinking Rouault's purposes here are less clear than in the case of the judges or the other themes. Does he mean to express "pity" or "mistake"? Mere "lewdness" or "human lewdness"?[22]

One possible solution that merits consideration lies in seeing the prostitute as a ransom for the sins of society. She is as much sinned against as sinner, and her depravity and her bearing of others' depravity serve to expiate the sins of a complacent bourgeois. We recall that the idea of vicarious suffering was very much in the

---

[17] *Op. cit.,* p. 447.
[18] Coquiot. *Les Indépendants* (Paris: Librairie Ollendorff, 1920), p. 72.
[19] *Le Nu, op. cit.,* vol. II, pp. 191-194.
[20] Quoted in Guenne, 1924, *op. cit.,* p. 5.
[21] Puy, 1920, *op. cit.,* p. 9.
[22] Jewell, *op. cit.,* p. 8.

air around the turn of the century, and perhaps Rouault meant to employ it in his *filles*. This was of course a central doctrine in the thought of Bloy. He wrote in 1907: "The Spirit prostitutes itself in order to come and save us."[23] Maritain specifically applied this doctrine to Rouault's prostitutes. He felt they were "the ransom for the bourgeois class. The reflection in the depths of the poverty of the saints." He saw in them "the stigma of corruption by money."[24] Suarès echoes this theme in his *Passion* which appeared in 1939 and which Rouault illustrated with 82 drawings. He says of the prostitute:

> You are sacred for those who are willing to understand. You are not sinner but victim, the receptacle of all our sins. Nor are you the guiltiest. Rather, you are the cesspool of our sins and lies. All other women, your sisters—the rich, the fashionable, the married, the highly esteemed, the very moral—you are the ransom for them all. Not one of them would possess the jewels and the gold she is so proud of— nor modesty, nor purity, nor vain plumage, nor the aigrette of her fair name, nor the hand-kissing and other marks of respect—if you, the victim, were not on the auction block for all women.[25]

The theological tenuousness of this doctrine notwithstanding, are Rouault's prostitutes rightly understood in this light? Rouault had no doubt breathed the atmosphere of this circle and perhaps had come to believe the doctrine himself. Yet we seriously doubt that he intended to import such a message into his *filles*. The painter's reactions to life and the world, we have remarked, were simple and emotional. They were not determined or prejudiced by specifics of religious dogma. Indeed the faith of the artist was less a standpoint taken on issues than a deep sympathy—even love—for a fallen world.

The gist of Rouault's intent may become clear in examining the affinity of Rouault's prostitutes with those of Dostoevsky. We say affinity rather than source, for by the painter's own statement he had not read *Crime and Punishment* before 1911. A friend, Baignères, recommended Dostoevsky to Rouault after a theatre presentation of *The Brothers Karamazov*.[26] Rouault found here an image of what his work was meant to be as he tells Suarès in a letter written on July 16, 1911. He was in the midst of reading *Crime and Punishment*,

---

[23] Quoted in Marchiori. *Georges Rouault* (Paris: Bibliothèque des Arts, 1965), p. 8.

[24] Quoted in Benoist, *op. cit.,* p. 447.

[25] Quoted in Courthion, p. 254. This reference suggests to what extent Suarès had himself been influenced by the world of catholic thought around him.

[26] Roulet tells us this, noting that it was before 1914 and the outbreak of the war; thereafter Rouault read *Crime and Punishment* and the *Idiot; op. cit.,* p. 229. The letter to Suarès indicates that this must have been in 1911.

and says of the experience: "I discover every minute new wonders, and what unknown and marvelous wonders they are ... (dwelling) in the midst of the most tragic and base realities ... transfigured by genius." His joy, he continues, was that of Columbus discovering the new world. "I carry within myself an infinite depth of suffering and melancholy which life has only served to develop, and of which my painting, if God allows it, will only be the flowering and imperfect expression."[27]

What could have been so moving in that great Russian novel? One could well select any one of several sections but perhaps the most striking in the present connection is that elegant scene where Raskolnikov is alone with the prostitute Sonia. He has come to confess to her that he is the murderer. He has just come from his mother and sister, for in his guilt he cannot abide their innocent intimacy. He takes Sonia's slight hand in his and then suddenly bows down and kisses her feet, saying:

> I did not bow down to you, I bowed down to all the suffering of humanity.... I said just now to an insolent man that he was not worth your little finger ... and that I did my sister honour making her sit beside you. It was not because of your dishonour and your sin I said that of you, but because of your great suffering. But you are a great sinner, that's true, and your worst sin is that you have destroyed and betrayed yourself *for nothing.* Isn't that fearful? Isn't it fearful that you are living in this filth which you loathe so, and at the same time you know yourself (you've only to open your eyes) that you are not helping anyone by it, not saving anyone from anything?[28]

The worst sin is that it is done not for her own sins, nor for the sins of others, but *for nothing.* Viewing her sins as a sacrifice lends her suffering a dignity it does not possess. And it is precisely this suffering, this hopeless suffering, that speaks most clearly of Rouault's prostitutes.

In order to show more plainly the suffering, Rouault avoids either blaming or excusing the error. For this he expresses pity; one does not pity sin or sacrifice. Cocagnac says of these defiled women: "He proceeds to make of them the image not of the error but of the pain of sin."[29]

Rouault's concern here as elsewhere is concrete rather than theoretical. He sees in life not the play of religious realities, as would

---

[27] *Correspondance,* p. 3.

[28] Fyodor Dostoevsky. *Crime and Punishment* (New York: Bantam Books, 1959), pp. 279, 280. Cf. Cocagnac who believes Rouault's thought "definitely betrays a spiritual experience as revolutionary as that of the Russian novelist." *Op. cit.,* p. 6.

[29] *Op. cit.,* p. 8. Italics his.

a theologian, but the frightful experience of real people. This he records without sermonic comment.

Women trapped by life having given themselves up to the concupiscence of hungry men find life a sink—impossible either to endure or to escape. They suffer from their sins without atoning for them. From this insight two Biblical implications, present in the simple recital of Rouault's vision, emerge. The first is that God uses sin to punish the sinner. Grundmann, writing in Kittel's *Theological Dictionary,* points out that the nerve of the Pauline doctrine of sin is self-assertion against the claim of God, which leads to "... the punishment of sin on the part of the God who punishes sin with sinning, i.e. to sexual perversity and expressions of the hatred which destroys fellowship."[30] Sin brings its own reward, and it is death (Romans 6:23). Man reaps what he himself has sown (Galatians 6:7,8). It is not so much that God punishes man for not keeping His law as that the law mocks man's attempts at righteousness, and he suffers for his failures. That is why Paul could say the law was a schoolmaster to bring us to Christ (Galatians 3:24).

Secondly, as righteousness is more than chastity, indulgence is worse than incontinence. Where one is the victory of love, the other is love's demise. This is the tragedy Rouault announces to all who pass by: that this woman of whom a hundred men have sickened should awaken in you a parody of love. The law against adultery is merely a feeble wall erected to preserve the delightful province of love. The law is positive.[31]

It is men who have invented the horror of lawlessness, the negative, in setting themselves up against the order of creation. Thinking themselves to be gods, they have lost the ability to be human. To quote once again from the theologian's discussion of sin:

> Men are as God when they set aside His prohibition. They do this the moment when they begin to doubt, first, that God's overruling is in their interests, and second, that God's will is unconditionally binding.[32]

In the process they have of course destroyed the very thing they set out to capture, and that is love. The love lost is more than the horizontal love of humanism, which is but a reflection of real love, but also includes love as a gift of God.[33]

---

[30] Gerhard Kittel, ed. *Theological Dictionary of the New Testament* (Grand Rapids, Michigan: Eerdmans, 1964), vol. I, p. 311.

[31] Bonhoeffer in recent years has stressed this positive nature of commandments as permission. In this light he sees prostitution as a denial of the freedom of bodily life which is fulfilled in love. Cf. *Ethics* (New York: Macmillan, 1955), pp. 183, 280, 281.

[32] Kittel, *op. cit.,* p. 282.

[33] Cf. Fierens who notes that Rouault's paintings here deal with both man

We admit that we too are reading into Rouault's prostitutes, though we hope we are reading correctly. The very least that can be said assuredly, as Cocagnac has put it, is that the very luminosity of Rouault's material appears as a reflection of the glory of God,[34] while at the same time the horror of the prostitutes' suffering is emphasized by the energy of the plastic expression. Venturi believes that, in spite of his faith or perhaps because of it, Rouault has realized the plastic expression of the nude[35]—not as an object of man's desire, but as a suffering creature made in God's image.

and God, wherein man is not the man of humanism. In this sense, he says, Rouault is closer to the middle ages than to modern skepticism. *Op. cit.,* 1933, p. 138.

[34] *Op. cit.,* p. 6.
[35] Venturi, 1948, p. 59.

Cirque (Pierrot, Punch, et Harlequin) — 1905
Circus (Pierrot, Punch, and Harlequin) — 1905

13. Clowns and Circus Life

Rouault's incurable skepticism of human progress was an extraordinary attitude in a millennial age such as the early 1900's. Why look for morals or lessons? he would ask. Who profits from them? "Human depths change so little," he wrote just after the war expected to end all wars was over.[1] The theme to which he returned more than any other to express his cynicism was the circus. We find 169 separate treatments of this subject, beginning already in 1902 and continuing until 1956, the last year he finished any work.

It is noteworthy that Rouault expresses this pessimism in the section of his *Souvenirs* on Daumier.[2] For this misunderstood designer was certainly a source of Rouault's circus motif. True, Toulouse-Lautrec, Degas, Seurat, Renoir, and Monet also treated the circus. But each had his own object in mind that set him apart from the lyrical vision of Rouault. Whether that object was to explore the intricacies of design, the compositional theories of Charles Henri, an idyllic dream, or the play of light, such aims prevented them from penetrating the trimmings of circus life. Unlike these artists, Daumier captured a reality behind the décor and uncovered the misery of those whose job it is to make us smile.[3]

Baudelaire, too, was Rouault's brother in spirit. Writing in 1861, he drew a parallel between the old decrepit buffoon leaning against the post of his shack and an old man of letters. As he describes it:

> I have just seen the picture of the old man of letters who has outlived his generation, after having been its most brilliant wit; of the old poet without friends, without family and without children, broken by his misery and public ingratitude, and in whose booth a forgetful world no longer wishes to enter.[4]

---

[1] *SI*, p. 83.

[2] *Ibid.*, pp. 81ff.

[3] Cf. Dorival, *Cinq études . . .*, p. 12.

[4] Charles Baudelaire. "Le Vieux saltimbanque." *Le Spleen de Paris* (Paris: Le Livre Club du Libraire, 1960), p. 55.

Le Pierrot sage — 1943
Reflective Pierrot — 1943

The circus has always had its devotées and apologetes. But Rouault's attachment was above all personal, and he mentions none of these influences specifically in connection with the circus theme. Here as elsewhere in studying Rouault, one is impressed with the folly of seeking artistic aetiology in an intellectual or even an artistic tradition. Visions such as Rouault's are not borrowed or inherited; they burn themselves upon the soul in a moment of insight. Just as one glance of a woman standing in a doorway was enough to open the whole awful world of the prostitute theme, so here too it appears a single experience—passing a traveling circus on the road—struck him with lightning-like force. In a letter written to Edouard Schuré in 1905, Rouault explains this experience. One day, he writes, a star had clutched my heart, and from that I was able to derive an entire system of poetics.

> That gypsy wagon stopped along the road, the emaciated old horse grazing on the thin grass, the old clown sitting on the corner of his wagon mending his bright many-colored costume. This contrast between brilliant and scintillating things made to amuse us, and this infinitely sad life, if one looks at it objectively, struck me with great force. I have expanded all of this. I saw clearly that the "clown" was myself, ourselves, almost all of us. This spangled costume is given to us by life. We are all of us clowns, more or less, we all wear a "spangled costume," but if we are caught by surprise, the way I caught that old clown, oh then; who would dare to claim he is not moved deeply by immeasurable pity? My failing (if it is one, in any case it is the source of immense suffering for me) is never to let anyone keep on his "spangled costume." Be he King or Emperor, what I want to see in the man facing me is his soul, and the more exalted his position, the more I fear for his soul.[5]

I have amplified all that, says Rouault, and it has become for me a system of poetics. It would be improper to place too much weight on this event, were it not for the fact that Rouault himself stressed the importance of it. Reflecting on it, he once mused: "To draw all of one's art from one experience of seeing an aging beat-up clown is complete arrogance, or perfect humility if that is the way you are made."[6] How can we enlarge upon this vision? What must we say is the circus and who are its clowns?

The circus. No child with as lively an imagination as Rouault's would have missed those itinerant circuses that crisscrossed the France of his day. These wandering troops—descendants of which are still seen today—were simple delights well suited to the child of the suburbs that Rouault considered himself to be. The painter

---

[5] Published in *Le Goéland*, Paramé, June 1952. Schuré was a symbolist author *(Les Grands initiés,* 1889), avidly read by Moreau.
[6] Quoted in Grenier, 1957, *op. cit.,* p. 34.

admits he felt a certain envy for these wanderers and their freedom. Their world, circumscript though it was, was free of all physical and of many spiritual boundaries. They were responsible, paradoxically, only to their diversion and the illusions they created. Rouault confessed, "I have always envied you, solitary as I am, attached to the pictorial land like a peasant to his field."[7]

Theirs was a spiritual freedom, even a superiority, that Rouault envied. As he expressed it in verse:

> I prefer to be the court jester
> And say freely
> Laughingly
> To immortal courtiers
> That I am not their servant
> In spiritual things.[8]

They are the fortunates who can wear their make-up without dissimulation. For their illusion is a part, perhaps the most important part, of who they are. Unlike the misplaced person, the performer has an itinerary that is chosen, accepted, even appreciated. Though they are always "misplaced," they are neither home nor away from home. Their life speaks of the inexorable impermanence of human existence. Their spiritual freedom, Rouault senses, is a parable of the freedom in which man was meant to live. As Edouard Muller reminds us, these wandering entertainers are the last to live in the condition of the true pilgrim.[9]

This spiritual liberty of the circus proclaims the supremacy of play. Jean Grenier has called Rouault's clowns "the foil of innocent children at play."[10] The clowns are the image of the man who, freed from guilt and eternal responsibility, can find his happiness completed and give himself up completely to the happiness of play. The clowns' antics have their delight in themselves and are their own reason for being.[11]

With play there is laughter as well. Baudelaire had said that as tears wash the pains of man away, so "sometimes it is the laugh that attracts and softens the heart; for the phenomena resulting

---

[7] *Cirque,* p. 10.

[8] *Soliloques,* p. 114.

[9] Edouard Muller. "Georges Rouault." *Labyrinthe,* 15 November 1944, no. 2, p. 4. The Apostle Paul urged upon the believer the kind of earthly detachment of the pilgrim, admitting that he knew both how to abound and to be abased materially. Cf. Philippians 4:12a.

[10] 1958, *op. cit.,* p. 65.

[11] This is the characterization as well of wisdom in the Old Testament, where especially in Proverbs it is likened to play. Rouault comments on the carefree nature of their life: "Clown, so visibly joyful, you sleep better than I." *Cirque,* p. 95.

Duo des frangins — vers 1947
Brother's Duet — about 1947

from the Fall can become the means of redemption."[12] The source of laughter, for Rouault, is as noble as its function. Not only does it afford enjoyment and soften the roughness of life's blows; it is necessary to man as man. In the *Cirque* he versifies: "The laugh is good to hear and to see, for it delivers us from so many miseries, real and imaginary."

> He who no longer knows how to laugh
> Or smile
> Is only waiting to die.[13]

The circus for Rouault is a picture of the world at peace with itself. But in reality all of its diversions are illusions and dreams, for the world man returns to after the performance is not at peace. Yet the circus remains a seductive farce for Rouault, somehow more real than the dark reality that lies around.

Here lies the painful, almost melancholy contrast for Rouault: not between the circus world and the lived world—the characteristics of the circus are often more essential to man as man than the acts of his real world—but between the act and the actor, between the laugh of the performer and the emptiness of his life. This contrast is reflected in the spectator by the gap between the chimera he shares briefly and the tight, tortuous sphere where his life is endured.

> Dream or reality, the wan child from the poor neighborhood will still find his way to the circus midway. One way or another, he will find there new and better ways to forget the long winters, the gloomy days, the hard and hostile faces, the depressed spirits and the callused hearts.[14]

Between the phantasm and the lived truth, what gulfs! A child of the suburbs, Rouault lived among such antitheses and sensed the hypocrisy of the city sophisticate. These awful differences were mirrored in the circus illusion. Critic Roger-Marx believes: "The circus for Rouault is the image of existence, the picture of grotesque and sublime mingled together, the possible and the impossible, the trivial and the exalted."[15] Venturi points out that others had seen in the circus a popular dramatic art, a type of ballet for the common person, while Rouault met it on its own terms, as a diversion.[16] And he loved it for itself, seeing in it a distorted reflection of the human dream.

---

[12] *Curiosités esthétiques,* pp. 245-6. Baudelaire goes on to betray his Jansenist heritage in stressing the diabolic origin of the laugh.

[13] *Cirque,* p. 52.

[14] *Ibid.,* p. 105.

[15] 1931, *op. cit.,* p. 98.

[16] Venturi, 1959, p. 21.

Qui ne se grime pas?
Don't We All Wear Makeup?
(Miserere, Plate 8)

The clowns. The members of the troupe, Rouault has told us outright, are all of us. In Rouault's treatment of the circus, the clowns were always the focal point. He has always sought to express the human concerns of the circus company rather than the flashy colors and bright lights. Even within the scope of this interest, however, a significant movement took place. Earlier, in the period from 1902 to 1912, the clown was often pictured with the objects he used in his act. Note, for example, "Clown with dog" cc. 35, 1903, "Clown with drum" cc. 36, 1903, "Clown with monkey" cc. 41, 1910. He also depicted the act at the circus, such as "Monsieur loyal and dancer" cc. 44, 1905, or "Circus Act" cc. 46, 1903. The emphasis on the illusion of the act continued into the next period, as seen in "Clowning" cc. 155, 1917. Slowly the emphasis changed from the clown playing his role to the clown as roleplayer, as human. In later periods, the focus was entirely on the clown as a person, and Rouault gave attention almost entirely to the head. Along with this shift of emphasis went another change: little by little the states of the soul became more and more visible on the faces of the clowns. Later works such as "Reflective Clown," p. 148, 1943, or "Dreamer" cc. 551, 1952, emphasize man caught by and in his illusion. One critic stresses the richness of color and warmth of the latter work, seeing in it "a sad and despondent feeling of reverie."[17] From showing the clown acting a part, Rouault had moved on to express the man behind the make-up. He asks, "In so many pleasures, evasions, dissimulations, tell me, realists and subjectivists, who really does not wear make-up?"[18]

Here is the moving conflict of which all great art is made: under the happily painted apparition dwells a stranger to happiness. Clowning may be necessary as a diversion, a fleeting vision of a lost frolic. Suarès admitted in an article on clowns: "He who can mock anything has the ability to hold himself above the world and himself."[19] But the comic, Suarès goes on, is at the same time "the comic mirror of tragedy." Ernest Hello explained how the tragedy viewed from without can become comical: "The situation which, seen in its depth from the inside, is pathetic can become comical when viewed from the outside...."[20] Humor is essential to life, but just as man is estranged from life so he is a stranger

---

[17] Dorival. "Rouault." *Le Bulletin des Musées de France,* May-June, 1947, no. 5, p. 20. Notwithstanding Courthion's date of 1952, Dorival saw it displayed much earlier. It was not unknown for Rouault to take a painting back and work on it after it had been displayed. Cf. Courthion, p. 406.
[18] *Cirque,* p. 14. Cf. also *Miserere,* plate 8, our p. 153.
[19] "Essai sur le clown." *Verve,* 1938, no. 4, pp. 101ff.
[20] *L'Homme, op. cit.,* p. 361.

to true humor. He sees it obliquely, afar off, as a spectator smiling at the antics of the clown. God, watching finite impertinency, can sit in the heavens and laugh, and on occasion man is invited to join in. Yet under the comic mask, life wears a tragic face.

It is this duality that gives to Rouault's clowns their melancholy depths. "Your clown is crying under his make-up," Suarès told the painter.[21] The humor of happiness is after all an illusion. The face of "Pierrot as aristocrat," p. 156, 1941, for example, is torn with this conflict. He stands self-assured with his hands on his hips, his habit fresh and well-fitting. A sun burns in one corner giving light but no warmth to the blue hues that dominate the picture. But it is the face, that unforgettable face, that reveals all the secrets. The set of his mouth and the dreamy eyes filled with a hundred wistful longings express better than words the contradiction of life. The comedy has fled with the crowd that came to laugh, and in its place are a question mark and an empty dream.

Empty dreams—does man hide them by his laughter, or does he find something he has missed in the farce? Rouault does not decide for us. His task was only to record this curious duplicity of life. Behind every sage is the fool and under the fool is often the sage. And who does not wear make-up?[22]

Yet Rouault's last word is one of compassion. "The clown is the victim of life, especially city life. As such he is a serf; he is miserable," wrote Suarès to Rouault. "He is an object of compassion and you have seen him with loving eyes."[23] One is not unkind to see sadness so much a part of life. Hello insisted: "Human passions are sad when seen in the perspective of their cause, which is error, and in the effect, which is unhappiness."[24] Yet pity has its limits, and man is the assailant as well as the victim. The greatest tragedy is that he should have to pretend to be something he is not but, somehow, was intended to be.

In the answer to Suarès' preface to his *Souvenirs Intimes,* Rouault calls those critics blind who have spent 30 years seeing only the bite of sin in his work. "We are fallen, it is true, but my clowns are really only dispossessed kings; their laugh is familiar to me; it reaches the realm of a million stifled sobs."[25] Man's deepest misery

---

[21] *SI,* preface, p. 8.

[22] This gap between the person and the personage has been exhaustively and perceptively considered by Swiss psychologist Paul Tournier in *The Meaning of Persons* (New York: Harper, 1957), which reads in places like a commentary on Rouault's clowns.

[23] *Correspondance,* p. 151, 1917.

[24] *L'Homme, op. cit.,* p. 361.

[25] *SI,* p. 14.

Pierrot Aristocrate — 1941
Pierrot as Aristocrat — 1941

lies not only in aspiring vainly for the heights but also in feeling a hidden affinity for their unattainable green pastures.

Who are the clowns? They are all of us. Like them, we all wear masks of what we would like to be, were meant to be, but cannot be. As Cocagnac notes, this gap between the mask and the man may be the most pointed trace of original sin.[26] It is a trace, moreover, that bears within itself the dream of that which we were created to be—and can yet become, when the joy of the fool and the wisdom of the sage unite in the bosom of the redeemed man.

[26] *Op. cit.,* p. 18.

SECTION B: THE THEME OF GRACE

*   *   *

14. The Supernatural

A French dictionary refers to "grace" as that "aid which God gives toward salvation." At first glance, neither "salvation" nor "God-given aid" are concepts especially suited to artistic expression, by contrast, for example, with a topic such as "degradation" which displays easily identifiable visible characteristics. Even religious art has not always been helpful in portraying such topics, for it has often confused "supernatural" with "transcendent" and settled for seraphim as safe religious subjects. Christian art has been most valuable when illuminating sacred history, though even here it has sometimes been insensitive to the presence of grace. And the twentieth century has been particularly hard on religious realities. Modern sentiment and its graphic expression, when they have not dismissed the supernatural as unverifiable, have attempted to remake it after their own Lilliputian image. Why, then, have we so persisted in using grace as an important characteristic of Rouault's work?

Let us ask first what is at stake artistically. Critics discussing Rouault's work have been notably silent on this aspect, except for occasional speculations in chapter endings.[1] The most helpful discussion is that of Venturi, who broaches this topic after a consideration of the friendship of Bloy and Rouault. He seeks to demonstrate that Rouault has succeeded in guarding the freedom of the artist both as craftsman and as person. Historically, he sees this

---

[1] The closing line of Courthion's valuable book is a classic in this regard. He claimed that Rouault had revealed the real function of art. "In the last analysis, this is to lose itself and to find itself transfigured in the concentrated act of prayer." P. 359.

tradition of freedom beginning in the late eighteenth century when Goya first opposed the "caractéristique" to the "beau idéal." We have already observed how Goya had imported moral and political ends into his work. At the same time, Venturi points out, he preserved an autonomy embodying a certain truthfulness and life that had been lost in the academic search for the "beau idéal." More importantly, this truth was not "abstract" but a truth to humanity. Baudelaire has said of Goya: "No one has dared more than he, in the sense of the 'absurd possible.' All of these contortions, these bestial faces, these diabolic grimaces are penetrated with humanity."[2]

With Daumier this is amplified. This painter's pity was a reaction to the corruption of society, but he represented, in Venturi's words, the liberation of the artist. It was in the freedom achieved by Daumier that Rouault worked throughout his life.[3]

In the rarefied atmosphere of modern art this is a warming ray. For in the name of freedom art has become a prisoner either of personal fancy—making freedom into anarchy—or of some particular artistic program. The century is cluttered with its "isms." But Rouault has demonstrated that true freedom of the artist is achieved only when place is left for human values, while the artist who turns his back on the infinite richness of the human situation is headed for slavery. Academicism, in many guises, has always been at odds with the nuances of humanity.

At first blush all of this may seem to have little to do with grace in its religious sense. Yet in the history of criticism the aesthetic and religious ideas of grace have always been associated; in many ways the former is derived from the latter. Artistic grace has been identified with a charming felicity that is freely bestowed by God and (later in the history of criticism) by nature, and never achieved by an act of the will.[4]

Venturi asserts that the "beau idéal" was basically a prejudice which had made grace sterile.[5] The world for the classicist had frozen. Grace, by contrast, liberates and renews. Rouault made this very point in criticizing both renaissance and modern art as he commented on Michelangelo's "Last Judgment." How inert all the figures seem, he declared: "They are incapable of going against the current of the new world. What a tragic epic of titans who will never complete the gesture they attempt. They wait. Who will

---

[2] *Variétés critiques* (Paris: 1924), pp. 142-143. Quoted in Venturi, 1959, p. 41. Italics his.
[3] Cf. Venturi, 1959, pp. 40ff.
[4] See on this: "A Grace Beyond the Reach of Art." *Journal of the History of Ideas* (1944), vol. V, pp. 131-150.
[5] *Ibid.*

deliver them? They are captives." But, Rouault adds, the trammels are not only on the canvas but in the painter as well. For their creator is himself captive.

> O Michelangelo, already when you create your figures, they have their eyes closed for eternity. That is why in the surrender of grace a Raphael and a Rubens, so much in love with life, seem like happy children at play.

Nor is this determent unique to these masters. Rouault goes on to suggest:

> Michelangelo is the somber ancestor of the lonely moderns for whom our beloved art has become a haven of rest where they flourish, even in the face of the fearful trials that assail on every hand from birth until death.[6]

Typically, Rouault concludes with reference to the trials with which human life is associated. For life as it is endured by rich and poor calls out with myriad voices for grace. Art which is true to its human condition must echo these harried calls. Only then will the real glory of life be seen. What is at stake, then, is both the freedom of the artist and the humanity of art. For if the artist is not open to grace, his art cannot be open to the moving pageant of human affairs.

How can grace be relevant to the artistic process? Grace is the presence and activity of God in the world. But for the artist, whose dictionary is the visible world, this presence is a kind of alien intrusion from another level of reality. Rouault was constantly aware of the mysterious depths of reality. He stood before the world with a genuine sense of mystery which engendered humility.[7] Yet his humility was impregnated with faith in the existence of an order in this depth:

> Everything is imponderable in the spiritual realms where the artist dares to dwell. Nevertheless there is an order that rules there more sure than the one controlling weights and measures.[8]

Moreau had taught his students to have respect for this mysterious inner order. Rouault recalls this counsel in his *Souvenirs* when he hails Moreau's insistence "on defending the rights of the imagination and the inner vision over against visible reality."[9] For Moreau, we noticed, the interior vision was primarily a vivid literary imagi-

---

[6] *Soliloques*, p. 74.

[7] Roger-Marx in one discussion on Rouault counts this aspect as one of the characteristics of great religious artists. Those who "bind man to man and the known to the unknown." *Rouault.* Séries: Médecines Peintures, no. 86, no pagination.

[8] *Stella Vespertina*, no pagination. He goes on to stress its inner orientation.

[9] *SI*, p. 44.

nation. Rouault followed his teacher in his stress on the openness to mystery and on artistic humility, but he went beyond Moreau's symbolism in locating the source of this vision. He explains in this context:

> I would go even further here. I would not dare to be an unworthy advocate for Gustave Moreau, but over against the reality that was able to satisfy Renoir or Degas, I would say, almost as the *surrealists* do, that there is a very lovely reality that is not always what the photographer sees in his dark room: Mother Nature hanging her head.[10]

What is this other "lovely reality" that Rouault believed in? It is not to be understood as something opposed to natural reality or as merely psychic and non-material. If the surrealists saw this other world as irrational and in some ways anti-natural, Rouault saw it rather as supernatural and super-rational. Though the presence of this higher order is manifest within man, it also infinitely transcends man. But we should not view this as an implicit pantheism. Rouault as an artist and believer set out to describe the Christian experience he knew. He affirms in the only terms at his disposition—artistic—that God exists, and everything must therefore be viewed in a divine light.

> In the darkness where Lazarus is raised
> The imagination races.[11]

It is here that the consideration of the sacred in art should begin: how does this other reality make itself manifest in art? A helpful discussion on the sacred in art appeared in 1947 in the journal *L'Art Sacré*. Joseph Pichard's introduction asserted that the sacred must be defined according to the Christian faith. The sacred, that is, does not include everything beyond the material but is determined by what God is in truth. This "truth" is the supernatural, radically "other" character of God. The creature coming into consciousness of this reality senses, on the one hand, a total annihilation of his being and, on the other, a fervent desire for union. This double aspect manifests itself as both reverence and servile love, both fearful awe and inescapable attraction.[12]

Entrance to the sacred must be accomplished by the rules, which in this case include participating in the redemption of Christ. This

---

[10] *Ibid.* Italics his. Cf. also Rouault and Suarès, "Moreau," *op. cit.,* April, 1926, p. 242. Art historians still debate Moreau's influence on surrealism. This much is certain: just as Moreau was able to open Rouault's perspective to that inner world which that student later believed to be the supernatural, so he suggested to surrealism that inner world which they explored as the sub- or pre-conscious.

[11] *Soliloques,* p. 120.

[12] April-May, 1947, *op. cit.,* pp. 100-102.

redemption, explains Pichard, is found "only around the great liturgic sacrifice that orders all sacred art." The end of sacred art, Pichard states in his conclusion, should be to serve the faithful in the realization of the sacred, that is, redemption. Paths to the sacred are available to the believing artist: (1) Terror, (2) Love and goodness beyond measure, (3) Symbolism and anthropomorphism of God, and (4) Divine peace.[13]

The kind of program implied by this statement has probably been best realized in the work of Albert Gleizes (1881-1953), who took part in this study. In his response he plainly states that research in the sacred should take one directly to the Church, the Scriptures and the sacraments. As the explanation of this world is found not in itself but in the Incarnation, that event must be the commencement of all journeys to the sacred. This means that the artist should serve the "living structures" provided for him by theologians and metaphysicians and embodied in Tradition as the living principle of divine order.[14]

Two characteristics of this research are worthy of special examination. The one is the incipient mysticism (Pichard has insisted that the realization of the sacred should "excite in our being a powerful desire for union"), and the other is the liturgical orientation. The concepts of "fearful awe" and "inescapable attraction" find a recent statement in Rudolph Otto's *The Idea of the Holy*. This book, to which Pichard makes specific reference,[15] identifies the sense of the holy as a human intuitive response in the face of ontological transcendence. But this concept as elucidated by Otto proves dangerously elusive. Identifying the sacred in "intuitive" terms threatens to dissipate any cognitive content in the realm of nonverifiable experience. Is the only human awareness of the sacred an emotional-mystical one? Despite his claims to the contrary, Otto imperils the rational, historical elements of the holy in human experience by stressing the importance of non-rational experience.[16]

In the second element, the liturgical, a place is left for the

---

[13] *Ibid.*, pp. 103, 104. Conclusion is on p. 131.

[14] Gleizes' aim earned for him the characterization of "an apologist for intellectual orthodoxy." Daniel Robbins. *Gleizes' Retrospective Exhibition at the Musée National d'Art Moderne*. Paris, 15 December 1964 to 31 January 1965, p. 25 of the exhibition catalogue. Gleizes' part in the research is described in Pichard, *op. cit.*, pp. 120ff.

[15] *Ibid.*, p. 101.

[16] Despite Otto's attempt to preserve the rational elements, in admitting the *discontinuity* of the spheres, p. 136, and removing the visible historical signs of Christ's ministry, p. 64, he does in fact disparage the rational components of religious experience. (New York: Oxford, 1958). Cf. also page 108 where he admits he is continuing the religious program begun by Schleiermacher.

objective (if not rational) component in the experience of the sacred. But this emphasis in Catholic art has its own peculiar danger. In the introduction[17] we made reference to Claudel's desire that modern religious art regain the imaginative power of the historical realities of the faith. But the lack of such power, especially apparent in Baroque art, is endemic to all religious art. For Catholic art must always serve the present expression of tradition which is celebrated liturgically in the Church. Revelation is not only the miraculous intervention of the supernatural in history and the record thereof but also God's present activity in the mass. Since, as Gleizes expresses it, the mission of the Church is a supernatural one,[18] the Church too is the proper sphere of grace and its artistic expression. The only justification for any work of art theologically, one writer on sacred art has said, would be to find in it "an expression of a need in the life of the Church."[19]

To add perspective to our discussion of the sacred in art it is instructive to recall Abraham Kuyper's 1888 lecture on Calvinism and art. He noted that the association of Catholic art with the Church is a remaining influence of the monolithic medieval culture. During that period, he points out, "scarcely a single art-style can be mentioned which did not arise from the center of divine worship and which did not seek the realization of its ideals in the sumptuous structure for that worship."[20] In Calvinism, he explains, the symbolical form of worship was transcended and a spiritual liberty was realized; an invisible priesthood replaced the visible one. A sterile religious monolith became open to the multiformity of life. The tutelage of the Church over all of life was ended; the whole world was seen as the stage for the mighty acts of God. Grace was liberated.[21]

---

[17] P. 12.

[18] Op. cit., p. 121.

[19] J. Paramelle. "Le Pèlerin et l'Absolu," in Victor-Henri Debidour, ed. Problèmes de l'Art Sacré (Paris: Le Nouveau Portique, 1951), p. 50. Cf. also J. Pichard. "Oeuvre de Georges Rouault." L'Art de l'Eglise, vol. 21, no. 1, p. 188. It must be granted that this is not true of much of Catholic art, which has often interpreted "the needs of the church" very broadly indeed. Still, the research we have just discussed and its emphases indicate this tendency is present and active, especially in "official" discussions of Catholic art.

[20] "Calvinism and Art." Six Stone Foundation Lectures (Grand Rapids: Eerdmans, 1943), p. 146. See also his The Antithesis between Symbolism and Revelation (Amsterdam-Pretoria-Edinburgh, 1899), where he identified the mystico-symbolic quest with an undue emphasis on liturgy which ignores the need for redemption.

[21] Ibid. Kuyper believes this accounts for Calvinism's failure to produce its own distinctive art style: it was against its very nature to do so.

More importantly, Calvinism gave art its own independent existence. It no longer had to serve the Church. Since for Calvin the world was beautiful but undone, art was free to roam over the entire created world, recording its contradictions and noting its past and future glory. There in the sufferings of men, art, given the eyes of faith, could discern a deeper "man of suffering." Comments Kuyper:

> Now we begin to understand that there was mystical suffering also in the general woe of man, revealing hitherto unmeasured depths of the human heart, and thereby enabling us to fathom much better still the deep depths of the mysterious agonies of Golgotha.[22]

Doubtless the atmosphere of the research of *L'Art Sacré* was that in which Rouault lived. His references to the unknown often reflect this influence. Yet his work extends beyond this single horizon and touches that referred to by Kuyper. His paintings of prostitutes and clowns evidence neither a mystical inclination nor a liturgical relevance. His was a vision that sought and discovered grace in the back streets of life as well as on its avenues. We cannot of course make of him a Protestant; we have often said we must avoid attempting to articulate specifically his religious thought. Protestantism, moreover, has often failed to fulfill Kuyper's program. But our very inability to place him firmly in any single artistic-religious tradition should serve as a signal reminder for us. Artistic greatness nourished on faith defies careful categorization, and no tradition has the monopoly on truth.

That grace exists meant for Rouault that its relevance was everywhere. No subject was secular or sacred. Christian realities were as much in evidence in the depressed suburbs as in the worship of the Church. Cocagnac recognized this in the same journal, *L'Art Sacré*, twenty years later. He felt with Rouault a strange harmony between sin and the love of God, between pain and redemption.[23]

---

[22] *Ibid.*, pp. 166, 167. That the Protestant tradition has not always been seen to hold such a broadened perspective can be seen from the words of Ernest Hello in 1872: "Protestantism has abandoned the imagination of man. It has not permitted the redeemer God to lay hold of it. It has forgotten that God the creator has made the sunsets and has called on the glowing evenings to tell man something of His splendour." *L'Homme, op. cit.,* pp. 22, 23. It is to be regretted that these two contemporaries could not have had occasion to learn from each other. A recent discussion of Protestant art in France opposes the Reformed tradition of a faith rooted in the "cross" to the Catholic-counter-reformation emphasis on "glory." Here, it would seem, Rouault lies in the former rather than the latter tradition. Cf. P. Romane-Musculus. "L'Eglise Réformée et l'art," in Victor-Henri Debidour, ed., *Problèmes de l'art sacré, op. cit.,* p. 93.

[23] *Op. cit.,* p. 27.

Suarès throughout his long friendship with Rouault struggled to comprehend these anomalous harmonies. In 1940 Suarès described the painter's faith as his refuge, adding: "Salvation resides somewhere else perhaps; in any case, this life is miserable and the present damned."[24] Yet the writer had to admit that grace shone through. Rouault was able to glorify even the material that was damnation itself. Suarès may have reflected his own puzzlement when he concluded: "Rouault oscillates between a mystical image of salvation and a biting satire on the world, which is one of perdition."[25]

Rouault had demonstrated in his work the *rapprochement* of sin and grace, though he was not always able to explain it verbally. In 1914 he tried to express his conviction to Suarès. Faith does not produce artistic miracles, he noted. A mediocre artist does not suddenly paint a great canvas. But he testified: *"As for me, I believe in a religious unfolding. I must tell you that."*[26] For grace is essential to man as man. Proceeding, he explained:

> The real nature of man dwells in the about-face of a conversion: He turns his love toward God, nor is his love less strong as a result, but rather the contrary. The emptiness of the creature is so great, the powerlessness of men toward one another so deep, so absolute . . . that in turning to God everything is transfigured.

But grace does not ignore human misery, as so-called religious persons often do. Indeed, it is grace that illuminates the depth of man's lostness. Rouault concluded:

> The enormous sufferings that many so-called superior natures in *the religious mold* often do not understand: just there is the starting point for many a man for whom life soon becomes a real desert, and human consolations . . . a perfect joke.[27]

Because grace exists the freedom of the artist is assured. Only then can the artist roam freely over life's multiplicity, and see it truly and see it whole.[28] It can call beauty and ugliness by their real names, because it knows them both by name. Fierens sums up Rouault's work in this way: "He leaves us some hope, but he destroys every illusion."[29] Grace is God's way of giving hope, but

---

[24] "Chronique de Caerdal." *La Nouvelle Revue Française,* 1940, vol. 54, p. 388.

[25] *Ibid.,* p. 389.

[26] *Correspondance,* p. 104. Italics his.

[27] *Ibid.* Italics his.

[28] Cf. Kuyper's contention that free grace and election have illuminated common life. *Op. cit.,* p. 164.

[29] *Op. cit.,* 1933, p. 139.

grace is also God's way of destroying all false hope and leaving us absolutely alone.

We have discussed grace without identifying its exact character in the work of Rouault. We have, however, tried to show its importance to art and the ways in which it might be expressed. Its character we must discern indirectly, from the way Rouault makes use of it in his treatment of nature and the Passion. It is to these topics, then, that we must turn.

15. Nature and Creation

G. K. Chesterton once answered in a masterful way the question of why an artist must know God in order to know nature:

> It is not only true that the less a man thinks of himself, the more he thinks of his good luck and of all the gifts of God. It is also true that he sees more of the things themselves when he sees more of their origin; for their origin is a part of them and indeed the most important part of them. Thus they become extraordinary by being explained.[1]

"Things" for Rouault were indeed extraordinary. One of the puzzles of Rouault's work that we shall examine in this chapter is why a painter with such a burning interior vision clamoring for expression should be tied in the strictest manner to the natural world around him. He practiced an intense observation that seemed to exhaust the meaning of every detail of the physical world. For it was there in the world that his own blazing insight found its physical image. His inescapable inner necessity always drove him toward the world and never away from it.

Who can forget Roulet's description of his walks with the painter on holiday in Geneva, Switzerland? They would wander leisurely down a street pausing at almost every step so that Rouault could read this bit of publicity or peer—utterly fascinated—into window displays. Often a full hour would not suffice for a single street. The painter would miss nothing, pausing here and there to pick some object up from the street, a piece of paper or a small box. Muttering, "Oh, that is nothing," he would toss it away.[2] "An ever more loving and precise observation of nature," he explained to Suarès, "will bring me to a more vibrant art."[3]

[1] *St. Francis of Assisi* (Garden City: Doubleday Image, 1962), p. 75.
[2] *Souvenirs, op. cit.,* pp. 227ff.
[3] *Correspondance,* p. 97.

His was not an idle, indifferent curiosity but an intense identification with the world, a passionate inquisitiveness that every person of imagination knows well. It recalls the simple delights of the child who sees a stick as a gun and who accompanies each discovery of the world with a flood of unanswered questions. As Rouault observed, "There is a child in every artist, for he cherishes the least little creature and 'every living thing' under the sky."[4] Art begins in this child-like wonder.

The same inquisitiveness applied to the flow of human events. For the sensitive artist, the quiet *atelier* where he works alone is no ivory tower. Rouault admitted: "It is impossible for me to isolate myself from the events of the day."[5] During the dark winter of 1939-1940 he told Suarès how events were affecting his work. They must, for "the most lively imagination needs various contacts with reality."[6] Beauty for Rouault, we recall, found its locus in the flow of human events. In the lived world, Rouault believed, "the beautiful rhythms are everywhere."[7]

Rouault was surely an expressionist. But the common conception of this is usually mistaken. We often understand an expressionist as a passionate artist who is anxious to express something of himself in his work. But it was Matisse who admitted he would stop painting if he had no audience; Rouault would paint with no hope of a viewer. For the communion the expressionist seeks is primarily with the subject. Compared to the intensity of this relationship, the audience matters little. Van Gogh has demonstrated this more clearly than anyone else in modern art. He once wrote to his brother Theo: "At bottom nature and a true artist agree. But nature certainly is 'intangible'; yet one must seize it, and that with a strong hand."[8] And again: "It sounds rather crude, but it is perfectly true: the feeling for the things themselves, for reality, is more important than the feeling for pictures. . . ."[9] Rouault, too, set as a part of his goal: ". . . to commune silently with nature, far from elaborate theories."[10]

---

[4] Rouault. "Enquête." *Beaux-Arts,* 1936, no. 198, p. 5.

[5] Quoted in Marchiori, *op. cit.,* p. 17.

[6] *Correspondance,* p. 330.

[7] *Stella Vespertina,* no pagination.

[8] *Dear Theo: The Autobiography of Vincent Van Gogh,* Irving Stone, ed. (New York: Signet Books, 1969), p. 61.

[9] *Ibid.,* p. 139.

[10] Quoted in Salmon, *op. cit.,* p. 184. It is perfectly true that many expressionists have not been so closely tied to natural reality. One thinks, for example, of Kandinsky. Roger Fry, in fact, sees Rouault as unique in this regard. He is a visionary, Fry says in one place, but "unlike most visionaries, his expression is based on a profound knowledge of natural appearances." *Vision and Design* (London, 1937), p. 193.

Such an artist's view of the external world is neither a mental cataloguing of objects nor a quasi-scientific analysis of their composition. It is a vital feeling with the things themselves, whether animate or inanimate. This is the basis for the observation made in chapter six above that Rouault's art was less physically exact than others' but at the same time true to life. As Brian O'Doherty expressed this, Rouault's reality is not that present to our senses but a psychological *intensification* of it. Rouault, dwelling within the subject he presents, revealed in his work the object's inner existence.[11] He was on intimate terms with the world and could share its secrets with those who remained strangers to it. We will ask shortly what these secrets might be.

Such communion must be the very heart of the painter's life. If nature and the true artist are one, there is always more that nature can teach the artist about himself and his work. As Rouault put it: "One is never finished seeing and watching. Our eyes are the door of our spirit and the light of our mind."[12]

Before seeking the import of Rouault's use of nature, let us note how it manifested itself in his work. The painter's interest in landscapes began early and, after outgrowing the initial classical style he demonstrated before Moreau's death, he painted several around the turn of the century. "The Plain," p. 170, shows a light, airy brushwork that recalls Turner or the Impressionists. He knew that nature was to be his starting point, but he did not yet understand its place. "Night Landscape" C. 43, painted just before Moreau's death, may be one of the few works which hint at the violence and intensity that was to come. His interest in portraying nature continued throughout his dark period, both in landscapes and in landscapes with figures.

But gradually the significance of this interest became clear to Rouault. In a letter to Suarès, written in 1913, he was emphatic as to the place nature and landscapes would play for him. He had just left the city (in 1911) and moved to Versailles, where he was freer to move about in the world of nature. Being here is helping the "delivery," he noted. "The landscapes (not understood in the way of the professional landscapists) will be my spring-board. They

---

[11] *Op. cit.*, p. 74. See Wright Morris' excellent article "The Violent Land: Some Observations on the Faulkner Country." *Magazine of Art*, March, 1952, vol. 45, pp. 99-103, where he compares the kind of expression exhibited in this American novelist with that of Van Gogh, Kokoschka, Munch, and Rouault. Says Morris: "Faulkner does not approach his subject—he is inside it. Being within, he works himself out." P. 100.

[12] Quoted in Guenne, *op. cit.*, p. 5.

La pleine — 1900
The Plain — 1900

will always be the basis of my work."[13] Here is the proper starting point: nature, not as a model, but as a living principle.

Dorival has observed that Rouault's landscapes in their maturity are innocent of all impressionism. Corot was more Rouault's father than Monet.[14] Rouault acknowledged a reaction common to his generation of painters. "Before knowing Gauguin, Cézanne, and

[13] *Correspondance*, p. 78.
[14] *Cinq études . . . , op. cit.*, p. 79.

Van Gogh, I already had a horror of this false copy of Nature. For it was usually a very ordinary copy and mediocre above all, though it was called shrewd."[15]

Later in another letter to Suarès he reflected on his independence from the impressionists. He disliked them because their vulgarization had become a formula, and formulae leave no room for the nuances of life, its laughter and its tears. Rouault adds: "But you can be sure that these fine 'naturists' are horrified as much of the word *caricature* ... as of the word *nightmare*." They are left: "... hanging by a rope like a chained watch dog."[16]

Nature cannot be neatly managed. Rouault's landscapes are marked with a strong sense of the autonomy of nature that seems in harmony with their consistent human orientation. As with other of his themes, one can trace an increasing importance given to the human elements in the composition. Near the end of his life, human values become central, and nature becomes a foil to them. "Christmas Landscape" C. 153, painted about 1920, preserves a warmth and, by the church tower reaching above the village, a strength despite the snowy chill and the lack of figures. On the other hand, "Biblical Landscape" C. 343, 1949, has been endowed with a richness of color that dominates the design, maximizing emotional impact rather than visual truth. Figures are present, but they are a part of the life of the composition and not separated from it. Human values have been extended to the whole surface (see our p. 176).

The importance of plastic concerns is demonstrated by Rouault's treatment of flowers, beginning in 1935. This interest should be seen more as a confirmation of Rouault's well-known attraction for rich colors, coupled with his constant preoccupation with nature, rather than as an arrival at happiness after the darkness of his earlier themes. His treatment of nature was never a celebration of an earthly paradise.[17]

If nature could never be merely a model as it was for the *"naturists"* though it was a constant source of inspiration, how in fact did Rouault make use of the lived world? His quarrel with the "objectivists" was their superficiality. They were, he felt, enchained by nature like oxen in a yoke. Give them a subject, he explains jokingly, and they are finished by the end of the week.

---

[15] *Correspondance,* p. 200.

[16] *Ibid.,* p. 330, 1940. Italics his.

[17] Dorival, though he admits in one place that there is both tragedy and joy in Rouault's use of nature (*Cinq études* ..., pp. 79ff.), claims the importance of his rich colored landscapes later reflected an appeasement. *Oeuvres inachevées,* 1965, p. 90.

This kind of advisor had warned him that he would soon have enough of nature. No indeed, Rouault answered them, for the visionary and the poet may spend a million years "investigating nature in varied and diverse ways, yet it will always be a springboard for renewal."[18]

Is nature then to be penetrated by and taken up into the intuition of the creative artist in the romanticist sense? Is nature but a vassal of the imagination? Commentators have tended to understand Rouault's use of nature in this way; the following is a typical view: "Ultimately he is a Romantic. The passion of his art derives from intense concentration on the object, often gained by hours of observation in obscure cafés."[19] This central use of the imaginative faculty recalls Baudelaire, for whom the imagination was an almost divine faculty able to perceive intuitively the intimate relationships or "correspondences" of things. "The 'correspondences'

---

[18] *Correspondance*, pp. 238, 239, in 1928.
[19] "Contemporary European Painters," 1939, *op. cit.*, p. 53.

Automne (Nazareth) — 1948
Autumn (Nazareth) — 1948

are between the outer and inner worlds: The natural and the supernatural; everything is a symbol, a 'hieroglyphic,' for poets to decipher by the faculty of 'imaginative insight.' "[20] What emerges here is the use of nature as a pretext rather than an end in itself. The spirit of the artist searches for its own image and reflection rather than for the premises of nature. Mysterious affinities with nature, moreover, easily become an excuse for artistic narcissism. The autonomy of nature is lost. None other than André Suarès accused Rouault of making this very mistake. You interpret and imagine, he wrote the painter. "Your temptation is to turn your back on nature. You go to it only for pretexts."[21]

Rouault knew nature was more than this. In fact, rather than being a "recreator" of nature, he confessed that it was nature that was remaking him: "The taste for delicate tonalities is a joy to the eye but also a millstone around the neck."[22] Roulet comments justly of Rouault: "Art is so difficult, bound up as closely as it is with life."[23] For Rouault always felt himself a captive to the sensible world. It was the condition of his art as it was of his life. In a response to a survey conducted on the *métier*, he emphasized that he felt each moment solicited by the vision of the sensible world. One advances in capturing this "sensible vision" little by little, not so much by the activity of the imagination as by the menial development of the means of creativity. This is an important relationship which Rouault made clear:

> We ought to be nourished on a mixture of classical and pictorial elements. We ought not to lean overmuch on the intellectual. There is an equilibrium, an order, a discipline to find little by little and step by step.[24]

Unlike the poet Baudelaire with whom he was identified, Rouault thought in pictorial terms. Sometimes, he admitted, it seems "that everything could be pictorial." But his point is nevertheless a significant one: the "means" for him involved in itself the accord between the sensible world and the interior light. After all, he

---

[20] Monroe C. Beardsley. *Aesthetics: From Classical Greece to the Present* (New York: Macmillan, 1966), pp. 255, 256. This has been recently illustrated by F. W. Leakey who has demonstrated that Baudelaire's concept of the supernatural was purely subjective. Cf. *Baudelaire and Nature* (Manchester University Press, 1970). See also the important article by Emile Bernard, "Charles Baudelaire, critique d'art et esthéticien." *Mercure de France.* 1919, vol. 135, pp. 577-600.

[21] *Correspondance,* p. 150.

[22] *Ibid.,* p. 239.

[23] *Souvenirs,* p. 73.

[24] "Enquête," *op. cit.,* p. 5.

concluded in his response, we are just getting to know form, color, and harmony.[25]

"Means," nourished on discipline and meticulous observation, strive after a unity that already exists. When he said: "The more the vision is an inner one, the more, it seems to me, one must ground himself in Nature," he meant more than that the imagination needs always to feed itself from nature. He sensed that the more closely one is tied to nature by observation and in spirit, the more there is of nature to be seen. Nature allows her secrets to be neither copied nor transferred by some artistic alchemy. They are there simply to be studied and and grasped in a loving courtship. Van Gogh expressed the same idea to his brother: "I believe that the way to acquire strength and power is to continue quietly to observe faithfully."[26] And Rouault confided to Roulet:

> They think that I am a "subjectivist." But actually I am both an "objectivist" and a "subjectivist." Those who say it is not necessary to look at nature are insensitive. It is very useful to be always on the alert, to observe nature constantly. There is always a reference point, even . . . in the poor quarter.[27]

Baudelaire's aesthetic is not definitive, but it is illuminating. For as man is not a slave of nature, the artist does not struggle only for imitation. Like musicians, Rouault explained, artists seek to transpose. The artist's creative imagination ought not to seek its own hidden dimensions in nature. Such a search has resulted in more than one sterile path for modern art. The artist's view is rather captive to nature because, like his own soul, nature points beyond itself to supernatural realities. These realities, insofar as man can know them at all, are not hidden but are revealed in and through nature itself.

This we must explore in more detail. But first let us ask what the artist's transposition of nature consists of. Modern art's most revolutionary innovation has been to consider a painting as a flat, colored surface rather than a rendering into three-dimensional pictorial space. This development, beginning with Manet, has stressed the integrity of the composition over against all representational elements. The growth of so-called non-representational art followed from this view.

Religious art has felt this influence. Some artists, following modern developments enthusiastically, have claimed to celebrate spiritual values with more purity in the midst of non-representational compositions. *L'Art Sacré* discussed this movement in religious art

---

[25] *Ibid.*
[26] *Dear Theo . . .* , p. 122.
[27] *Souvenirs*, p. 71.

in a 1958 issue. The writers point out that even in the middle ages the images taught emotionally as well as doctrinally. With the introduction of perspective came a temptation to be merely marvelous instead of profound. But now, with what the article calls "a non-figurative evocation," art is able to search out secret rhythms and harmonies of the visible world. Man thus has a new-found means to probe the heart of nature in which, we are told, the sovereign God keeps "the infinite imaginativeness of divine Ideas and the powerful ordering force of the First Harmony." This fullness of the silent life abstract art can introduce into the churches.[28]

But to say art has experienced the temptation to reduce the supernatural to naturalistic-realistic terms is not to say supernatural reality is *better* expressed in non-representational terms. This risks making spiritual values into something opposed to nature, a Kantian *Ding-an-sich* which is subject to neither discussion nor observation. G. Mercier, in a scholarly discussion of abstract religious art, addressed himself to the question of "what" can be expressed in this way. He maintained that in both representational and non-representational art, though different means are employed, there is a single end in view, viz. "émouvoir ou transmettre un message" (to move or transmit a message).[29] But to separate "moving" and "communicating" seems to destroy the conception of a unified goal. Does not art rather move *and* transmit a message? In fact, is not its essence made unique by a blending of both elements? Mercier's discussion seems to further the confusion. He attempts to show how Christianity itself has been the means of the discovery of a large amount of symbolism as, for example, in the catacombs. This is true enough, but what is patently false is his assertion that these symbols were developed to express what is hidden in reality: dynamism, glory by rhythms and colors.[30] The symbols in the catacombs were clearly to *communicate*—not what was hidden but what had become abundantly clear in the Incarnation. One has only to take, for example, the fish, the Greek letters of which stand for "Jesus, Christ, God, Son, Savior," to see how much theology was hidden in those early symbols. William Neil comments in studying this very symbol:

> To the Christians of the second century *no symbol said so much.*
> It stood for Incarnation, Redemption, Resurrection—the whole scheme
> of Christian salvation. But it was historically linked with the miracle

---

[28] "L'Image, la représentation, et l'évocation non-figurative." *L'Art Sacré,* 1958, September-October, nos. 1 and 2, pp. 17-20.

[29] *L'Art abstrait dans l'art sacré* (Paris: Editions de Boccard, 1964), p. 9.

[30] *Ibid.,* p. 26.

Paysage biblique — *1938 ou 1939*
Biblical Landscape — *1938 or 1939*

of the Loaves and the Fishes and apostolic vocation to become fishers of men.[31]

One could hardly conceive of an aesthetic symbol laden with more cognitive baggage. To say that all of this has nothing to do with the appreciation of the symbol as form, as would the purist, is to betray the intent of the artist.

The scope of this discussion extends beyond our present purposes. Suffice it to observe that the alliance of modern non-representational art with Christian art is at best tenuous. Christian art has always been concerned to explore the plastic and emotional components of historical and created reality. But how did Rouault come to terms

---

[31] *2000 Years of Christian Art*, p. 31. Italics mine. If further emphasis were needed, it could be noted that along with the "symbols" there were a large number of written inscriptions in the catacombs stressing Biblical teaching, especially in the light of the resurrection. Cf. Philip Schaff. *History of the Christian Church* (Grand Rapids: Eerdmans, 1951), vol. II, pp. 297ff.

Les fugitifs — 1911
The Fugitives — 1911

with the problem of abstract and non-abstract art? How did this particular Christian artist seek concretely to express Christian realities?

In spite of Rouault's attraction for nature, it was inevitable that he should feel the impact of the freedom of modern art. We have observed already that he championed this very freedom. Through the example of Cézanne, he came to recognize the importance of the internal coherence of his composition. As his work matured we have seen an evolution toward a single emotional impact and away from concern with visual detail. Compare, for example, "Fugitives," p. 177, 1911, with "Biblical Landscape" C. 343, 1949. Venturi points out that in the later work the lines and colors take on a symbolic quality (see also p. 176). The form is simplified to give a unity that succeeds in expressing his religious concentration in the pictorial surface.[32] The impact Rouault achieves, however, is not foreign to the subject but inherent in it. It has not been imported into the picture so much as discovered there and enlarged upon. One hesitates to employ the word "abstraction," with its connotation of unreality, but Venturi's judgment is a sound one: "It is by abstraction from visible reality that one can reach this more profound reality, which is the reality 'beyond.' "[33]

But we come to recognize this "beyond" as the mysterious depth of reality from evidences of supernatural reality deposited in and displayed by reality. The "beyond" and the ineffable belong to God; no artistic symbol can penetrate their secrets—not because their reality is imprecise but because our human capacities are inadequate. Infinitude must remain veiled to the finite. But Rouault, abstracting elements from reality, was able thereby to bring us closer to the universal and essential characteristics displayed in that reality. He was taking us not so much beyond nature as within it.

Living as he did in the closest communion with the world, Rouault was able to interpret its depths in his artistic language by abstraction, use of colors, and other means. In nature his work found its meaning. Inevitably this continuity between nature and his work has brought the accusation that he was being literary. In a letter to Suarès he noted that some complained the minute he put "omens" under the pictures of his Miserere. According to their point of view, "it belongs to literature or worse yet . . . to ethics, and therefore it has nothing to do with painting." The world is simple when, like them, you limit everything to form, color, and harmony. Their frontiers are more limited, noted Rouault, than those envisioned by messieurs Hitler and Mussolini.[34]

---

[32] Venturi, 1948, p. 97.
[33] Ibid.
[34] Correspondance, p. 322.

For Rouault art and life made a single whole. In using nature in his art he aimed to capture—we repeat—its essential meaning and its drama, not to seek something beneath and beyond it. Rouault was wary of the abstract. As Grenier notes, "He was afraid of stifling his sensitivity in its rarefied atmosphere. Thus he always stayed in the realm of the figurative."[35] Waldemar George affirms that Rouault avoided being either abstract or literary. Instead "he takes a portion of reality and transforms, transposes and recreates it without idealizing it."[36] He sought out those elements of the human drama that celebrated the truth and meaning of nature. Though later in life he was less concerned with physical details, the vision he recorded was one in which even those details found a meaningful place. He was seeking the truth of which Van Gogh wrote: "...My great longing is to learn to make those very incorrectnesses, those deviations, remodelings, changes of reality, that they may become—yes, untruth if you like—but more true than literal truth."[37]

Rouault was virtually alone in his quest for the truth that fitted his intense identification with life. He differs greatly from the modern artist, as Herbert Read has characterized him:

> But there is no doubt that the modern artist, feeling himself no longer in any *vital* contact with society, performing no *necessary* or *positive* function in the life of the community, retreats upon himself and gives expression to his own states of subjectivity, limiting himself to this expression, and not caring whether expression is also communication.[38]

Such solipsism must be judged a blind alley for art, as it has been for philosophy. It is a condition in which art cannot live. Like all human expressions, art is intensely relational. Religious art separated from life cannot help but suffer spiritual deprivation.

But ultimately, in being estranged from life, art suffers more than a poverty of its own resources. It suffers and is poor because it cannot exist without the plenitude of spiritual nourishment which nature embodies. Here, finally, lies the significance of Rouault's use

---

[35] "Les Idées de Georges Rouault." *Op. cit.,* p. 38.

[36] "Georges Rouault." *Le Bulletin de la Vie Artistique,* May 15, 1924, p. 229.

[37] *Dear Theo . . . ,* p. 301.

[38] *Art Now* (London: Faber and Faber, 1960), p. 84. Italics his. Ironically, critic Read's statement notwithstanding, many artists do care whether or not they are "communicating." In the midst of their views of art and the human predicament, art is the last vestige of meaning and relatedness that life offers. Matisse has already been quoted above: he would not continue to work without an audience. Picasso likewise could be called to witness. Even in the eighty-eighth year of his life he works long hours admitting: "I have not said all I have to say, and I do not have much time." Quoted in Jacques Michel, *Le Monde,* 3 July 1969, p. 17.

of nature. There is something that binds man in the same fabric of meaning with nature, and that something is their divine source. Nature and man both point beyond themselves, for Rouault, to their creator.

Critics have without fail spoken of the spiritual and religious function of Rouault's work, especially in his treatment of landscapes. Cocagnac talks of Rouault's interior world of faith illuminating his exterior world of nature. His streets are often somber and lonely; the only light is the sun or the moon, seeming to glow as the light of his faith.[39] Dorival shows that when happiness is present it is embodied in the very openness of the sky, which seems to lift the human figures and make them a part of its magnificence. When, however, there is tragedy, as in his "social landscapes," nature itself becomes a part of the tortured human existence.[40]

Even in nature the simultaneous presence of the themes of degradation and grace mark the canvases of Rouault with their special pathos. This juxtaposing of light and darkness prompted Venturi to remark: "It is an apocalyptic vision of nature."[41] Suarès added, "His landscapes are meditations on dreams. In them he frees himself from the age and from the demon."[42]

Both Venturi and Dorival point out that in 1930 a new aspect was added to his treatment of nature: the figure of Christ appears. After this he begins what have been called his "Biblical landscapes," one of the most beautiful of which is reproduced on p. 176. Venturi says of these: "The tragedy of Christ is associated with the announcement of death and of night, under a glowing Palestinian sky."[43] Dorival comments: "The only persons who belong there are sacred personages. The sacred exalts the concrete as a cloak of architectural abstraction. The concrete orchestrates the sacred."[44] What is it that makes nature particularly suited to the divine presence despite its tortured condition? Waldemar George believes it is because God, for Rouault, is more than a general idea: "He manifests himself in all his creatures. The universe of appearances is itself nothing but a manifestation of the divine presence."[45] Nature is in some important sense related to the sacred presence. But it is at the same time distinct from that presence. The world is not

---

[39] *Op. cit.,* 1964, pp. 21, 22.
[40] *Cinq études . . . ,* p. 79, and "Autoportraits," *op. cit.,* p. 238.
[41] Venturi, 1948, p. 93.
[42] "Chronique de Caerdal," p. 389.
[43] Venturi, 1959, p. 105.
[44] *Cinq études . . . ,* p. 83. Both stress the opportunity these offered for Rouault to exercise his rich sense of color, which emphasized the presence of a transcendent reality in the world of nature.
[45] "Georges Rouault: oeuvres inédites." *Op. cit.,* 1937, p. 5.

simply the sensible appearance of the divine, for this cannot account for its broken state. For Rouault there is light in the sky but not always on the earth. His landscapes are sacred not because nature is sacred but because it is a creation of God who in Christ has identified himself with man.

How are we to understand Christ's appearance among men? Like the symbol of the fish, it carries a large meaning. As he had sought The Clown, Rouault was seeking to find The Landscape in itself. This inevitably led him to Christ, who not only gave nature its original image but came to restore that image when it had been lost. Thus the meaning, the symbolic reference, of Christ among men is not some secret metaphysical or imaginative harmony. It is an Incarnation, a Redemption, and even a Resurrection. To this we turn next.

De Profundis — 1946

16. The Person of Christ and the Passion

Rouault was above all the painter of the Incarnation. In fact, his religious interest consisted almost wholly in a preoccupation with the presence and sufferings of Christ. Of the 160 works of a distinctly religious nature,[1] some 33 are heads of Christ, 12 are of the Passion, and the balance are mostly figures of Christ with others. Christian hospitality is Christ in the home of Mary and Martha. Christ is pictured welcoming the little children, speaking with the fishermen, the lepers, the sick man, the poor, the doctors, or a single small child. In Rouault's famous "Biblical landscapes" (as for example p. 176) the figure of Christ stands out. In works of church interiors (as C. 273 and cc. 418) the crucifix is usually the focus of the composition. In his treatment of death, such as "De Profundis" ("Out of the depths"), p. 182, it is the Christ on the cross or the Holy Countenance hanging above the dying man that gives content to the portrayal of death. Only a few religious compositions, some of which we will consider in the next chapter, include no reference to Christ.

After his conversion around 1900, Rouault attempted only two religious compositions before 1910: "Christ and Disciples" cc. 16 and "Head of Christ" cc. 21.[2] The latter is important for the hints it gives of all of Rouault's future emphasis on the Passion. Already much less importance is given to visual accuracy. As Venturi points out, the contours and the shading do not at all coincide with the contour of the form. But if the image is less clean, it is more alive with a kind of spiritual energy. The bright and clear contrasting colors pick up the intensity of emotion reflected in the dark brood-

---

[1] Only 128 are listed in Courthion, but he lists only a selection of 5 prints from the *Miserere*, which collection would bring the figure up to around 160. We stress again the tentative nature of these figures.

[2] This latter work Venturi, 1959, p. 44, calls "Christ Scourged."

La Sainte Face — 1912
The Holy Countenance — 1912

ing eyes. Though the subject is Christ, the context is human brutality. Rouault increasingly portrayed Christ in a human context, enlightened by his presence.[3]

There is little doubt that the events of World War I did much to deepen Rouault's faith. During those clouded days he did some of the work on the plates that compose the *Miserere*. After this, Dorival goes so far as to say, the painter seemed to concentrate on the Passion almost exclusively, as if in gratitude.[4] His output of religious works was greatest in the decade 1930-1940. Like other themes, the Passion underwent a simplification of form. Typically Rouault was less interested in pictorio-historical research than in what Venturi calls a mystical meditation on the meaning of the event. He considered more the essence than the accidents. Thus the form itself, rather than the gestures or expressions of the figure, became expressive.

The heads of Christ reflect the same restraint. "Holy Countenance," p. 187, is typical of the impassive nature of Christ's visage. Resignation, suffering, and commiseration appear more by the absence of aggression and revenge than by any expressive value of their own. The man of sorrows is seen as a simple, kindly, and at times pleading figure. Simplicity of form, gravity of contours, and heavy but luminous colors all contribute to this single effect. Rouault's ability to give his images a spiritual quality has led some to call him the last painter of Christian icons, a strangely apt designation.[5]

It remains for us to discuss the Incarnation as Rouault conceived it pictorially to see why it occupied such a place of importance. One student has remarked: "With Rouault there is no Annunciation, very little Resurrection, only a grand and permanent Incarnation, the indelible trace of the Holy Countenance on the veil of Veronica."[6]

Rouault conceived of and painted Christ in the same flesh as that of the clowns and prostitutes. His was always a human portrayal of Christ. And as man is shown in perpetual pain and suffering due to sin—Rouault, we recall, avoids any forensic speculation as to the guilt or innocence of any given individual—so the presence of Christ can be a perfect identification with man: he, too, came to bear the awful pains of sin. Rouault throughout seems to assume the sinlessness of Christ, more to add pathos to his suffering than to add

[3] Cf. *ibid.*, pp. 45, 46.

[4] *Oeuvres inachevées*, p. 98. Only after World War II did he turn to the saints.

[5] Benoist, *op. cit.*, p. 462.

[6] *Ibid.*, p. 462.

efficacy to his sacrifice. The pity appropriate to human suffering is raised to hieratic proportions.

As in all the work of Rouault, the focus here is human rather than cosmic, experiential rather than theoretical. Cocagnac is one of the few critics who have tried to draw out more theology and stress Christ's mediation between the two worlds. On the cross, he points out, Christ is shown hanging between the light of the sky and the darkness of the earth. He is, Cocagnac believes, the way of grace between man's misery and the love of God.[7] Theologically this is valid, and it is not inconsistent with Rouault's other work, but the fact remains that Rouault emphasized the sufferings more than the death of Christ. And he did so for a very important reason: to make the presence of Christ at once more relevant and more all-pervading with respect to the human situation. It was the misery and loneliness of man that was Rouault's personal and Christian starting point. Rouault's allusions are quite clear at this point. In a litany of *"longues peines"* he mused once: "Deep down inside the most unfriendly, unpleasant or impure creature, Jesus dwells."[8] Whatever the outward aspects of Christ's earthly identification, its basis and justification for Rouault is Christ's espousal of human suffering. In his *Soliloques* the painter reminisces that Christ no doubt looked much like a fisherman.

> His friends were fishermen
> Understood in the best sense.
> Clearly he could do no better
> In taking on our suffering
> Than going where it was most severe.[9]

Christ's presence is a presence of suffering in and with our sufferings.

Here, more clearly than in any other portion of his work, it is obvious that Rouault was a product of a literary tradition rather than a theological one. While much of his view of suffering and the Passion can be traced back into the Catholic tradition,[10] it is more immediately in the Catholic literary milieu around the turn of the century that the painter's roots are to be found. It was here that his sensitive and intense feeling for human weakness found its religious *raison d'être*.

We recall that Bloy, under the influence of Hello and especially Tardiff de Moidrey, came to view the sufferings of Christ as reflected in all of history and shared mystically by all Christians.

---

[7] *Op. cit.,* p. 28.
[8] "Visages réels ou imaginaires." *Verve,* 1939, vol. II, nos. 5-6, p. 120.
[9] *Ibid.,* p. 125.
[10] A fact we attempted to show in the case of Bloy, chapter 3 above.

La Sainte Face — *1933*
The Holy Countenance — 1933

Suffering for Bloy was as inevitable as it was all-pervasive, to the degree that not only man's condition but his very nature is defined by suffering. Bloy's starting point was the orthodox doctrine of the vicarious suffering of Christ, which he recounted in his own unmistakable manner. Christ in being made flesh came in order to make suffering the perfect penitence. Bloy spoke of this vicarious suffering in *Le Désespéré,* putting these words in the mouth of Christ:

> I have created you, beloved vermin, in my thrice sacred resemblance, and you have responded by betraying me. Thus instead of punishing you, I have punished myself. It was not enough that you resembled me. I, the Impassible, felt a great desire to make myself like you, so that you would become my equals. Therefore I have made myself vermin in your image.[11]

Christians are to recognize that all suffering is taken up into the suffering of Christ and has received divine sanction. Christ so identified himself with man that he took on their image, bearing with them the pains of sin. This thought achieved such an importance for Bloy and those around him that the timeless mystical aspect of Christ's anguish took precedence over his historical death. François Mauriac reveals his debt to this movement when he claims that wherever the police interrogate a prisoner and beat him, there Christ is suffering.[12]

With Huysmans and Bloy especially, this doctrine took on the added facet of vicarious sufferings by Christians for the world's sin. Veronique, the mistress of Marchenoir in *Le Désespéré,* found it difficult to separate her lover and her Savior since both were in agony for love of her. They both, she believed, fulfilled the vocation of saving others.[13] Huysmans illustrated this idea in a concrete way in his reaction to the tragic fire at the Charity Bazaar in Paris in May, 1897. Many leaders of charitable organizations perished in the blaze. Baldick tells us that Huysmans looked on the victims as having been chosen by God to redeem their country.[14]

Huysmans believed there was justification for this doctrine in Church history and tradition. He claimed: "All the saints practiced it, and it is the *raison d'être* of certain contemplative orders ... who expiate the sins of others every day."[15] An interesting experience reveals something of the insistence and irrationality with which they defended their position. In 1901 a Catholic doctor in Munich

---

[11] P. 375.
[12] "Pâques: passion et résurrection." *Plaisir de France,* April-May, 1949, p. 57.
[13] *LD,* p. 387.
[14] *The Life of J.-K. Huysmans,* p. 248.
[15] *Ibid.*

wrote Huysmans suggesting that if he were right, no Christian doctor could practice medicine in good faith. Huysmans responded
that both sickness and health lie in God's hands; the idea of
vicarious suffering, though much abused, "still remains the *essence
of Catholic belief,* the lesson taught us at Calvary, (and) the purest
mystical theology."[16]

The elaborate symbolic hermeneutics of Bloy and his intricate
apologetic imagery did not appeal to the intuitive Rouault in its
detail. But its illumination of human suffering was impressive to
the young painter. It was to find a semblance of meaning in human
misery that Rouault instinctively turned to the sufferings of Christ
and was attracted to Bloy and Huysmans. He did not bother to
develop a logical schema to understand this; he wanted simply
to know where man's sufferings could find succor. One could almost
say the Cross became for Rouault an emotional reference point.
As one critic has put it: "Rouault has stripped to the bone the
human flabbiness of his figures in order to reach the wood and
iron of Calvary's agonies."[17]

Yet his faith was not merely an escape, for it included the problem of sin as well as suffering. It was his own infirmity that made
him look to Christ on the cross. In 1938, amidst great weariness
of spirit, he wrote to Suarès:

> So little righteous
> And certainly helpless, the poor wretch
> With the best of intentions,
> Trips and falls more than once.
> Like Jesus on the road to Calvary
> Under the weight of the cross
> Wanting to take on our sufferings.[18]

Yet his sense of sin at the same time gave him a keen desire to
share in the sufferings of his Savior: "May God help me, or Jesus
Christ, if I have sinned; may he punish me, stray dog that I am
on this miserable earth."[19] Still it is doubtful that Rouault ever
adopted the idea of vicarious suffering by Christians in the extreme
form of Bloy and Huysmans.

Other sources may help to illuminate Rouault's view of the Pas-

---

[16] *Ibid.,* p. 291. Italics mine. It is of course true that this idea is not new
to Catholic tradition. Huysmans tried to demonstrate this by tracing it back
to Calvary in *L'Oblat,* which was published in 1903.

[17] J. R. Thomé. "Georges Rouault." *Le Courrier Graphique,* May-June, 1952,
p. 22. "It was in suffering, the sweat of man, and his own tears that the
painter found the road to the Incarnation and Redemption." *L'Art Sacré,*
March, 1965, p. 22.

[18] *Correspondance,* p. 312.

[19] *Le Cirque,* p. 135.

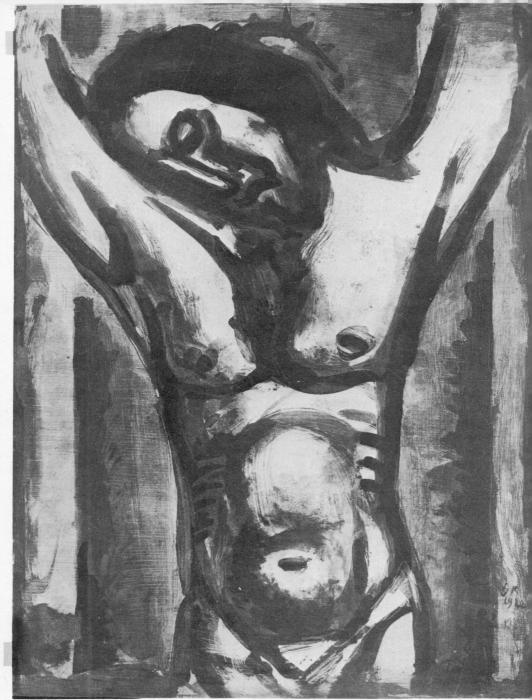

Jésus sera en agonie jusqu'à la fin du monde
Jesus Will Be in Agony Until the End of the World
(Miserere, Plate 35)

sion. One of these drawn from the history of Catholic thought in France is Blaise Pascal. Rouault borrowed from this great believer the title he employed for plate 35 of the *Miserere:* "Jesus will be in agony until the end of the world." The phrase is taken from the section of the *Pensées* entitled "The mystery of Jesus," which is a meditation on Christ's prayer in the garden of Gethsemane (Matthew 26:36-46). The Lord had brought certain disciples with him for comfort, but they slept. The pain of Jesus, Pascal muses, was a secret only he and heaven knew; his human friendship could not accompany him to its height. Though Christ had sought human company as a support, they slept. Comments Pascal: "Jesus will be in agony until the end of the world; we must not sleep during that time." While his disciples were sleeping Christ sweat drops of blood in anguish over bearing their sins. But, Pascal implies, do not all of us sleep while Christ suffers? "Are you content that it is costing me the blood of my humanity, if you do not give at least of your tears?" Do not be afraid, Pascal has Christ say, you would not search for me if you had not already found me. Christ reassures us: your salvation is my affair.[20]

Cocagnac addresses himself to this word of Pascal in relation to Rouault. Rouault wants to stress that this combat Christ has waged for us was fought alone. "He continues to wage battle against the anguish born of sin." Rouault does not ignore the resurrection, Cocagnac insists; but it is the eternal efficacy of his Passion which is the origin of his victory. God has opened his flesh to all the evil and ravages of sin.[21] It is true that Rouault does not ignore the resurrection but, we shall observe shortly, it occupies a minor place compared with the Passion. Rather it is the continuing nature of Christ's abuses that attracts Rouault, as can be seen in themes such as Christ mocked, for these experiences answer best to the continuing misery of man.

Another source of Rouault's inspiration lies in the iconography of the Church. This influence is typified by his interest in Saint Veronica. Rouault painted her at least twice: in 1938, cc. 386, and in 1945, C. 248. M. 33 also makes reference to this holy woman ("Veronica with her soft linen still passes along the road"). This last-mentioned picture features a detached head of Christ with his crown of thorns, seemingly impressed on a piece of cloth. Veronica, which means literally "the true icon or image," is a fictional saint identified in the New Testament Apocrypha with the woman with the issue of blood whom Christ healed and also with a woman who

---

[20] Cf. fragments 553-555, Léon Brunschvicq, ed., *Oeuvres, op. cit.,* vol. XIII, pp. 434-441.
[21] *Op. cit.,* p. 30.

encountered Christ on his walk to Calvary. Seeing him sweating under his super-human burden, this woman is believed to have wiped off his face with a piece of linen. The traits of Christ's face remained miraculously visible on the cloth. "The veil of Veronica" was thus the Holy Countenance, generally presented by Veronica herself. The tradition is legend,[22] but the symbolism is significant. Rouault may well have been impressed with Bloy's radical belief in the exchange of the images and found in Veronica a moving example. In picturing Christ's espousal of human misery, Bloy even went to the extreme of making Christ become filthy to redeem man from his filth.[23] Rouault himself wrote in Le Cirque: "The mulatto called Agnus Dei became ugly with age so as to become frightening."[24]

It is clearly the humiliation of Christ that is the heart of the Passion for Rouault. Christ's emptying is conveyed in Rouault's symbolism by bowed head, eyes resigned to suffering and death. Marois has well said of Rouault's Veronica: "Her face is radiant with faith and love, as if she has recognized her God only on account of his sufferings."[25] The neck of the Savior is not lifted up but ready to be offered. Through it all he never opens his mouth to protest. The supposed extremes caused Roger-Marx to see in Rouault's Christ not a Redeemer but an executed criminal. Rouault offers no "alleluia."[26] Seillière's description of Bloy's image of Christ is relevant to Rouault's as well: "Jesus often seems to him too enfeebled by his continuing crucifixion to react to the insults he receives at the hands of degenerate Christians."[27]

Yet at the same time Rouault's use of Veronica indicates he believed the reverse as well. As Christ took on the image of human misfortune, so a Veronica could take on the image of her Savior by sharing in his humiliation.

> Hard trials, ephemeral joys
> Are we not all condemned?
> The hours fly away
> —Inexorable flight—
> And may the last be blessed
> If the task seems finished.[28]

---

[22] Cf. Louis Réau. L'Iconographie de l'art chrétien (Paris: Pr. Univ., 1959), vol. II, pt. II, chapter III, p. 19.

[23] See above, p. 39, n. 54.

[24] P. 135.

[25] Pierre Marois. "La Foi et l'art religieux." Hommes et Mondes, August, 1951, no. 61, p. 418.

[26] Séries: Médecines Peintures, op. cit., no pagination.

[27] Op. cit., pp. 50, 51. In the case of Rouault "degenerate Christians" should be replaced with "feeble and suffering humanity."

[28] Le Cirque, p. 76.

Rouault refused to see suffering as an end in itself, as Bloy often had. Pain is necessary in order to reach a peace, a peace that many believe Rouault came to understand more deeply near the end of his life. In this sense Christ is not only the model but also the Savior. The apathy and hostility of the world Christ faced is the same we must all face. That he suffered is the only hope for us in the midst of our own difficulties. Human tragedy made Rouault more and more see the love of Christ as the unique hope. In identifying such hope in his vision of Christ, Rouault painted him, especially later in his work, as victor as well as victim. In this note of triumph we too can share—we too can wear the veil of Veronica. Dorival puts it: "Christ will make all those who have suffered as He has share in his triumph."[29]

It is in this hope and triumph that Rouault's view of the resurrection must be found. Grenier perceptively points out that Rouault's later Christs expressed more of the resurrection than of the Passion.[30] Resurrection for Rouault is but an instance of the general truth that all hope is located in the sufferings of Christ. Because of this, resurrection hope can become a present Christian reality. Mauriac is not denying the fact of the historical resurrection in noting that, as there are many sufferings, so there are many resurrections. "The executioners always succeed in making the most ordinary human face to shine."[31] The importance of this hope is pointed out by André Malraux in discussing tragic expression in Rouault. Death, he says, gives to life a tone tending to absurdity, not to lamentation. For Rouault there is no way to express love except through Christ, and that, we could add, through his suffering. As Christ is the hope in trials, so he is the answer to the absurdity of death. "Christ—and not God—delivers from the absurd those who believe in him."[32]

In a very personal way Rouault was able to translate this hope into a Christian reality in his paintings. "Out of the depths," p. 182, pictures a man dying alone. The only activity, clashing strangely with this central drama, appears through the window. Hope is represented by a Crucifix that hangs over the suffering and impassive man. Here the hope of resurrection is shared by two who appear

---

[29] La Table Ronde, October, 1952, op. cit., p. 178.
[30] "Idées de Georges Rouault." Op. cit., p. 38.
[31] Op. cit., p. 57.
[32] "Notes sur l'expression tragique en peinture, à propos d'oeuvres récentes de Georges Rouault." Les Formes, 1929, no. 1, p. 5. M. 31 portrays Christ on the cross and below is the sermon that is demonstrated by the suffering pictured: "Love one another" (see p. 194).

Aimez-vous les uns les autres
Love One Another
(Miserere, Plate 31)

to commune in their agonies, waiting together for the blessedness of paradise.

The vision of this future state is only obliquely present in Rouault's work. It is a mystical hope offered because of Christ's work. Rouault meditates about his own work of painting:

> O crucified Jesus!
> He paints to forget the "pursuing boredom" of life
> Far from this world of shadows and appearances
> He has departed quietly for the land of peace
> Which has haunted him day and night,
> Toward the land of peace
> Where all is harmonious
> To the eyes, the mind and the spirit.[33]

What can be said by way of evaluation? Seillière had accused Bloy of replacing the theology of the fathers with sentimentalism, "his brand of moralism having supplanted revelation."[34] Must we make the same judgment of Rouault? Rouault was of course far less explicit about his opinions than was Bloy, and he avoided the extremes to which the latter was prone. But beyond that we feel somehow hesitant to suggest a critique of a painter's faith, especially of a faith so deeply felt.

In M. 32 Rouault draws a man, perhaps blind, with his head down, reaching out to touch Christ who stands beside him. The title reads: "Lord, it is you, I recognize you." Here is summed up the faith of Rouault: neither intellectual nor hesitant, but as certain as the sense of touch. He sees the living Christ in the same way he sees the judges and prostitutes: with a clear, penetrating, intuitive vision. His view of the Passion is a combination of such a faith with a deep feeling for the awful contradiction of the human failure. He achieves a mystical vision, an identification with the work of Christ rather than an explication of his person.

But although Rouault did not share Bloy's excesses, it must be admitted that his sensitive nature made him prone to depict the emotional aspects of Christian realities. There is undoubtedly a broader meaning in Christ's death and resurrection than the illumination of human misery; just as the problem of sin is not exhausted by a consideration of human suffering, so the efficacy of Christ's death does more than give sense to human suffering. Rouault may have known this, and yet it was the latter aspect that captured his artistic imagination. He admits that his vision was as simple and untheological as was his painting, saying of himself:

---

[33] *Stella Vespertina*, no pagination.
[34] *Op. cit.*, p. 94.

He was chained
To such legendary misery
That he painted and repainted
With emotion
Jesus at Calvary
On the cross.[35]

---

[35] *Soliloques,* p. 142.

17. Human Figures as Religious Themes

While the Incarnation was the focus of Rouault's religious draw-ing, certain other subjects are worthy of mention. These are the saints and religious personages. Here the choice of subjects is traditional, but the style of the painter's characterization demands careful attention. As elsewhere, the iconography of the subjects is taken up into the life of the composition itself, and the form becomes a part of the matter treated. We have observed how Rouault worked at all times in the most intimate communion with nature. He sought the depth of meaning that nature *presents*, not by going beyond nature but by seeking that which is most significant in nature. His method was presentational rather than representational.

This strategy resulted in a kind of symbolism that has been pointed out by several commentators but which has yet to be studied in detail. Dorival's excellent study suggests that, seeing the true prostitute, or judge, or clown, he gives their character in the form of a symbol.[1] Venturi speaks of Rouault raising the pictorial scene to a supernatural level.[2] Thus the image itself takes on a spiritual quality; the locus of the impact is to be found within the composition itself, not elsewhere in some symbolized "content."

The roots of Rouault's symbolism ought perhaps to be traced to the symbolists of the end of the last century. Courthion, while he does not elaborate, mentions the probable influence of artists Puvis de Chavannes and Jean Carrière, and of Schuré's *Les Grandes initiés,* on the one hand, as well as that of Paul Gauguin and Emile Bernard on the other.[3] We touched above on Denis' desire that the pictorial elements themselves become expressive of states of

---

[1] *Cinq études . . . ,* p. 93. Cf. Malraux, *op. cit.*
[2] Venturi, 1959, p. 65.
[3] Courthion, pp. 35ff.

the soul. This indirect symbolism must be clearly distinguished from that of Moreau and Odilon Redon, for whom fantastic subjects became the means of expressing preternatural realities. The difference between the two types of symbolism is similar to that between allegory and metaphor. Denis himself warned against confusing "the mystical and allegorical tendencies which search for expression by means of the subject (e.g. Moreau and Redon), and the symbolist tendency which searches for expression by means of the work of art."[4] It was the latter quest on which Gauguin had set modern art: expression by means of the pictorial elements rather than the subject.

Rouault's symbolism more nearly resembles that of metaphor than that of allegory. If Moreau stimulated his respect for the unknown depths of consciousness, Gauguin taught him his aesthetics. But even here his independence is evident, for we have seen in the section on Denis how Rouault distrusted artificial attempts to "record" feelings or ideas. Rouault set out less to record a vision than to capture an emotional reality.

It is interesting that, in spite of his constant emphasis on the human elements of every scene, Rouault painted relatively few portraits and self-portraits. In this he seems to be in harmony with a more general tendency to de-emphasize the individual, evidenced by the fact that the few portraits undertaken by modern artists are highly stylized. Jean-Paul Sartre believes this trend reflects our spiritual maturity in outgrowing the primitive sorcery called transcendence.[5] Waldemar George, in discussing the same phenomenon, suggests that we have ceased to believe in what Sartre calls "sorcery." He comments: "If the portrait be for us a dead letter, it is because the individual himself has ceased to be the active figure in contemporary life." The alternative which modern portraiture suggests is a negative value, the mask.[6]

Is Rouault then succumbing to the modern surrender of man's hard-won individuality to the Greek conception of the mask? Why, especially in the light of his human concern, was he so uninterested in the individual? Bernard Dorival asks these questions in an important article about the painter's portraits and self-portraits. He understands Rouault's interests as two-fold: architectural and symbolic. The first preoccupation forced the painter to search in the human face for what Dorival calls "plastic rhythms." The line of the jaw, for example, is seen not as the key to the soul so much

---

[4] Denis. *Théories*, p. 17. See especially Rookmaaker, *op. cit.*, pp. 79ff., where this distinction is definitively elucidated.

[5] Special issue on heads and portraits. *Verve*, 1939, nos. 5, 6, p. 44.

[6] "Masks or Faces." *Apollo*, 1931, nos. 13-14, p. 280.

Le vétéran (en souvenir d'H. Rupp) — **vers 1946**
The Veteran (in Memory of H. Rupp) — *about 1946*

as a plastic rhythm analogous to that of every human jaw. It is thus a reminder of man's common physical denominator.[7]

But the head is expression as well as form. So Rouault attempted to establish a relationship between the head of his subject and all men. From the individual, Dorival explains, he wants to move at once to the species. The humanity of Christ, the clown or the judge forges a link between his condition and our own. He is more interested in *man* than in *men*.[8]

Withal Rouault succeeds in striking very near to each individual person. For it is the universal arising out of the particular that gives sense to reality and distinguishes great art. This could be illustrated by his portrait entitled "Veteran" cc. 501, painted in 1946. It was done in memory of H. Rupp, Moreau's executor. But its relevance is much larger, extending to all those of age and experience who view life with a knowing eye.

Waldemar George illuminates the matter further by his discussion of the life and vitality of Rouault's faces. The glance, he points out, is what makes vacant eyes come to life in a way which he compares with Aeschylus' birth of tragedy and the "know thyself" of Socrates. Contemporary painters have difficulty making eyes come alive. The reason, suggests George, lies in the divorce between man and the universe, which has reduced art to the dehumanized arena of visual pleasures. Rouault succeeded where others failed because he ended that divorce. His world is alive with real people living in dialogue with other people and with nature.[9]

With Rouault, moreover, the plastic elements themselves take part in the presentation of the human values; that is, they become symbolic. Let us seek to illustrate this symbolism by a study of certain figures he has chosen. As all human figures find plastic and human meaning in the figure of Christ, so one could say all of the studies of women Rouault undertook find their meaning in the figures of Eve and Mary. Beneath the accidents he sought the *woman*. The Biblical characters themselves are seldom objects of study.[10] But in a sense they lie at the heart of all of Rouault's studies of women. The atmosphere, derived from Catholic tradition, is that described by Emile Bertand. From Genesis 3:15-16, he points out, women were subject to special grief in giving birth. Mary is the personification of womanhood. The pains she endures

---

[7] "Autoportraits et portraits." *Op. cit.,* pp. 234-236.
[8] *Ibid.*
[9] "Georges Rouault and the Birth of Tragedy." *Formes,* March, 1931, p. 41.
[10] Eve is treated only once indirectly, "Fallen Eve" cc. 176, 1930, and Mary once in cc. 383, 1937, and elsewhere indirectly in Biblical scenes such as the "Flight into Egypt," in Nazareth and other Biblical landscapes.

in childbirth are those she endures in participating in the sacrifice of her son. She joined Christ in his suffering, though she did not sin. She is a picture of the Church suffering at the foot of the cross, actively accepting and participating in its own redemption.[11]

Like her son, Mary represents hope. Rouault prays in *Soliloques:*

> Kind Mother
> Take me by the hand
> Like an obedient child
> Beside the invisible cliffs
> That run along the path.[12]

She too is the new Eve, recapturing by grace what the first Eve had lost.

> Eve knew not
> What sin was
> Nor sainthood
> She wanted to be pretty
> To conquer man
> And life.
>
> But blackest fate
> One fine day
> The wrinkles came
> The man passed and smirked
> Eve wept and soured
> It is the game of life.[13]

The fall (who can separate the moral defects from the physical?), the deformed prostitute beholding her face in a mirror, and on the other hand those women who are lit by the interior glow of grace, Veronica whose faith resulted in the image restored by Christ—all of this is reflected in the faces of Rouault's figures and in the emotional vigor of his forms. All record the single divine-human drama of sin and grace.

Rouault's religious inspiration finds expression in other ways worthy of note, but each in its own way elaborates the single theme. There is St. Martha, who recalls the woman whom Christ loved (John 11:5) but whom Christ also reproved for being distracted from himself with much serving (Luke 10:40). Joan of Arc appears as a subject twice (1949, p. 202); 1951, C. 345) and exudes a religious fervor as well as intense patriotism. Of this subject Venturi says: "Rouault knew how to make of this motif one of the most intense mystical expressions imaginable, where the colors

---

[11] C. Baumgartner, ed. Le *Dictionnaire de spiritualité: aescétique et mystique* (Paris: 1932 to the present), "Notre Dame des sept douleurs," pp. 168ff.

[12] P. 155.

[13] *Soliloques,* pp. 161, 162.

Notre Jeanne — 1948-49
Joan of Arc — 1948-49

had an astonishing phosphorescence."[14] In the 1951 version, the luminous light of the sun seems to be reflected in the strength and determination of the figures, even in the stepping of the horses.

Rouault's plastic symbolism is especially evident in the pictures last mentioned. The composition, especially in its contours and colors, is not merely the means of suggesting a horse and rider. It is itself a part of the strength and emotion those figures are to represent. This is not only true of the symbolic use of color— Baucher points out the obvious iconology in the cold blues, the oranges offering hope, and the gray misery[15]—but also in the very sensuous nature of the pigment itself. In this instance the painting as an end in itself extends even to the physical elements of the canvas. Rouault's use of paint and color is intended not only to suggest the figures but also to present a universal quality, in this case emotional depth and determination. Rouault's technique diminishes the perceptual *likeness* but reinforces perceptual *reality*. The impact of the picture is therefore larger and more profound than any verbal discussion of faith and patriotism.[16]

Among other religious subjects, we have already discussed Veronica, the image of the believer's restored likeness of the Savior. We have also discussed the Exodus and the flight into Egypt, two differing pictures of the single motif of flight, picturing man as "birds of passage as we are here below."[17] As Christ in his suffering gave meaning to human suffering, so the flight of the Holy Family sheds meaning upon all human flight.

All of these are simply particular instances of the single religious message which informs all of Rouault's work, whatever the subject. For he was as much a religious painter in his prostitutes as in his Christs. It must all be understood together, for each part illumines the rest. Degradation, as modern existentialism has shown, is absurd when seen alone, and grace by itself is unreal. Seeking

[14] Venturi, 1959, p. 96. Rouault's love for his country is well known. He confessed once to Suarès: "This France so often disparaged (sometimes by ourselves) is still, in spite of it all, *like a rare work of art* in this black and barbarous world." *Correspondance,* p. 107. Italics his.

[15] *Op. cit.,* p. 222.

[16] Cf. a classic discussion of such universal qualities in painting: T. M. Greene. *The Arts and the Art of Criticism* (Princeton: Princeton University Press, 1940), pp. 279ff. He calls these adjectival universals which are related to substantive universals "as the perceptual qualities, states, and relations of a perceptual object are related to the object itself..." p. 279. Among those discussing this symbolism in Rouault, see Charensol, 1926, *op. cit.;* Carol Seeley, "Notes on the Use of Symbols in Contemporary Painting," *Art Quarterly,* 1948, vol. II, p. 327; and Donald Goodall, "Rouault's Passion Cycle," *Art in America,* 1962, vol. 1, no. 4, pp. 75-79.

[17] Rouault. *Soliloques,* p. 191.

the universal, Rouault succeeded in being relevant to all men without yielding to the incidental and the banal. He maintained a real sense of the supernaturalness of grace without being fanciful. Dorival comments on Rouault's blending of peace and pain: There is "always a connection between immanence and transcendence, and in this totality he denies nothing to nature or to supernature."[18]

Rouault was a religious painter not because he had faith and chose religious subjects. Rather, he was a religious painter, or rather a Christian painter, because his faith was real and deep and extended to every part of his artistic sensitivity. He was one in whom the image of Christ had been restored, enabling him to add to the intense observation of the artist the insights of faith. And he created in his own image.

---

[18] *La Table Ronde,* 1952, *op. cit.,* p. 179.

18. Conclusion

The religious implications of modern art have been much debated. Some believe modern art celebrates the demise of religion, while others see in its liberty a reflection of the freedom and omnipresence of the divine. Régine Pernoud is one who believes the wonder and marvels of grace are reflected in the contemporary artistic revolution. The talent of classicism had frozen into rules, and revolution was inevitable. Coming like a breath of fresh air, abstraction has opened the way for imagination to regain its rights from the intellect.[1] And Jacques Maritain assures us, "It is only in the light of theology that art today can achieve self-knowledge and cure itself of the false systems of metaphysics which plague it."[2]

Among those who have vociferously debated the relevance of religion to art is the English critic Clive Bell. In 1913 he stated unequivocally:

> The representative element in a work of art may or may not be harmful; always it is irrelevant. For, to appreciate a work of art, we need bring with us nothing from life, no knowledge of its ideas and affairs, no familiarity with its emotions. . . .[3]

All that is relevant is "significant form" realized and enjoyed by the viewer in aesthetic exaltation. Not only is religion unimportant to this experience, but for a moment all human interests are shut off. The purism[4] that Bell and others such as Roger Fry publicized has been implicit in much of recent art; indeed, there is a sense

---

[1] "Devant l'art moderne." *L'Art Sacré*, 1950, nos. 5-6, pp. 11-19.

[2] *Art and Scholasticism and the Frontiers of Poetry*, p. 139.

[3] *Art* (New York: Capricorn Books, 1958. First published in 1913), p. 27.

[4] We wish to use the term "purism" in a broad sense, which should be distinguished from the shortlived movement which followed cubism and was championed by Ozenfant and Edouard Jeanneret (better known as the architect Le Corbusier), beginning in 1918.

in which Bell was simply putting his finger on an element latent in art ever since impressionism. Maritain was certainly guilty of wishful thinking when he claimed in 1927 that purism of this sort was entirely a thing of the past.[5]

In 1935 Bell had occasion to comment on an exhibition of Rouault's work at the Mayor Gallery in London. "Rouault is not an artist easily appreciated," Bell begins, and he appeals to most people as a psychologist. The critic goes on to wonder with Roger Fry whether the same good fate would not befall Rouault that has befallen other dramatists: that the literary interest would evaporate and leave behind a residue of "pure aesthetic significance." Bell admits that he has always been bored and irritated by Rouault's "tragic characters." Still, he sees some beautiful expressive painting, illustrating plastic values which have nothing to do with moral and intellectual issues.[6] But is it possible to separate the "issues" from Rouault's "expression"? Does not his very success lie in his ability to blend these two aspects, so that each reinforces the other without compromising a whit of its forcefulness?

On the other hand, can art ever be an amoral affair, totally divorced from life, as Bell insists? Are the only proper criteria formal ones? Questions like these loom large in any discussion of Christian aesthetics. They extend beyond the scope of our essay, but it may be possible in closing to offer tentative lines of approach which are suggested by the present study of Rouault. The entire life and work of Rouault stands as a monument to the bearing of Christian faith upon Christian artistic expression. In the brief scope of this conclusion we will attempt to suggest this relation of faith to four major aesthetic concerns: (1) The nature of the creative process,

---

[5] Against this statement of Maritain's it is instructive to place one of Susanne K. Langer, who followed in the path Bell blazed. She said in 1942: "There is a strong tendency today to treat art as significant phenomenon rather than as a pleasurable experience, a gratification of the senses." *Op. cit.*, p. 175. It is here, she goes on to say, that a new philosophy of art is to be found, to which all metaphysical questions of first cause and substance are totally irrelevant. Cf. p. 80 of the same work. If truth were decided by election, as some moderns prefer to think, the returns received to date despite the reaction of Pop Art favor Bell and Langer rather than Maritain. That purism remains popular, however, does not deny the fact that art always has a religious choice to make. Cf. Maritain, *op. cit.*, p. 138.

[6] "Two Exhibitions." *The New Statesman and Nation*, October 19, 1935, p. 558. To Bell's testimony of discomfort could be juxtaposed one of Samuel A. Lewisohn who answers Bell in an article on "Drama in Painting." Says he: "In studying a Rouault with friends I have found no discomfort in admiring alternately the drama and the jewel-like qualities." *Creative Art*, September, 1931, pp. 185-198.

(2) Art as expression and as representation, (3) The extent of art as religious expression, and (4) The form-content distinction.

(1) *The nature of the creative process.* Explicitly in Chapter 6 above and implicitly throughout our study, we have observed the determinative nature for graphic art, first, of the human conditions of its creation and, secondly, of the concrete and menial nature of its production. If the artist's vision is intuitive and personal, his work is the patient application of physical processes. If either of these aspects is overstressed, the crucial balance is lost and painting becomes either aesthesia or mere craftsmanship.

In the first place, the work of art derives wholly from the person of the artist in all the material and human relationships that define his personality. This is its human condition, as inescapable as it is vital to creativity. It is here as well that the question of Christian aesthetics centers, not in the discussion of subject or literary purpose.[7] This means that the end the artist serves as a person in creating will be reflected in his work. Part of man's nature as *imago Dei* is that he must create after his own image. One cannot simply claim to reject all ends outside of art itself. For it is the artist and not the art that is the primary cause, not by decision of the artist but by the nature of creation.

On the one hand, since human art reflects human values, the Christian's work will reflect Christian values because of who the artist is. This is true not because he decided it should be so but because of what it means to be a Christian, that is, remade in the image of Christ, and because of what it means to be an artist, one who shapes in his own image. Here the doctrine of the Christian life, carefully and Biblically conceived, can contribute much to the discussion of a Christian aesthetic. It is very likely that artists who set out to be both Christians and artists, as two conscious ends, fail in making Christian art at all and make only an imitation of it. One need not look far for illustrations. At the same time, since man is created in the image of God, all of art—Christian and non-Christian—will speak something of human dignity and beauty. Christian values are merely the realization of what all men strive after.

But on the other hand, since man's nature is marred by moral failure, Christian and non-Christian art must inevitably reflect this

[7] Cf. Maritain: "If you want to make a Christian work, then be Christian, and simply try to make a beautiful work, into which your heart will pass; do not try to 'make Christian.' " *Op. cit.*, p. 66.

[8] *Ibid.*, p. 97. See the useful discussion of the modern artist's commitment in relation to that of the audience. H. R. Rookmaaker. *Art and the Public Today* (Huemoz, Switzerland: L'Abri Fellowship, 1968).

condition as well. Degradation is just as much a part of the human condition as is grace. Thus a Christian aesthetic must come to terms with the reality of sin, which is a universal but imaginary freedom from God. The Bible makes clear that "no one understands, no one seeks for God. All have turned away, together they have gone wrong; no one does good, not even one" (Romans 3:11, 12). This broken primary relationship, as we have seen, results in the misery of hopelessly severed relationships on the human level as well.

A Christian aesthetic must not only recognize brokenness but also indicate that healing is possible only in a genuine conversion. Joy and truth are to be found not merely in choosing God over against sin, but, as Rouault has stressed, in experiencing the presence and power of God. Only God through Jesus Christ can restore the broken fellowship. Only a real conversion, a work of God, can regain for the artist the struggle for righteousness and goodness which, through the fruit of the Holy Spirit, can become creative. Professor Rookmaaker in his excellent discussion of these matters might have been referring to Rouault when he wrote: "Though the Christian has been freed from the bondage of his sin by Christ, yet so long as he is in a sinful world he has to do battle against sin, hungering and thirsting after righteousness, seeking peace, helping the oppressed—and fighting against his own sin, too, in order to have the freedom and openness that belong to the fruit of the Spirit."[9] The struggle is for true freedom, for, as the Apostle Paul testifies, "the law of the Spirit of life in Christ Jesus has set me free from the law of sin and death" (Romans 8:2).

If the artist as person is the primary cause of the work of art, the material means of creating is the secondary cause. As all that appears in the work derives from the artist's personality, so all must be done through the physical process of creation. Above we referred to the Christian life as a relevant theological category; here the doctrine of creation must be considered. Properly speaking, only God creates. He spoke and the world was made immediately without means external to himself. In the same way he spoke and life began. To man, on the other hand, was given the authority to name, care for, and arrange the world of things. It is in this sphere that his creativity must be exercised. He does not create in the sense of the original creation, since he must always begin with the physical world. Between man tilling and tending the earth and man painting and forming there may be a difference in quality

---

[9] H. R. Rookmaaker. *Modern Art and the Death of a Culture* (Chicago/London: Inter-Varsity Press, 1970), p. 226.

but there is none of function. It is all a part of a single office of man: dominion.

This office is not, however, unrelated to the original creation. Though different in kind and starting point, Adam's task of naming the animals continued in an important sense the creation God had begun. He confirmed and determined its order. All of man's creativity is precisely of this sort: arranging, ordering, and naming the original creation. That which is novel is always relative to the material conditions in which art must perforce be located. Absolute novelty belongs to God alone.

Maritain distinguishes similarly between the workman and the instrument, but in his distinction he does not make sufficient allowance for the significance of the material conditions. The instrument he terms a virtue: "Art is a *habitus* of the practical intellect."[10] This "instrument" has no other end than the good of the object.[11] The meaning of the virtue, he allows, is realized only in the activity of creation. Pure act belongs to God alone: *unus est artifex, Deus.* Thus human art must always be subject to its human conditions. So it is true that the virtue of art is immanent within the human creator. But art as a virtue, he admits, is in some way inhuman. Thus at times he speaks of art as having an almost transcendent character. The end rules and values of art, for example, are not those of man but those of the work to be produced. "The work is everything for Art; there is for art but one law: the exigencies and the good of the work."[12]

In the *Frontiers of Poetry* Maritain discusses this distinction between the nature and the condition of art in more detail. Art, he insists, must not reject the servitude of its human condition but must try ceaselessly to overcome it. Only in this way can art achieve its true spirituality. Thus Maritain appears to disparage the humanity of art. He admits there is what he calls an antinomy between the demands of the essence of art "taken in itself transcendentally" and the conditions of existence called for on earth. Once again it is evident that there is something almost essentially incompatible between the nature of art and its human conditions.

Nevertheless, after having struck the transcendent note, Maritain returns to acknowledge the immanence of art within man. Art's existence always depends on man and always ends by displaying the weakness of man. He concedes, however, that a frank acceptance of its conditions may bring about a renewal in art's life, im-

---

[10] *Op. cit.,* p. 12.
[11] *Ibid.,* p. 94.
[12] *Ibid.,* p. 9.

plying that something in the essence of art may respond to its human condition.[13]

It would seem that art as an intellectual virtue, outside its scholastic framework, is as elusive as the spirituality of the purist. For the humanity of art, rather than being a part of its glory, is its shame, a kind of prison-house of the soul. Professor Maritain's scholastic categories, it would seem, have led him to attribute to art the kind of *aseitas* that belongs to God.

We have seen that Rouault's means were intrinsic to his artistic vision. The process of bringing the work of art into existence is not a necessary evil but a part of the work itself. As an artist thinks with his hands and in the material, so the artifact is itself the material existence of the artistic vision. Art is no more "essentially" spiritual than man is essentially spirit.

The theological category, we repeat, that can be helpfully elaborated in this connection is that of creation and the mandate given to the first man to cultivate the earth (Genesis 1:28; 2:15). All of man's activities must be in an immediate relation with the created world which was part of the human condition in which man was to live. To attempt to create apart from these conditions is to covet that absolute creativity that belongs only to God. Only God creates *ex nihilo;* for man *ex nihilo nihil fit.*

(2) *Art as expression and as representation.* If art must always count the physical world as the environment of its existence, what has this to do with the subject art chooses? Must art always follow nature?[14] Maritain insists that expression in art proceeds from the work itself and the means employed rather than from the subject represented. Since the Renaissance the subject has achieved undue importance, and Maritain believes this accounts in large measure for the failure of modern religious art. Maritain notes that Maurice Denis—among others—has made this imbalance one of his major concerns and has restored the spiritual superiority of the artist over nature.[15]

Subject to the very human foible of excess, modern art was quick to take this superiority to extremes and banish from art any material or human reference at all. Indeed though he did not foresee or intend it, the whole development of Abstract Expressionism is but a logical extension of Denis' position. This has resulted on the one hand in what could be called an idealist vertigo which ignores the material and subjective conditions art is obliged to satisfy. The end of this quest is an aesthetic exaltation, as difficult to pre-

---

[13] *Op. cit.,* pp. 122-124.
[14] We use nature in the sense of created reality.
[15] *Op. cit.,* p. 198, n. 131.

pare for as it is to define. It calls on the viewer to exult, not because he sees something on the canvas he recognizes and can identify with, but because the significant form displayed there must somehow communicate with his spirit, lifted above the stream of life. Bell says of this experience: "(The viewer) feels an emotion for his speculations which arises from no perceived relation between them and the lives of men, but springs, inhuman or superhuman, from the heart of an abstract science."[16]

On the other hand art has elevated to the status of works of art, at the whim of the "creator," the most mundane objects of everyday life. This has brought about the kind of pop art that characterized the 1960's. Such an ignoring of the spiritual aspects of art recalls H. Wheeler Robinson's characterization of "modern" life some fifty years ago: "For all of us, and inevitably, the handicap of the imagination is with the body and against the spirit, and the material seems more real than the spiritual."[17]

The unique problem facing art then is to break up this formidable alliance between the senses and the imagination without ignoring altogether the subjective context of art. For the Christian this involves exercising proper humility before creation without lapsing into imitation, which is documentation and not art.

Rouault sensed this problem throughout his life. He perceived in nature something that most men do not see. He saw intently, patiently, all that nature contained. Because he saw with the eyes of faith he was able to see a depth of radiance to which others are blind. He said: "The one who makes a melodious beauty is the one who delivers himself of the object that inspires him, while transforming and transfiguring it."[18] But in transforming the object, we have emphasized, the artist does not make it into something other than itself. He does not import the meaning into the subject. Rather he finds in the object the sense that is in harmony with the material and human conditions of the artist and with those of the production of the work.

Put simply, this means that Rouault transformed nature because it is transformable. It pointed beyond itself, for the universe as created bears the image of its divine creator. Moreover, the immanence of God assures a continuing relationship. He is everywhere active in the created world through the sustaining presence of God the Son (Colossians 1:17). As Clyde S. Kilby has put it, the morality,

---

[16] Loc. cit., p. 27. Bell is in fact describing a mathematician engrossed in his speculations, an experience, Bell believes, similar if not identical to aesthetic experience.

[17] Christian Experience of the Holy Spirit (London: Collins, 1962), p. 45.

[18] Stella Vespertina, no pagination.

and we might add the meaning, of the universe is built-in; art can therefore be moral without stating morals.[19] Thus there is a sense of genuineness to all that Rouault portrayed. Cogniat has well observed that the monsters Rouault has created are not pure invention, but if man were perceptive he would recognize himself in them.[20]

It is true that religious art must concern itself with a reality that transcends nature, namely the supernatural. But the empirical nature of art compels it to record the supernatural only in its relation with creation, as it makes itself manifest in and through history. It must abandon any search for primordial or extra-sensory reality; it is no more equipped than any other human function to probe the mysteries of infinity. As Gerardus van der Leeuw expresses it in his book, *The Holy in Art,* though religion seeks an "other" reality, as long as it does not surrender to asceticism it does not seek the supersensual. What is wrong with the world is not its materiality but its sinfulness.[21] And just as degradation can be concretely presented, so grace is not a vague mystical presence but has been made perfectly clear in the visible, material, historical life and work of Jesus Christ.[22]

But Rouault as an expressionist was not only probing nature's secrets in his work, he was also telling his own. Leon-Martin goes so far as to claim the merit of Rouault is that he painted because

---

[19] *Christianity and Aesthetics* (Chicago: Inter-Varsity Press, 1961), pp. 30, 31.

[20] *Georges Rouault,* p. 10. He gives to art a function it does not possess, however, in claiming that man's faults therefore find an expiation in the monsters Rouault has painted.

[21] *Sacred and Profane Beauty: The Holy in Art* (New York: Holt, Rinehart, and Winston, 1963), p. 179.

[22] With painterly insight Albert Gleizes discussed how the work of Christ accomplished in his father's carpenter shop was part of the same road that led to Calvary. *Op. cit.,* p. 126. The wood of both was equally physical. This is the answer to the contempt with which aestheticians are apt to consider the relevance of a supernatural reality to painting. John Hospers, a leading American aesthetician, notes: "Even if the notion of a 'transcendent reality' 'beyond' the pale of experience made sense, how could it ever be experienced through art or anything else? And if on the other hand we could experience it, then how could it be transcendent?" At all events, he concludes, even if it did exist it would be of no help in art. "What art reveals is certainly something *within* the realm of (actual or possible) human experience ... within our spatio-temporal universe—something relevant to the rest of our experience and illuminating that experience. But how a 'transcendent reality' could do this is difficult to see." *Meaning and Truth in the Arts* (North Carolina: Univ. of North Carolina Press, 1946), p. 221, italics his. Difficult it is, unless that "transcendent reality" made itself known in physical and historical terms. This, of course, is exactly what happened, according to the Christian doctrine of Incarnation and Revelation.

he had something to say. Quoting Rouault, he reminds us that the human factor evident in the creative process is likewise determinative of the subject painted: "The most noble subjects are debased by a base spirit, but modest and simple realities can be raised and magnified."[23] Rouault paints, Leon-Martin adds, not only because his eye is moved but also because his intelligence is touched. What his brush produced was therefore not only a motif emotionally moving—though it was that—but also a part of a cognitive message that Rouault believed with his mind as well as his heart.

Thus nature displays a sense that answers to the human condition of art, and the artist has a vision that matches those same conditions. But most importantly, the sense and the vision match. There is a harmony between the artist's message and the world. For the human creator, remade in Christ's image, shares in a deepened way the image of the handiwork of God in the world. The harmony is not always perfect, for the creature, like the Christian, waits to be freed from his bondage to decay.[24] But this correspondence allows art to fulfill its true nature. For good or ill, art is always true to humanity. Though its splendor points beyond the human world it never leaves that world behind, just as the supernatural transcends the natural without being anti-natural. Sensitive individuals always feel at home in the world of great art, just as Christians feel at home in the world of the supernatural, for just as the great artist makes hidden harmonies manifest so Christ has brought the mysteries of God to light through the Gospel.[25]

Rouault sensed this harmony. "Our art finds its equilibrium between two realms, the contemplative (a rather outmoded word) and the objective."[26] For the believer there is no conflict in being true to both. Expressionism in the sense that Rouault was an expressionist lies neither in the spirit of the artist nor in the subject alone but in both together. Charles Morgan, discussing the part the artist can play in the community, stated that the artist's impact lies in the force he imparts to his work. "The fertilizing power is not the subject, but the aesthetic passion which the author pours

---

[23] "Georges Rouault," p. 113.

[24] Romans 8:19-21.

[25] II Timothy 1:10. Hospers has even admitted the existence of this nature within nature, noting that essence is revealed by art which a mere surface realism does not touch, though he refuses to see in it a metaphysical entity. *Op. cit.*, p. 169. Art is true to the real human nature. The "essence" Christian art reveals is not the divine realm, but the human as it is invaded and pervaded by the divine activity. Christian art is concerned with the immanence, not the transcendence, of God.

[26] *Stella Vespertina*, no pagination.

into it; and this aesthetic passion is expressed not in subject alone or in treatment alone, but in a harmony between them."[27] As that author succeeds in showing in his useful essay, and as we have intimated in this section, art viewed in this way is rich with implications not only for theology but for society and its tiresome quest for the "good life." Man and nature, for those who observe closely, can be seen to bear the same image. And that image is divine.

(3) *The extent of art as religious expression.* Rouault often called attention to the uniqueness of art as a means of human expression. He detested all attempts to explain verbally what he was seeking to say. He believed, "Art is not subject to explanation, for it is a marvellous language."[28] Yet he also knew that art expressed the inmost being of the artist better than words. "We express very clearly what we are: art is an ardent confession."[29] These insights, to which we have often returned in our study, sketch the limits of religious expression that art can achieve.

We have noted that art proceeds wholly and entirely from the person of the artist. Picasso is speaking for many modern artists when he admits: "It is not what the artist does that counts but what he is."[30] The identity of the artist furnishes the context of expression as well as the conditions of the life of the artifact. It follows then, as we have seen, that the artist can succeed in transmitting to his creation no more than who he is. This is the first limit of artistic expression: the commitments and values of the artist. Art shares the artist's bias and faith as surely as a child resembles his parents. Moreover, the artist need not set out to make it so, but this limitation results from the intimate and personal nature of creativity. Thus Rouault's faith determined the nature of his religious expression. His was a faith as deep-seated and all-pervading as it was verbally unexpressed. It was as simple as the belief of a child, yet as deeply rooted as the faith of an aged warrior for God. Abbé Morel testified aptly at the funeral of the artist: "Rouault was truly a Christian even in his reflexes."[31] His art was an utterance of his whole person and of all his faith; it bore the strengths and weaknesses of both. As Marcel Arland affirms: "His religious

---

[27] Charles Morgan. *The Artist in the Community* (Glasgow: Jackson, 1945), p. 26.

[28] "Enquête," *op. cit.,* 1936, p. 5.

[29] *SI*, p. 14.

[30] Quoted in John Berger. *The Success and Failure of Picasso* (Middlesex: Penguin, 1965), p. 9.

[31] "En Souvenir de Georges Rouault," *op. cit.,* p. 65. Cf. Leon-Martin's characterization of the artist: "He reacts spontaneously yet thoughtfully by reflex." *Op. cit.,* 1930, p. 113.

works are only the natural culmination of his spirit and of his art."[32]

This is the essence of expression in Christian art as well as the deathblow to artificially conceived Church art. A Christian artist produces Christian art, naturally, from a plenitude of faith that overflows into his work. The art betrays the man.

But there is a second limit that follows from the nature of art. Art is first and foremost a visible and empirical statement. Rouault emphasized: "The greatness is not in the compass of the designer but in the eye of the artist."[33] However interior and spiritual the vision, art is finally a visible combination of material elements. It can be a physical extension of the artist's interior life, as we have demonstrated. Yet the domain of the artifact is inescapably visual.

Yet art is also non-discursive and intuitive, not to say irrational. Rouault stressed that he intended to make beautiful form expressive, but far from the discussions of the critics.[34] Though, as we mentioned, art can be a part of a rational whole, its communication is as immediate and pre-cognitive as it is concrete.

This being the case, we cannot expect logical or articulated completeness in its religious expression. The language of art is presentational rather than suasive. Its "truth" is more a personal hymn of faith than the recitation of a creed. It is true that the Word has a place of priority in Biblical theology. It was the Word that was given to Moses on Mt. Sinai and spoken through the prophets, and the Word was made flesh in Christ. Yet throughout Christian history this importance has been quite consistent with the personal realization and expression of the spiritual values embodied in the Word. There is room for both theoretical discussion and passionate artistic expression of one and the same reality. Despite the pronouncements of modern theology, there is no contradiction between the objectivity of the Word and the subjectivity of the Christian experience of that same Word.

This ought to put religious art in its proper place of value as Christian testimony. Faith alone is not enough, but when the gifts are added to it, Arland claims: "The work takes on a resonance that no other inspiration is likely to give."[35] And since, as Professor Rookmaaker reminds us, God is the source of the gifts as well as of the faith, we can praise him for the beauty of each artistic testimony.[36]

The testimony of all art is, of course, an end in itself. But Chris-

---

[32] "L'Art sacré." *Hommes et Mondes*, February, 1951, no. 55, p. 297.
[33] "Enquête," *op. cit.*, p. 5.
[34] *Ibid.*
[35] "L'Art sacré," *op. cit.*, p. 296.
[36] Rookmaaker, *op. cit.*, p. 248.

tian art may succeed in bearing the same fruit that comes from the presentation of the Word. One critic, Jacques de Laprade, admitted in 1936 that it was time to make a frank evaluation of Rouault and his method. "The careful, detailed critic falls flat before his subject." We are forced rather, says Laprade, to ask of his entire work: is he right or wrong? As we stand before his canvases, we are brought to the most intimate part of ourselves and forced to revise everything.[37]

(4) *Form and content*. This distinction dear to classical aesthetics may serve as a focal point to help us bring these ideas together. We have seen that some have used the non-discursive nature of art as an excuse to banish any extra-pictorial considerations from the idea of "content." Rouault's rejection of such purism has prompted at least one critic to call him frankly a terrible pamphleteer.[38]

Hidden behind such purism is often, though not always, an assumption it would be well to recognize. The fact that, for these artists, there is no continuity between life and work is a result of the fact that there is no overriding continuity to life itself. If the heavens are deaf it follows that the earth is dumb. Though some purist aestheticians have no intention of furthering this hypothesis (Bell is one of them), their theories tend to support it. Meanwhile practicing artists such as Sartre, Camus, Ionesco and Beckett are only too happy to have their creations understood in this way.

Rouault was a man, to borrow the phrase of Cogniat, who could not abide the divorce between the heavens and the earth. The synthesis he achieved between form and content was a result of the communion he felt between these two realms. The explication of this harmony we believe to be of great theological significance as the very basis of all Christian aesthetics. Let us look once more at the work of the artist for an illumination of this thesis.

The first point to be underscored is that there is no inherent conflict between the sensory and the intellectual components of the artist's vision. We have led up to this point in our discussion of the Word above. To say that creative or aesthetic experiences are primarily sensory is not to say they are non-intellectual. Maritain discusses this in a footnote in *Art and Scholasticism* and suggests that every perception of beauty is accomplished by the presence of a concept, even if it be unclear and confused. This follows from the very nature of the intellect. In fact, he claims,

---

[37] 1936, *op. cit.*, p. 8.
[38] Robert Heitz. "Les Tendances de la peinture moderne." *La Vie en Alsace*, January, 1936, p. 178.

it is intelligentiated sense that gives rise to aesthetic joy.[39] It is
this, we would add, that sets aesthetic joys apart from merely sensual delights such as a pretty piece of colored cloth or a warm
evening breeze.

A second point is that every great work of art displays the
double art of poetry: the movement of both form and idea. René
Baucher has described Rouault as a poet in this sense, for he
juxtaposes two different and apparently heterogeneous orders of
reality: the plastic or sensory and the intellectual. The movement
of idea and of meaning in the work of Rouault harmonizes with
the plastic, material conditions of its artistic presentation. Baucher
illustrates this in Rouault's presentation of the sufferings of Christ:
"At the same moment that we imagine ourselves being moved by
the sufferings of his martyrdom, we exult in the representation of
the martyr."[40] As the material environment of creativity is not
incidental but a vital part of the art itself, so the material conditions of the painting are not to be seen through but form a part
of the meaning of the artifact. Only God, we have said, brings
meaning into being from nothing; man must work with creation
and bring out of it its greatest glory.[41]

At the base of it, Albert Gleizes has recognized, the problem of
art is that of reality. The split between the kingdom of God and
the kingdom of men is painfully apparent in art as in life. This
accounts for both the uniqueness and the loneliness of a figure
like Rouault. For he had sought and found an answer for the
problems of art and life in the Incarnation. We agree with Gleizes
that only in taking the Incarnation seriously will men understand
the sacred. For this, once and for all, has healed the split between
the earth and the heavens, between the material and the spiritual.
False gulfs these were from the beginning, for God had sealed
the world from the start with his stamp of value, both spiritual
and material: It was good. Then God chose the stage of the world
on which to perform his drama of sacred history,[42] climaxing in

---

[39] *Op. cit.,* pp. 163-165.

[40] *Op. cit.,* p. 220. But Baucher goes on to say that the purity of form
leaves us free to go beyond the form itself to pure emotions, p. 221. This
is to re-introduce a division between the intellect and the emotions that
we wish to deny.

[41] It may be argued that an artist in the end has created a different being
in making his artifact. Still there is a spiritual-physical continuity that we
wish to stress.

[42] From this Claudel understands that only the Christian can portray real
drama. For if there is no joy or sense (the emotional and intellectual) there
can be no drama "because there is no struggle." But for the Christian the
actions of men are set on a large stage. *Pages de prose,* p. 122.

the physical appearing of Jesus Christ. The Christian looks for
meaning not to the sky but to creation and history, explained
and restored by Christ. In this perspective even the most simple
reality takes on a religious dimension. Says Gleizes: "Thus from
the profane he moves, of necessity, into the area where the purity
of the spiritual will appear as the perfectly normal conclusion."[43]
This is a normal process because the harmony of the world is no
longer mysterious but has been made plain. It is moreover a harmony which takes seriously our creation in God's image and our
need for rebirth in Christ's.

In closing it is worth noting one aesthetician who has pointed
out the fallacy in distinguishing radically between form and content: Morris Weitz. The artist starts with his experience, says Weitz,
as it converges upon a theme or idea. This he unifies in an imaginative way while embodying it in a sensuous medium. All of this
together makes the artistic content. To this he puts a name or
title, which is not a part of the content but is intended to direct
attention to that content. It is not illegitimate that there be an
extra-pictorial association in this way, i.e. that the content should
refer beyond the canvas while remaining true to itself (though
most people unfortunately regard the content of the work as a
springboard to *their* associations). For, concludes Weitz, "just as
there is no artistic distinction between form and content, so there
is no antithesis between form and ideas, representations and emotions."[44] In principle the harmony can be achieved, but Weitz says
that the problem which Bell raised remains: can these elements
integrate *successfully* with each other? We submit the entire work
of Georges Rouault to testify that they can.

---

[43] "Recherche du sacré." *Op. cit.,* p. 126. Cf. Gilson's statement: "Ever
since the birth of Our Lord, the birth of every child is a nativity." *Op. cit.,*
p. 272.

[44] "The Form-Content Distinction." *Art and Philosophy, op. cit.,* pp. 348,
349.

Biographical Notes

A Chronology of the Life of Georges Rouault

1871	May 27: Born during the Commune in a cellar of Paris during bombardment of Paris by Versailles Government. Father: Alexandre Rouault from Montfort in Brittany, 31. Mother: Marie-Louise Alexandrine Champdavoine, Paris, 27.
1881	Rouault is under the influence of Grandfather Champdavoine and aunts. The former a great admirer of Daumier, Courbet, and Monet.
1885/90	Apprentice in stained glass: first Tamoni, then Hirsch. Evenings at the *Ecole des Arts Décoratifs.*
1890	December 5: Enters the *Ecole des Beaux-Arts* under Elie Delaunay.
1891/2	September 5, 1891: Delaunay dies and is succeeded by Gustave Moreau. Rouault begins a series of religious subjects in a Rembrandtesque style.
1893	Competes for Prix de Rome and fails with "Ordeal of Samson."
1894	"Child Jesus Among the Doctors" receives Chenavard Prize.
1895	Fails again for Prix de Rome with "Dead Christ Mourned by the Holy Women."
1896	Exhibited at Salon des Artistes Français.
1898	April 18: Gustave Moreau dies at 72 years.
1901	Retires to Benedictine Abbey at Ligugé where J.-K. Huysmans wanted to found brotherhood of artists. — Paints romantic landscapes, religious compositions, and Paris scenes.
1903	January 14: Inauguration of Musée Gustave Moreau. — Salon d'Automne is founded; Rouault sends 2 paintings.
1904	Meets Léon Bloy in March. — Public sneers at "gloomy" paintings shown at Salon d'Automne. — Does watercolors of prostitutes and clowns.
1905	Displays "M. et Mme Poulot" at Salon d'Automne.
1906	Displays at Salon d'Automne and the Berthe Weil gallery.
1907	Meets Ambroise Vollard.
1908	January 27: Marries Marthe Le Sidaner, by whom he was to have 4 children: Geneviève, Isabelle, Michel, and Agnès. — Paints a series of Judges and Tribunals. Granier takes him to Tribunal de la Seine.
1910	February 24-March 5. First one-man show at Galerie Druet. — Paints poor people and peasants.

1911 Moves to Versailles, rue de l'Orangerie, where Maritains are neighbors. — Second show at Galerie Druet, December 11. — Meets André Suarès.

1913 Vollard buys all Rouault's works to date.

1917 Vollard becomes Rouault's dealer.

1917-1927 Works on books for Vollard. Rarely exhibits.

1918 Abandons watercolor and gouache. Paints in oil: religious subjects, the Passion. Palette becomes more colorful.

1919 First Museum representation bought by the government: "Child Jesus Among the Doctors," displayed in Colmar.

1920 Exhibition by collector D. Girardin at Galerie La Licorne.

1921 First monograph on Rouault by Michel Puy.

1922 Exhibition at Galerie Barbazanges.

1924 April 22-May 2: Retrospective at Galerie Druet. — First appearance of J. Maritain's article on Rouault, "Frontières de la Poésie," in *La Revue Universelle*.

1926 Published *Souvenirs Intimes*. — Publication of book on Rouault by Georges Charensol.

1929 Does settings and costumes for Diaghilev's ballet "The Prodigal Son," score by Prokofiev. — Badly burns hands while playing Santa Claus.

1930 Begins series of etchings for *Cirque de l'étoile filante* and for Suarès' *Passion*. — First exhibitions outside France: London (St. George Gallery); New York (Brummer Gallery); Munich (Neumann Gallery); Chicago (Art Club).

1932 Mrs. Chester Dale gives to Musée de Luxembourg its first Rouault.

1937 June-October: Retrospective at Petit Palace. Venturi, upon seeing this, decides to do his study on Rouault.

1938 Rouault's graphics on display at Museum of Modern Art in New York. — *Le Cirque de l'étoile filante* is first published.

1939 Ambroise Vollard dies in an auto accident, July 22.

1940 Venturi's first study on Rouault is published.

1940/41 Exhibitions in Boston, Washington and San Francisco.

1943 *Divertissement* published.

1945 Retrospective in Museum of Modern Art in New York. 161 items. Catalogue by James Soby.

1946 April: Braque-Rouault exhibition at the Tate Gallery, London.

1947 March 19: Rouault wins case against Vollard's heirs. Meanwhile 119 canvases had not been returned. — June: *Stella Vespertina* published.

1948 April-June: Retrospective in Kunsthaus, Zurich, 166 items. — First presentation of *Miserere* at gallery Odette des Garets (Nov.-Dec.).

1949 First maquettes for enamels executed at Ligugé.

1951 June: "Tribute to Rouault" at Palais Chaillot. Film on *Miserere* released.

1952-6 Retrospectives in Brussels, Amsterdam, and Paris. Other shows at Cleveland, New York, Los Angeles, Osaka, Tokyo ('53), Milan ('54), Albi ('56).

1958 February 13: Rouault dies at 87 years. State Funeral.

Bibliographical Notes

1. *Primary Sources: Writings by Rouault.*
   "Anciens et modernes." *Verve.* 1938, vol. 1, no. 4. Pp. 104-106.
   "Art et beauté." *L'Intransigeant.* February 8, 1932. P. 5.
   "Ce qu'ils pensent de l'art sacré: Georges Rouault." *La Croix.* May 11, 1952. P. 5.
   Le Cirque de l'étoile filante. Paris: Ambroise Vollard. 1938.
   "Claude Monet." *L'Amour de l'Art.* 1927. No. 8. Pp. 200, 201.
   and André Suarès. *Correspondance.* Paris: Gallimard. 1960.
   Divertissement. Paris: Tériade. 1943.
   "En Marge des doctrines." *L'Intransigeant.* November 15, 1932. P. 6.
   "Enquête." *Cahiers d'Art.* 1935. No. 10. Pp. 5-14.
   "Enquête: l'art peut-il utiliser la photographie?" *La Revue de l'Art Ancien et Moderne.* 1936. Vol. 69. P. 88.
   "Evocations sur Matisse." *Les Chroniques du Jour.* April, 1931. No. 9. P. 8.
   "A Feu Debureau." *Les Funambles.* December 1, 1926.
   and André Suarès. "Gustave Moreau." *L'Art et les Artistes.* April, 1926. Pp. 217-248.
   "Une Lettre de Georges Rouault." *Cahiers d'Art.* 1928. No. 3. P. 102.
   Miserere (Preface). New York: Museum of Modern Art. 1952.
   Miserere (Preface). Paris: L'Etoile Filante aux Editions du Seuil. 1963.
   Paysages légendaires. Paris: Editions Porteret. 1929.
   "Le Pêcheur de perles suivi de bâtons rompus." *Les Saisons.* Summer, 1945. Pp. 29-36.
   "Pour ou contre." *Les Chroniques du Jour.* January, 1931. No. 8. P. 3.
   "A Propos de Forain." *La Vie.* January 25, 1913. No. 3. Pp. 410, 411.
   "Réponse à notre enquête sur le métier." *Beaux-Arts.* 1936. No. 198. P. 5.
   Soliloques. Neuchâtel: Ides et Calendes. 1944.
   Souvenirs Intimes. Paris: Frapier. 1926.
   "Souvenirs du jeune âge sont gravés dans mon coeur." *Le Point.* August-September-October, 1943. Nos. 26, 27.
   Sur l'art et sur la vie. Paris: Denoël/Gouthier. 1971.
   Stella Vespertina (Preface). Paris: Drouin. 1947.
   "Trois artistes." *Mercure de France.* February 16, 1910. Vol. 83. Pp. 654-659.
   "Le Visage de la France." *Verve.* 1940. Vol. 2. No. 8. Pp. 12-21.
   "Visages réels ou imaginaires." *Verve.* 1939. Vol. II. Nos. 5, 6. P. 120.
2. *Secondary Sources.*
   Marcel Arland. "L'Art sacré." *Hommes et Mondes.* February, 1951. Vol. 6. No. 55. Pp. 294-298.

"Premier regard sur l'exposition des maîtres de l'art indépendant."
   La Nouvelle Revue Française. 1937. 25th year. Pp. 350-352.
"Rouault et Kandinsky." *Hommes et Mondes*. March, 1947. No. 8.
   Pp. 582-586.
"Rouault." *La Nouvelle Revue Française*. July 1, 1931.
"Sur Georges Rouault." *Formes*. 1931. No. 16. Pp. 96-97.
Adolphe Basler. "Le Problème de la forme depuis Cézanne." *L'Amour de
   l'Art*. 1930. No. 11. Pp. 361-366; 431-433.
René Baucher. "Rouault et la peinture religieuse." *Synthèses*. January,
   1951. No. 56. Pp. 218-225.
Germain Bazin. "Existe-il un art expressioniste en France?" *Art Présent*.
   1945. No. 1. Pp. 40-47.
Clive Bell. "Two Exhibitions." *The New Statesman and Nation*. October
   19, 1935. Vol. 10. P. 558.
Luc Benoist. "Georges Rouault." *Tendances*. 1965. No. 37. Pp. 441-464.
Pierre Berthelot. "Rouault." *Beaux-Arts*. 1931. No. 8. P. 24.
Anne Bettems. "Rouault." *Pour l'Art*. 1950. No. 14. Pp. 23-24.
Léon Bloy. "Notes sur Georges Rouault." *Cahiers d'Art*. 1928. No. 3.
   Pp. 102-104.
Albert Boime. "Georges Rouault and the Academic Curriculum." *Art
   Journal*. Fall, 1969. Vol. 29. No. 1. Pp. 36-39.
Georges Borgeaud. "Un évènement capital." *La Vie Intellectuelle*. March,
   1949. Pp. 303-304.
Robert Boulet. "L'Art modern et l'art religieux." *L'Art Sacré*. October,
   1937. No. 3. Pp. 94-96.
Marquette Bouvier. "Georges Rouault: expresionista y místico." *Goya*.
   1958-60. Nos. 25-30. Pp. 18-24.
M. Brillant. "Ce qu'ils pensent de l'art sacré: Georges Rouault." *La Croix*.
   May 11, 1952. P. 5.
Marcel Brion. *Georges Rouault*. Paris: Braun. 1950.
J. A. Cartier. "Rouault artisan." *Le Jardin des Arts*. 1955-56. No. 2. Pp.
   479-484.
Georges Charensol. "Georges Rouault." *L'Art Vivant*. 1926. No. 28. Pp.
   128-130. Included in book published in 1926.
   "Georges Rouault." *La Revue des Deux Mondes*. 1958. No. 2. Pp.
   148-153.
   Georges Rouault: L'homme et l'oeuvre. Paris: Editions des Quatre
   Chemins. 1926.
   "Rouault: peintures inconnus ou célèbres." *La Revue des Deux
   Mondes*. 1965. No. 2. Pp. 451-455.
A.-M. Cocagnac. "Rouault." *L'Art Sacré*. January-February, 1964. Pp. 3-31.
Raymond Cogniat. *Georges Rouault*. Paris: Editions G. Crès. 1930. Col-
   lection: Les Artistes Nouveaux.
   "Georges Rouault." *Le Point*. 1937. No. III. Pp. 115-116.
Gustave Coquiot. "Georges Rouault." *Cubistes, futuristes, passéistes*. Paris:
   Librairie Ollendorff. 1914. Pp. 156-160.
Les Indépendants. Paris: Librairie Ollendorff. 1920. Pp. 72-3.
"Georges Rouault." *Les Peintres maudits*. Paris: André Delpeuch. 1924. Pp.
   115-123.
Pierre Courthion. *Georges Rouault*. Including a Catalogue of works pre-
   pared with the collaboration of Isabelle Rouault. Paris: Flammarion.
   1962. English Edition: London: Thames and Hudson; and New York:
   Harry N. Abrams. 1962.

M. A. Couturier. "Rouault et le public ecclésiastique." *L'Art Sacré*. September, 1938. Pp. 244-247.

Enrico Crispolti. *Georges Rouault: I maestro del colore*. Milan. 1965. No. 112.

Pierre Descargues. "Les Chefs de file de l'expressionisme français." *La Connaissance des Arts*. July, 1961. No. 113. Pp. 68-75.

Bernard Dorival. "Autoportraits et portraits de Georges Rouault." *La Revue des Arts*. December, 1953. No. 4. Pp. 229-238.

Cinq études sur Georges Rouault. Paris: Témoins du XXe siècle, Editions Universitaires. 1956.

"Georges Rouault." *Le Bulletin des Musées de France*. 1947. Vol. XII. No. 5. Pp. 19-22.

"Georges Rouault." *La Table Ronde*. October, 1952. No. 58. Pp. 175-180.

Georges Rouault. Notes on Paintings in the National Museum of Modern Art. Paris: 1956.

"Présence de Rouault." *Art de France*. 1961. No. 1. P. 390.

Rouault. Paris. 1942.

Rouault. Geneva: Editions René Kister. 1956.

"Rouault, peintre tragique de la condition humaine." *L'Education Nationale*. May 22, 1958. No. 19. Pp. 16-18.

Marie Dormoy. "Georges Rouault." *Arts et Métiers Graphiques*. August 15, 1935. No. 48. Pp. 23-30.

"*Le Cirque de l'étoile filante* de Georges Rouault." *Arts et Métiers Graphiques*. May 15, 1939. No. 68. Pp. 35-40.

Raymond Escholier. *La Peinture française: XXe siècle*. Paris: Floury. 1937. Pp. 31-35.

Anon. "L'Exposition du Pavillon de Marsan." *L'Art Sacré*. January, 1939. No. 4. Pp. 21-26.

Anon. "Exhibitions: London. Rouault and the Middle Age Spirit." *The Studio*. 1938. No. 116. Pp. 167-168.

Paul Fierens. "Georges Rouault." *L'Amour de l'Art*. 1933. No. 14. Pp. 136-139.

"Georges Rouault au Musée d'Art Moderne." *Le Bulletin des Musées Royaux des Beaux-Arts*. December, 1953. No. 4. Pp. 163-168.

Henry S. Francis. "A Head of Christ by Georges Rouault." *The Bulletin of the Cleveland Museum of Art*. 1951. Vol. 38. Pp. 71-72.

Roger Fry. "La Peinture moderne en France." *L'Amour de l'Art*. 1924. No. 5. Pp. 141-160.

Gilbert Ganne. "Georges Rouault: peintre mystique et réaliste." *Le Jardin des Arts*. 1958. No. 41. Pp. 392-396.

Maximilien Gauthier. "Notice bio-bibliographique: Georges Rouault." *L'Art Vivant*. May, 1930. No. 130. Pp. 410-417.

Waldemar George. "Georges Rouault." *Le Bulletin de la Vie Artistique*. May 15, 1924. Pp. 229-230.

"Georges Rouault and the Birth of Tragedy." *Formes*. March, 1931. P. 41.

"Georges Rouault: oeuvres inédites." *La Renaissance*. October-December, 1937. No. 5. Special issue on Rouault.

L'Univers de Georges Rouault. With Geneviève Nouaille-Rouault. Paris: Scrépel Cabinet de Dessin. 1971.

"Masks or Faces." *Apollo*. 1931. No. 13-14. Pp. 271-278.

Anon. "Georges Rouault et Ambroise Vollard." *Beaux-Arts*. 1933. No. 24. P. 6.

Louis Gillet. "Trente ans de peinture au Petit Palais." *La Revue des Deux Mondes*. 1937. No. 4. Pp. 319-339.

Donald B. Goodall. "Rouault's Passion Cycle." *Art in America*. 1962. Vol. I. No. 4. Pp. 75-79.

Jean Grenier. "Les Idées de Georges Rouault." *L'Oeil: Revue d'Art*. April, 1957. No. 28. Pp. 31-40.

"Georges Rouault et La Bible." *Les Preuves*. April, 1958. No. 86. Pp. 64-65.

Jacques Guenne. "Georges Rouault." *Les Nouvelles Littéraires*. November 15, 1924. Vol. 3. No. 109. P. 5.

Robert Heitz. "Le Rouault du Musée de Colmar." *La Vie en Alsace*. November, 1935. No. 11. Pp. 250-251.

"Tendances de la peinture moderne." *La Vie en Alsace*. January, 1936. Pp. 174-178.

Anon. "Hommage à Georges Rouault." *Mizue*. Special issue in Japanese. 1958. Tokyo.

Michel Hoog. "La Donation Rouault au Louvre." *Etudes*. September, 1964. Pp. 215-219.

Russell Warren Howe. "An Impasto Dream: Georges Rouault." *Apollo*. 1950. Vol. 52. Pp. 36-37.

Agnès Humbert. "Georges Rouault." *The Scottish Art Review*. 1958. Vol. VI. No. 4. Pp. 2-6.

René Huyghe. "Histoire de l'art contemporain: le Fauvism, les Coloristes." *L'Amour de l'Art*. 1933. No. 14. Pp. 97-102; 129-132.

Pierre Imbourg. "Les Grandes peintres chez eux: Georges Rouault." *Le Journal Amateur de l'Art*. 1954. No. 123. Pp. 8-9.

Georges Izard. "Le Droit moral de l'artiste dans les procès de Bonnard et Rouault." *Art de France*. 1961. No. 1. Pp. 209-210.

Edward Alden Jewell. *Georges Rouault*. Paris: Editions Hypérion. 1947. Introduction by Georges Rouault. Translation of the English edition.

Una E. Johnson. "Georges Rouault and His Prints." *The Bulletin of the Brooklyn Museum*. 1951. Vol. XIII. No. 1. Pp. 6-12.

Marcel Jouhandeau et al. "Making Raids on Faces." *Verve*. 1939. Nos. 5-6. Pp. 67-68.

Gustave Kahn. "Georges Rouault." *Mercure de France*. January 16, 1912. Vol. 85. P. 409.

Jacques de Laprade. "Georges Rouault." *Beaux-Arts*. 1936. No. 163. P. 8.

Jacques Lassaigne. *Rouault: les trésors de la peinture française*. Geneva: Skira. 1951.

Léon Lehmann. "L'Art vécu, Georges Rouault." *Beaux-Arts*. 1935. No. 136. P. 2.

Louis Leon-Martin. "Georges Rouault." *Art & Décoration*. 1930. Vol. 57. Pp. 111-114.

Jacques Lethène. "Les Salons de la Rose-Croix." *Gazette des Beaux-Arts*. 1960. Vol. 56. Pp. 363-374.

Samuel A. Lewisohn. "Drama in Painting." *Creative Art*. September, 1931. Pp. 185-196.

André Lhote. "L'Exposition Georges Rouault aux 'Amis de l'Art Contemporain.'" *La Nouvelle Revue Française*. Vol. II. No. 43. 1934. Pp. 303-304.

Parlons peinture. Paris: Editions Denoël et Steele. 1936. Pp. 257-262.

"La Peinture, le coeur et l'esprit." *L'Amour de l'Art*. 1923. No. 4. Pp. 779-782.

André Malraux. "Notes sur l'expression tragique en peinture à propos d'oeuvres récentes de Rouault." *Formes*. 1929. No. 1:5-6. D.

Giuseppe Marchiori. *Georges Rouault*. Paris/Lausanne: Bibliothèque des Arts. 1965.

Jacques Maritain. *Art and Scholasticism and the Frontiers of Poetry*. New York: Charles Scribner's Sons. 1962. Translated from the third edition of *Art et Scolastique*. 1935.

"Les Frontières de la poésie." *Cahiers d'Art*. 1927. No. 3. Pp. 93-95. Published with *Art et Scolastique*.

"Georges Rouault." *La Revue Universelle*. May 15, 1924. Vol. 17. No. 2. Pp. 505-508.

Georges Rouault. New York: Abrams, 1954.

and Georges Chabot. "Georges Rouault." *Cahiers d'Art*. 1928. No. 3. Pp. 97-112.

Raïssa Maritain. *Les Grandes amitiés*. New York: Editions de la Maison Française, Inc. 1941: Vol. 1. 1944: Vol. II. English Translations: Vol. I. *We Have Been Friends Together*. New York: Longmans, 1942. Vol. II. *Adventures in Grace*. 1945.

Pierre Marois. "La Foi et l'art religieux." *Hommes et Mondes*. August, 1951. No. 61. Pp. 414-424.

Roger-Marx. "Salon des Champs-Elysées." *La Revue Encyclopédique*. 1896. Pp. 297-306.

Jerome Mellquist. "Georges Rouault: Christian Painter." *The Commonweal*. December 23, 1938. Vol. 29. Pp. 232-234.

Anon. "The Modern Romantic: Contemporary Painting in Europe." *The Studio*. 1939. Special Autumn issue. P. 53.

L'Abbé Maurice Morel. "En Souvenir de Georges Rouault." *Etudes*. April, 1958. Nos. 296-297. Pp. 64-66.

"Georges Rouault." *Art et Industrie*. 1946. No. 3. Pp. 63-64.

"La Physionomie de Rouault." *Etudes*. 1947. No. 253. Pp. 188-191.

Wright Morris. "The Violent Land: Some Observations on Faulkner Country." *The Magazine of Art*. March, 1952. Vol. 45. Pp. 99-103.

Edouard Muller. "Georges Rouault." *Labyrinthe*. November 15, 1944. No. 2. Pp. 4-5.

Brian O'Doherty. "Georges Rouault." *Studies*. Spring, 1956. Pp. 67-76.

Régine Pernoud. "Devant l'art moderne." *L'Art Sacré*. January, February, 1950. Nos. 5, 6. Pp. 11-19.

Henri Perruchot. "Georges Rouault: l'insatisfait." *Le Jardin des Arts*. June, 1967. No. 151. Pp. 2-11.

Joseph Pichard. "L'Oeuvre de Georges Rouault." *L'Art d'Eglise*. 1953. Vol. xxi. No. 1. Pp. 177-189.

et al. "Recherche du Sacré." *L'Art Sacré*. April-May, 1947. Nos. 4-5.

Michel Puy. *Georges Rouault*. Paris: Nouvelle Revue Française: Les Peintres Français Nouveaux. 1920.

Jean-François Revel. "Le Misérabilisme tué par Buffet." *La Connaissance des Arts*. 1960. No. 100. Pp. 52-61.

Robert Rey. "Georges Rouault et Edouard Vuillard." *Le Bulletin des Musées de France*. June, 1929. Vol. 1. Pp. 123-127.

André de Ridder. "La Naissance de l'expressionisme." *L'Amour de l'Art*. 1934. No. 15. Pp. 385-388.

Claude Roger-Marx. "L'Oeuvre gravée de Georges Rouault." *Byblis*. Autumn, 1931. Pp. 93-100.

Rouault. Arcueil (Seine): Innothéra. Laboratoire Chantereau. No date. Séries Médecines Peintures. No. 86.

"Rouault, le pathétique." *Le Spectateur*. February 18, 1947. No. 90. P. 5.

John Rothenstein. "European Painting: 1893-1943." *The Studio*. 1943. No. 125. Pp. 109-110.

Anon. "Rouault." *Beaux-Arts*. 1939. No. 322. P. 4.

Anon. "Rouault: peintures inconnues ou célèbres." *L'Art Sacré*. March-April, 1965. Vol. 7. No. 8. Pp. 22-25.

Claude Roulet. *Georges Rouault: souvenirs*. Paris: Bibliothèque des Arts. 1961.

Georges Rouzet. "Le Courrier de Paris: Georges Rouault." *Le Thyrse*. 1938. No. 40. Pp. 245-252.

André Salmon. *L'Art vivant*. Paris: Crès & Company. 1920. Pp. 30-32. *"Le Miserere* de Georges Rouault." *L'Amour de l'Art*. 1925. No. 6. Pp. 182-186.

Gérald Schurr. "Rouault: un des peintres modernes les plus chers." *La Galérie des Arts*. July-August-September, 1964. No. 18.

Carol Seeley. "Notes on the Use of Symbols in Contemporary Painting." *Art Quarterly*. 1948. Vol. II. Pp. 324-334.

Raoul Sertat. "Le Salon des Champs-Elysées." *La Revue Encyclopédique*. 1895. Pp. 185-190.

James Thrall Soby. *Georges Rouault: Paintings and Prints*. New York: Museum of Modern Art. 1945. With "Notes received from the artist."

Robert Speaight. "Hommage to Rouault." *The Dublin Review*. July, 1941. Vol. 209. Pp. 59-68.

André Suarès. "Chronique de Caerdal." *La Nouvelle Revue Française*. 1940. Vol. 54. Pp. 388-391. *"Yorick: essai sur le Clown." Verve*. 1938. Vol. 1. No. 4. Pp. 101-104.

Angelico Surchamp. "Un Art sacré pour notre temps." *Zodiaque*. October, 1952. No. 2. Pp. 3-35.

Walter Tappolet. "Georges Rouault." *Du*. September, 1948. No. 9. Pp. 39-42.

J. R. Thomé. "Georges Rouault." *Le Courrier Graphique*. May-June, 1952. No. 58. Pp. 19-26.

Louis Vauxcelles. "Ambroise Vollard, curieux homme." *Beaux-Arts*. 1939. No. 343. Pp. 1-2.

Lionello Venturi. *Georges Rouault*. Paris: Skira. 1948. Second edition. *Rouault: étude biographique et critique*. Geneva: Albert Skira. 1959.

Ambroise Vollard. *Souvenirs d'un marchand de tableaux*. Paris: Club des Librairies de France. 1957. English Translation: *Recollections of a Picture Dealer*. London: Constable, 1936.

Alexander Watt. "Paris Commentary." *The Studio*. July, 1952. Vol. 144. Pp. 186-188.

R. H. Wilenski. "Georges Rouault." *Apollo*. 1930. Vol. II. Pp. 473-474.

M. Zahar. "Georges Rouault ou le retour au grotesque dramatique." *Formes*. 1933. No. 31. Pp. 354-355.

Christian Zervos. "Approches de l'oeuvre de Georges Rouault." *Cahiers d'Art*. 1952. Vol. 27. Pp. 101-164. *"Dernières oeuvres de Rouault." Cahiers d'Art*. 1960. Nos. 33-35. Pp. 175-188.

3. *General Works.*

Robert Baldick. *The Life of J.-K. Huysmans*. Oxford: Clarendon Press. 1955.

Charles Baudelaire. *Les Curiosités esthétiques: l'art romantique*. Paris: Garnier et Frères. 1962.

C. Baumgartner. *Le Dictionnaire de spiritualité: aescétique, doctrine et histoire.* Paris: Beauchesne. 1932 *et seq.*

Monroe C. Beardsley. *Aesthetics: From Classical Greece to the Present.* New York: Macmillan. 1966.
Aesthetics: Problems in the Philosophy of Criticism. New York: Harcourt, Brace and World. 1958.

Clive Bell. *Art.* New York: Capricorn. 1958. First published 1913.

John Berger. *The Success and Failure of Picasso.* Middlesex: Penguin, 1965.

Georges Bernanos. *Le Journal d'un curé de campagne.* Paris: Plon. 1936. English Translation: *The Diary of a Country Priest.* London: Boriswood. 1937.

Emile Bernard. "Charles Baudelaire, critique d'art et esthéticien." *Mercure de France.* 1919. Vol. 135. Pp. 577-600.

Léon Bloy. *Belluaires et Porchers.* Paris, 1905.
Le Désespéré. Paris: Mercure de France. 1967.
La Femme pauvre. Paris: Mercure de France. 1937. English Translation: *The Woman Who Was Poor.* London: Sheed and Ward. 1939.
L'Invendable. Paris: Mercure de France. 1919. "Journal," 1904-1907.
Quatre ans de captivité à Cochons-sur Marne. Paris: Mercure de France. 1959. "Journal," 1902-1904.

Mary Rosalie Brady. *Thought and Style in the Works of Léon Bloy.* Washington: Catholic University Press. 1945.

Guy Chastel. *J.-K. Huysmans et ses amis.* Paris: Bernard Grasset. 1957.

Kenneth Clark. *Le Nu.* Paris: Livre de Poche. 1969. 2 Volumes. Translated from the English: *The Nude: A Study of Ideal Art.* London: John Murray, 1956.

Paul Claudel. *Pages de prose.* Paris: Gallimard. 1944.

Hubert Colleye. *L'Ame de Léon Bloy.* Paris: Desclée de Brouwer. 1930.

Victor-Henri Debidour, ed. *Problèmes de l'art sacré.* Paris: Le Nouveau Portique. 1951.

Maurice Denis. *Journal.* Paris: La Colombe. 1959. Vols. I and II.
Nouvelles théories: 1914-1921. Paris: Rouart and Watelin. 1922.
Théories: 1890-1910. Paris: Bibliothèque de l'Occident. 1912.

Lucien Descaves. *Les Dernières années de J.-K. Huysmans.* Paris: Albin Michel. 1941.

Michel Drucker. *Renoir.* Paris: Editions Pierre Tisné. 1944.

Stanislas Fumet. *La Mission de Léon Bloy.* Paris: Desclée de Brouwer. 1935.

Charles Garside. *Zwingli and the Arts.* New Haven: Yale University Press. 1966.

Etienne Gilson. *Painting and Reality.* New York: World, Meridian Books. 1959.

T. H. Greene. *The Arts and the Art of Criticism.* Princeton: Princeton University Press. 1940.

Richard Griffiths. *The Reactionary Revolution: The Catholic Revival in French Literature, 1870-1914.* London: Constable. 1966.

Ernest Hello. *L'Homme.* Paris: Librairie Académique. 1921.

John Hospers. *Meaning and Truth in the Arts.* Chapel Hill, North Carolina: University of North Carolina Press. 1946.

Louis Hourticq. *L'Encyclopédie des Beaux Arts.* Paris: Librairie Hachette. 1925.

Johann Huizinga. *The Waning of the Middle Ages.* Middlesex, England: Penguin Books. 1965.

Anon. "L'Image: la représentation et l'évocation non-figurative." *L'Art Sacré.* September, October, 1958. Nos. 1, 2. Special issue.

H. W. Janson. *The History of Art: A Survey of the Major Visual Arts from the Dawn of History to the Present Day.* Englewood Cliffs: Prentice Hall, Inc.; New York: Abrams. 1962.

W. E. Kennick, ed. *Art and Philosophy: Readings in Aesthetics.* New York: St. Martin's Press. 1964.

Clyde S. Kilby. *Christianity and Aesthetics.* Chicago: Inter-Varsity Press. 1961.

Abraham Kuyper. "Calvinism and Art." *Calvinism: Six Stone Foundation Lectures.* Grand Rapids: Eerdmans. 1943. Pp. 142-169.

P. A. Lemoisne. *Degas et son oeuvre.* Paris: Paul Brame and C. M. De Hauke. 1946. 4 volumes.

Jacques Maritain. *Creative Intuition in Art and Poetry.* New York: World, Meridian Books. 1954.

"Quelques pages sur Léon Bloy." *Cahiers de la Quinzaine.* Paris. 1927. Tenth issue of the eighteenth series.

François Mauriac. "Pâques: passion et résurrection." *Plaisir de France.* April-May, 1949. No. 141. Pp. 54-59.

G. Mercier. *L'Art abstrait dans l'art sacré: la tendance non-figurative dans l'art sacré.* Paris: Editions E. de Boccard. 1964.

André Michel, ed. *L'Histoire de l'art.* Paris: Librairie Armand Colin. 1926. Vol. VIII.

Jacques Michel. "Picasso toujours neuf." *Le Monde.* July 3, 1969. P. 17.

William Neil and Eric Newton. *2000 Years of Christian Art.* New York: Harper Brothers. 1966.

Fritz Novotny. *Cézanne.* Paris: Editions du Phaidon. 1948.

Rudolph Otto. *The Idea of the Holy.* New York: Oxford University Press. 1958.

Herbert Read. *Art Now: An Introduction to the Theory of Modern Painting and Sculpture.* London: Faber and Faber. 1960.

The Philosophy of Modern Art. New York: World, Meridian Books. 1954.

Louis Réau. *L'Iconographie de l'art chrétien.* Paris: Presses Universitaires de France. 1959. 4 volumes.

H. R. Rookmaaker. *Art and the Public Today.* Huemoz, Switzerland: L'Abri Fellowship. 1968.

Modern Art and the Death of a Culture. London: Inter-Varsity Press, 1970.

Synthetist Art Theories. Amsterdam: Swets and Zeitlinger, 1959.

George Santayana. *The Sense of Beauty.* New York: Dover Publications, Inc. 1955.

Ernest Seillière. *Léon Bloy: la psychologie d'un mystique.* Paris: Editions de la Nouvelle Revue Critique. 1936.

Irving Stone, ed. *Dear Theo: The Autobiography of Vincent Van Gogh.* New York: Signet. 1969.

Gerardus van der Leeuw. *Sacred and Profane Beauty: The Holy in Art.* New York: Holt, Rinehart, and Winston. 1963.

W. A. Visser 't Hooft. *Rembrandt and the Gospel.* New York: Meridian Books. 1960.

Alfred North Whitehead. *Science and the Modern World.* New York: Mentor Books. 1948.

4. *Selected Exhibition Catalogues.†*

Brussels: Retrospective exhibition, 1952, Palais des Beaux-Arts. March 21-May 1. Text by G. Salles and Lionello Venturi. Brussels: Editions de la Connaissance. 1952.

Colmar: Musée d'Unterlinden. July-September, 1965. Preface by Gaëton Picon.

Dieppe: Musée de Dieppe. May 22-September 16, 1963. Introduction by Jean Lapeyre.

Geneva: Musée d'Art et d'Histoire. October 26-November 24, 1957. Cabinet des Estampes.

Hamburg: Kuntsverein. April 2-May 1, 1965. Preface by Ewald Rathke.

Metz: Le *Miserere* de Georges Rouault. Musées de Metz. Summer, 1965. Preface by Bernard Dorival.

New York, Cleveland: The Cleveland Museum of Art and The Museum of Modern Art. 1953. Introduction by Georges Salles and Lionello Venturi. New York: Museum of Modern Art.

Paris: Catalogue des oeuvres de Gustave Moreau. Paris: Musée Gustave Moreau. 1966. Preface by Jean Paladilhe.
Georges Rouault. Galerie des Garets. February 7-March 1, 1947.
Musée Nationale de l'Art Moderne. July 9-October 26, 1952. Paris: Editions des Musées Nationaux. Introduction by J. M.
Musée Nationale de l'Art Moderne. May 27-September 27, 1971. Catalogue by Michel Hoog.
Oeuvres inachevées données à l'Etat. Musée de Louvre. June 23-November 9, 1964. Paris: Ministre d'Etat Affaires Culturelles. Preface and text by Bernard Dorival.

Québec, Montréal: Musée de Québec. January 28-February 28, 1965. Musée d'Art Contemporain de Montréal. March 19-May 2, 1965.

Strasbourg: Edvard Munch. Musée des Arts Décoratifs. March-April, 1969. Strasbourg: Cabinet des Estampes. 1969. Texts by Ragna Stang and Paal Hougen.

Tokyo: *Oeuvres inachevées données à l'Etat.* 1965. Tokyo: National Museum of Western Art.

Zurich: Kunsthaus. April-June, 1948. Texts by Abbé M. Morel and W. Wartmann.

†All exhibitions of Rouault unless otherwise noted.

Index

231